# THE AGRARIAN QUESTION IN
# SOCIALIST TRANSITIONS

# THE AGRARIAN QUESTION IN SOCIALIST TRANSITIONS

Edited by
ASHWANI SAITH

FRANK CASS

*First published in Great Britain by*
FRANK CASS AND COMPANY LIMITED
Gainsborough House, 11 Gainsborough Road,
London E11 1RS

*and in the United States of America by*
FRANK CASS AND COMPANY LIMITED
c/o Biblio Distribution Centre
81 Adams Drive, P.O. Box 327, Totowa, NJ 07511


Copyright © 1985 Frank Cass & Co. Ltd.

British Library Cataloguing in Publication Data

Special issue on The Agrarian question in
socialist transitions.
1. Agriculture—Economic aspects—
Communist countries
I. Saith, Ashwani     II. Journal of development
studies
338.1′09171′7     HD1415

ISBN 0-7146-3276-7


This group of studies first appeared in a Special Issue on
'The Agrarian Question in Socialist Transitions' of *The
Journal of Development Studies*, Vol. 22, No. 1, published
by Frank Cass & Co. Ltd.

Typeset by Williams Graphics, Abergele, North Wales
Printed in the U.K. by
John Wright & Sons (Printing) Ltd. at The Stonebridge Press, Bristol

which accompanied it). Rather, as the economy became more industrially developed and more complex, expansion became more sustained while the cycles became somewhat less severe.

## V. METHODS AND RESULTS

To what extent did the expansion of public sector investment and employ-ment depend on squeezing peasant farm incomes through manipulation of the price 'scissors'? Table 1 shows that by 1925/6 the scissors were as much as 56 per cent less favourable to the peasant than in 1913, but this was not the result of government policy. Higher operating costs in Soviet industry meant that the regime was far more preoccupied with trying to force down industrial product prices, in order to squeeze costs and realise reserves of slack capacity, than with letting them rise in order to squeeze the peasant.

TABLE 1

THE 'SCISSORS', 1925/6–1928/9

| 1913 = 100 | 1925/6 | 1926/7 | 1927/8 | 1928/9 |
|---|---|---|---|---|
| The 'scissors' | 156 | 151 | 137 | 128 |

Note: The 'scissors' are measured by the ratio of an index of retail prices of industrial products to an index of planned delivery prices of agricultural products, based on 1913. Divergences between state planned delivery prices and free market prices for foodstuffs did not become substantial until 1928/9.

Source: Carr and Davies [1974: 1024].

Moreover, the immediately subsequent trend favoured the peasant, not public sector industry − by 1928/9 the adverse shift in the terms of trade compared to 1913 had been reduced from 55 per cent to 28 per cent. Retail prices of industrial goods were reduced in 1927 and held at the lower level, while procurement prices for agricultural goods were being allowed to drift up.

Table 2 shows price indices for 1928−32 in all the main markets in which urban−rural trade took place. Only in 1930 did state and co-operative retail prices for manufactures retailed in the village begin to rise significantly by comparison with state procurement prices for farm products. From this it might be supposed that the conservative public sector pricing policy pursued up until collectivisation stemmed from an appreciation of Preobrazhensky's dilemma − that pushing up industrial prices would spark off a peasant grain strike; once this fear had been lifted by the first wave of collectivisation in 1929−30, industrial prices in the village could be allowed to rise. Both suppositions would be wrong.

First, it is true that before collectivisation peasants had begun to withhold sales of foodstuffs (especially grains) from state procurement agencies, but the reason was not the adverse terms of trade, which were improving. The reason was that the ambitious public sector investment programme was inflating household purchasing power in both town and country beyond the

TABLE 2

PRICE INDICES, 1928–32

| 1928 = 100 | 1929 | 1930 | 1931 | 1932 |
|---|---|---|---|---|
| Producer prices for agricultural goods: | | | | |
| Centrally planned procurements | 111 | 116 | 119 | 109 |
| Decentralised procurements | - | - | - | 354 |
| Free market sales | 233 | 525 | 814 | 3006 |
| Weighted producer prices | 117 | 180 | 199 | 314 |
| Rural purchase prices for industrial goods: | | | | |
| Investment goods | 100 | 100 | 100 | 100 |
| State and co-operative retail | 101 | 110 | 134 | 292 |
| Free market retail | 111 | 174 | 313 | 674 |
| Weighted user prices | 101 | 110 | 171 | 241 |

*Source*:  Taken or calculated from A. A. Barsov [*1969*], *Balans stoimostnykh obmenov mezhdu gorodom i derevnei*, Moscow: 108, 112–113, 115, 123.

capacity of consumer industries to satisfy it. Lack of availability of consumer goods forced the seller of foodstuffs to accumulate useless cash, and constituted a disincentive to sell. One solution would have been for the authorities to restrain public sector investment, but this had been ruled out by Stalin. Another option would have been to allow public sector industrial prices to rise. This would have restored macroeconomic equilibrium and food producers' marketing incentives, at the cost of making explicit the reduced living standards required by the public sector investment programme; again this was politically unacceptable.[7] While ruling out both of these options, the authorities instead followed a third alternative which made matters still worse. This was to try to reduce peasant incomes and the cost of public sector investment by pushing down the demand price of grains in the grain market, which they largely controlled through procurement agencies, although they could not prevent the demand prices for other kinds of agricultural outputs from rising in the comparatively unregulated markets for livestock and dairy produce, vegetables etc. As a result farmers diverted resources from grain cultivation into these other, more profitable activities; the agricultural system benefited, farm incomes were not reduced, and the supply of grains to the public sector was disproportionately hindered [*Davies, 1980: 40*].

Second, was collectivisation the decisive factor which allowed the authorities at last to squeeze the peasantry by manipulation of the scissors? It is true that after 1930 the public sector retail prices for industrial goods rose faster than state procurement prices for farm products, but the impact of this development upon the supply of funds for public sector accumulation in industry was more than offset by other changes. One offsetting factor lay in unregulated exchanges within the private sector which persisted (at times illegally) throughout this period. Prices for private sales of foodstuffs and purchases of manufactures both multiplied several times between 1928 and 1932, absolutely and relative to prices obtained in the public sector. But (see Table 2) the free market price of foodstuffs rose by 30 times, compared to only six or seven times for free market manufactures. The persistence of a private sector within agriculture and trade was to have a major effect on the flow of funds between agriculture and industry. For, although virtually all households became worse off, those households which still had access to private supplies of foodstuffs or artisan products could trade on advantageous terms with households reliant on the public sector for their incomes, and best of all was to have food for sale.

The other offset to public sector manipulation of the scissors lay in the fact that, with the creation of a public sector in agriculture, investment in farm capacity now became a charge on public sector resources. At the same time the damage done by collectivisation, in particular widespread losses of draught livestock, had to be made up by the transfer of farm machinery at subsidised state wholesale prices to new public sector agricultural enterprises called 'machine and tractor stations'; these transfers were not compensated by immediate reductions in farm household purchasing power.

Why, then, was collectivisation undertaken? Since it was not required to resolve Preobrazhensky's dilemma, and did not increase the resources available to finance industrialisation, it has been argued that the only remaining motives were to back up Stalin's struggle for personal power and to suppress the consequences of leadership blunders such as the attempt to hold down grain prices from 1926 onwards [e.g. *Millar, 1976: 53–5*]. This view exaggerates what could have been achieved within the NEP framework. The high level of public sector investment being pursued in the late 1920s was increasingly incompatible with NEP, given the right (enshrined in NEP) of the peasant farmer to command resources for agriculture and consumption. To this extent the growing state of shortage and macroeconomic disequilibrium was inevitable [*Wheatcroft, Davies and Cooper, 1982: 32*]. The Soviet regime was in the process of formulating a definite intention to make the transition away from a demand-constrained economic system to a resource-constrained economy characterised by 'expansion drive' and 'investment hunger' [e.g. *Kornai, 1980: 191–5*], and the market relation with the peasantry would have suffered under any policy design, no matter how finely calculated. At the same time the choice of methods and rate of collectivisation undoubtedly reflected specific features of nascent Stalinism – its impatient desire to get things done, its intolerance of constraints and pragmatic willingness to substitute coercion for consent – with results tragic for agriculture and the rural population. The collectivisation drive was also characterised by highly exaggerated expectations about what would prove technically possible in a large-scale, socialised agriculture given the short time horizon and extremely limited public sector investment resources available for farming, and these expectations would be disappointed in a most brutal clash with reality [*Davies, 1980: Chapter 10*].

When we take into account the volumes of resources being transferred between the different sectors through different markets, what was the net impact upon Soviet primary accumulation? Research has concentrated on the net transfer between agriculture and industry, rather than between the private and public sectors. The pioneer in this field, the Soviet economist A. A. Barsov [*1969: Table 10 (facing p. 112) and p. 118*], has calculated that during collectivisation the commodity terms of trade moved in favour of agriculture, although the extent of this movement proved highly unstable in the short term. When the resource transfers themselves are valued in constant 1928 prices, it is claimed that agriculture received subsidies from industry throughout the period 1928–32, and that the net subsidy tended to increase while collectivisation proceeded. This result should no longer be considered surprising, given that 17 years have passed since its first publication in a Soviet journal in 1968.

Barsov's findings have been criticised on various grounds. Alec Nove [*1976: 58*] has called into question whether such flows are in principle measurable, given the turmoil of Soviet economic reality in these years. Another area for criticism has been Barsov's reliance (understandable, however, under the circumstances) on Soviet official statistics [*Morrison, 1982: 577–80*].

On a more practical level, R. W. Davies and S. G. Wheatcroft have suggested that Barsov neglected the role of rural non-agriculture in claiming agricultural resources and supplying the agricultural population. Empirically, Barsov may have conflated agriculture with the village and the private sector, and public sector urban non-agriculture with non-agriculture as a whole. The importance of this lies in the role played by private sector rural non-agriculture before 1930, and its rapid elimination in the course of farm collectivisation.

The impact of adopting Davies and Wheatcroft's revisions is shown in Table 3. The role of rural non-agriculture emerges as a set of residuals between two sets of data which may not be fully comparable in other ways than those of which we are aware, so it is important not to place too much weight on their accuracy. The table suggests, however, that before collectivisation rural non-agriculture made a substantial net contribution to agriculture – much larger than the urban non-agricultural subsidy – when product flows are measured in 1928 prices. Thus, Barsov greatly understated the flow of resources from industry as a whole to agriculture in 1928–30. The subsequent elimination of rural industries may thus be said to have had two negative consequences – it was a directly retrograde step from the point of view of industrialisation; indirectly it must have increased the dependence of the agricultural population upon the products of public sector urban industries, without increasing the availability of agricultural products. From the point of view of primary socialist accumulation the trade-off between living standards and public sector investment was worsened. But at the same time the elimination of rural industries directly increased the economic weight of the public sector.

Barsov [*1969: 130–31; 1974*] has also prepared an alternative evaluation of the transfer of resources between agriculture and industry for 1928–32 and 1937–38 in terms of what Michael Ellman [*1978*] calls 'labour adjusted roubles'. This involves correction of 1928 prices for the overvaluation of a unit of industrial labour-time in 1928 compared to a unit of agricultural labour-time and for changes in labour productivity after 1928 in both sectors. The prices of 1928 are rejected as a measure of value because they still incorporated the pre-revolutionary heritage of exploitation of the agricultural producer by state monopoly capital by means of adverse terms of trade. Barsov estimates the extent of this discrimination as an overvaluation of industrial commodities (and of the labour-time embodied in them) at 1928 prices by a factor of two. In subsequent years this factor would be increased by an increase in labour productivity in agriculture, and reduced by an increase in the same in industry, so Barsov makes appropriate adjustments in the valuation of commodities

TABLE 3

AGRICULTURE'S SALES AND RECEIPTS, 1928–32

| Billion 1928 roubles | 1928 | 1929 | 1930 | 1931 | 1932 |
|---|---|---|---|---|---|
| Agriculture's sales to non-agriculture: | | | | | |
| To urban non-agriculture (1) | 3.2 | 3.5 | 4.0 | 4.2 | 3.2 |
| To all non-agriculture (2) | 3.4 | 4.0 | 3.9 | - | - |
| Residual attributable to rural non-agriculture (2-1) | 0.2 | 0.5 | - | - | - |
| Agriculture's purchases from non-agriculture: | | | | | |
| Investment goods from urban non-agriculture (3) | 0.6 | 0.7 | 0.9 | 1.4 | 1.4 |
| Consumer goods from urban non-agriculture (4) | 3.4 | 4.1 | 4.4 | 3.7 | 3.3 |
| Consumer goods from all non-agriculture | 5.8 | 6.4 | 6.4 | - | - |
| Residual attributable to rural non-agriculture (5-4) | 2.4 | 2.3 | 2.0 | - | - |
| Agriculture's net transfer to non-agriculture: | | | | | |
| To urban non-agriculture (6) | -0.8 | -1.3 | -1.3 | -1.0 | -1.6 |
| To all non-agriculture (7) | -3.0 | -3.1 | -3.4 | - | - |
| Residual attributable to rural non-agriculture (7-6) | -2.2 | -1.8 | -2.0 | - | - |

Source: Rows 1, 3, 4 and 6 are from A. A. Barsov [1969], Balans stoimostnykh obmenov mezhdu gorodom i derevnei, Moscow: Table 10 (facing p. 112) and p. 118. Rows 2 and 5 are from R. W. Davies and S. G. Wheatcroft [1983], 'Soviet National Income Accounts (Balances) for 1928–30: A Rare Historical Source', Centre for Russian and East European Studies, University of Birmingham: 21–2.

produced in both sectors in subsequent years (this would be equivalent to correcting the 1928 correction by an index of the double-factoral terms of trade).[8] Table 4 shows the results. When commodity flows are revalued in this way, it emerges that agriculture suffered from unequal exchange throughout the period, but an adverse shift in the terms of trade (the 'ratio of non-equivalence') was secured only for 1929–31; by 1932 the labour-adjusted 'scissors' were already more favourable than in 1928, and the favourable trend persisted to the late 1930s. Industry did after all receive a net 'tribute' from agriculture throughout the inter-war period (this is the result of Barsov's radical downvaluation of industry's sales to agriculture), and the tribute was larger in 1929–31 than in 1928. But the increase in the tribute during collectivisation was only small and temporary. By 1932 it had fallen back to below the 1928 level, and was smaller still in 1937–38 – there was no recovery after the post-collectivisation famine. As a proportion of industrial accumulation the agricultural tribute declined steadily, from 54 per cent in 1928 to only 18 per cent in 1932 and 16 per cent in 1937–38.

The main emphasis of Barsov's research was placed on resource transfers between industry and agriculture. This is not the same as the focus of primary

TABLE 4

AGRICULTURE'S LABOUR-ADJUSTED SALES AND RECEIPTS IN 1913, 1928–32 AND 1937–38

| Billion labour-adjusted roubles | 1913 | 1928 | 1929–31 average | 1932 | 1937–8 average |
|---|---|---|---|---|---|
| Agriculture's sales to non-agriculture (1) | 5.54 | 3.71 | 4.76 | 3.78 | 3.49 |
| Agriculture's purchases from non-agriculture (2) | 1.72 | 1.84 | 2.17 | 1.95 | 2.15 |
| Ratio of non-equivalence (1 ÷ 2) | 3.22 | 2.02 | 2.19 | 1.94 | 1.63 |
| Agriculture's net transfer to non-agriculture (1 - 2) | 3.82 | 1.87 | 2.58 | 1.83 | 1.35 |
| (1 - 2) as share of agricultural output | 0.36 | 0.19 | 0.29 | 0.22 | 0.16 |
| (1 - 2) as share of industrial investment | - | 0.54 | 0.37 | 0.18 | 0.16 |

*Note*: Labour-adjusted roubles are defined in the text.

*Source*: A. A. Barsov [*1974*], 'NEP i vyravnivanie ekonomicheskikh otnoshenii mezhdu gorodom i derevnei', in *Novaya ekonomicheskaya politika: voprosy teorii i istorii*, Moscow: 96, 99.

socialist accumulation which rests on the public sector and its relation with the private sector. However, Barsov's research has been extended to reveal major aspects of primary accumulation. One aspect of this lay in the differential treatment of different sectors within agriculture. In 1928 almost all of agriculture was in small peasant hands. In 1929–30 a large but at first highly unstable socialised sector was formed. By 1932 more than 60 per cent, and by 1937 more than 90 per cent of peasant farms had been collectivised; a substantial nationalised farming industry had also been created. Table 5 shows that in 1930–31 the labour-adjusted (double-factoral) terms of trade were only marginally less favourable to agriculture as a whole than in 1928, and those for the private sector tended to follow those for agriculture as a whole or remain slightly more favourable. Nationalised state farms were far more favourably treated; their terms of trade were twice to four times as advantageous. Collective farms were enormously discriminated against; taking into account the unfavourable terms on which they rented machinery services from the state-owned machine and tractor stations attached to them, their terms of trade with non-agriculture were 14 times less advantageous than those facing state farms in the worst year of 1931, and more than three times as bad as those facing agriculture as a whole. In subsequent years (we have only 1932 and 1938) this pattern of discrimination moderated. But by 1938, although state farms had lost their advantage, the private sector had improved its position and collective farms were still twice as badly treated as agriculture as a whole. In short, although collectivisation failed to secure more than a small and short-lived increase in the net transfer of resources (measured in labour-adjusted roubles) out of agriculture as a whole, it created new sectors within agriculture and treated them differently. State-owned farms and

TABLE 5

THE LABOUR-ADJUSTED TERMS OF TRADE, 1930–32 AND 1938

| Ratios of nonequivalence | 1930 | 1931 | 1932 | 1938 |
|---|---|---|---|---|
| State farms | 0.82 | 0.55 | 0.51 | 1.92 |
| Collective farms (including machine and tractor stations) | 4.22 | 4.46 | 2.82 | 1.37 |
| Collective farms alone | 4.75 | 7.75 | 4.64 | 3.17 |
| Private farms | 1.90 | 2.11 | 1.91 | 1.23 |
| All agriculture | 2.04 | 2.31 | 1.94 | 1.64 |

*Note*: The ratio of non-equivalence is defined as sales divided by purchases when both are measured in labour-adjusted roubles.

*Source*: Barsov [1974: 101].

machine and tractor stations were subsidised at the expense of collective farms; an incidental, and unintended beneficiary was the remaining private sector.

Ellman [*1975: 856*] has also extended Barsov's research to examine changes in relations of production within industry, but covering only the years 1928–32. He starts from the proposition that if the net transfer from agriculture to industry fell over the period of the first Five Year Plan, then the increase in industrial investment over the period must have been financed in some other way. He finds its source in the increase in the industrial workforce, coupled with the decline in the real wage cost of output (the latter mainly accounted for by the decline in the real wage). In labour-adjusted value terms it transpires that 30 per cent of the increase in industrial accumulation resulted from the increase in absolute surplus value resulting from increased employment; the increase in relative surplus value resulting from the lower wage cost of output was sufficient to make good both the remaining 70 per cent of the increase in industrial accumulation, and a further 31 per cent short-fall resulting from the decline in the agricultural surplus. The increase in employment was made possible by the administrative mobilisation of resources into public sector capital construction, the imposition of an obligation to work upon the adult able-bodied population of the towns, and the flood of former peasants who left the village to seek work for a wage income.[9] The lower wage cost of output was made possible by a reduction in the real wage paid to both existing and newly employed workers, enforced through inflation, queues, ration cards and the differentiation of rewards for more skilled and responsible grades. All this took place in the context of restructuring of public sector managerial relations of production on the basis of more hierarchical, centralised authority.

Associated with the resource flows and reorganisation of the period were large-scale social mobility and migration. Between 1928 and 1940 state employment almost tripled, with the creation of 20 million new jobs. Until some point in the late 1930s, most new recruits to public sector industry were of peasant origin; of the rural recruits, most were young and without previous experience of non-agricultural wage employment. Other recruits to urban non-agriculture were predominantly women, who increasingly added jobs in the public sector to housework and childcare responsibilities; and school-leavers, who contributed to the natural increase in the workforce.

The mobilisation of rural labour for public sector capital construction was an exceptionally bewildering affair for those participating in it. Permanent migration from country to town could hold many advantages for the migrant. In general urban living standards were higher than in the countryside, not least because supplies were more assured in times of shortage. Thus, even when living standards were collapsing everywhere, as in the early 1930s, the rural – urban migrant could still benefit. Opportunities for advancement and promotion were also far more numerous in the urban setting, and the hard-working, politically conscious would-be official would almost inevitably leave the village at some point. However, movement to the towns was also fraught with obstacles. Employment as a gang labourer on a building site in a new town which might still be no more than mud and fields was likely to carry more privations than privileges. Opportunities for individual advancement might still be beyond reach. The regime had a multiplying need for cadres and officials, but there was a need for scapegoats too. At lower levels the chance of promotion exceeded the likelihood of personal disaster by some margin, but with rapid advancement up the public sector administrative hierarchy the margin disappeared or at times became negative.

Many were mobilised involuntarily, and entered the field of public sector capital construction as forced labour. Again, the peasantry provided the first echelon for the large-scale application of forced labour – those interned in the course of collectivisation and the agricultural campaigns of the first Five Year Plan. Unfortunately this is a subject where quantification is most difficult. For the most precise estimates tend also to be the most exaggerated, and more sober experts are reluctant to be precise (e.g. Rosefield [1980] and accompanying discussion).

In summary, what were the defining features of Soviet primary accumulation after 1928? First, in labour-adjusted roubles agriculture financed a significant but declining proportion of public sector accumulation through unequal exchange. Second, the price 'scissors' or terms of trade between industry and agriculture proved resistant to administrative controls and failed to move in a way which would pay for the increase in industrial investment, although they were successfully manipulated to benefit nationalised enterprise at the expense of collective farming within public sector agriculture. Third, trends in the exchange of commodities and terms of trade were incidental to establishment of the decisive condition for Soviet primary accumulation – the administrative mobilisation of resources – products and labour – into public sector capital construction of large-scale industrial projects, which was carried out regardless of the consequences for market equilibrium or incentives for small producers. Fourth, the administrative mobilisation of products on this scale would have necessitated changes in agricultural organisation whatever happened, and farm collectivisation was itself a major act of primary accumulation; however, contrary to received opinion, the collectivisation process did not additionally give rise to the expanded flow of products to be mobilised. Fifth, the main constituents of Soviet primary accumulation were the collectivisation of peasant farming and its subordination to state enterprise within public sector agriculture, the elimination of private sector small-scale rural industries, the rationing of industrial investment resources exclusively to the public sector and their denial to private enterprise, and the associated movement of millions of workers out of the household and private sector to employment in public sector capital construction at a reduced real wage. From this point of view, the real process of Soviet primary accumulation had more in common with the mobilisation of labour envisaged by Bukharin in 1920, than with the products transfer urged by Preobrazhensky in 1924–26. Sixth, the viability of public sector expansion on this basis was underpinned by the transformation of public sector managerial relations of production and of the economic system as a whole on hierarchical, authoritarian lines.

## VI. LESSONS

The experience of Soviet primary accumulation contains several lessons of significance for other developing countries engaged in a transition to socialism. First, primary socialist accumulation goes far beyond the issues of industry versus agriculture, worker versus peasant or town versus village. Soviet primary accumulation brought about radical change within industry and within agriculture, not just in the relations between them; it drastically altered the lives of both workers and peasants, and of both town and country. Even the issue of public versus private enterprise does not sum it up because the nature of the public sector was also profoundly transformed. Thus, even if primary socialist accumulation sometimes appears to narrow itself down to comparatively technical issues such as the pricing of industrial and agricultural commodities, decisions taken on such a narrow basis may turn out to have implications reaching far beyond what was anticipated.

Second, primary socialist accumulation is not a deterministic concept. There is no one course which all developing countries must follow. Within Soviet experience the concept of primary socialist accumulation acquired several different meanings. However, primary socialist accumulation from below, relying on a mixture of worker and community initiatives, co-operative forms and economic methods, appeared less attractive to those in charge of the Soviet political system than primary socialist accumulation enforced from above through administrative mobilisation of resources and the centralisation of authority.

Third, the Soviet pattern of primary socialist accumulation proved viable and had a number of beneficial results. Bukharin and others who had argued that the Soviet state could not launch a confrontation with a hundred million peasants and dispense with their goodwill were proved wrong by Stalin and his colleagues. In the short term this primary accumulation pattern was associated with a sharp deterioration in the quality of life for most Soviet citizens. In the long term, however, an economic system was built which gave rise to full employment, rising living standards and a high degree of economic security for nearly everyone, at least in peacetime conditions. What is more, a Soviet military–economic counterweight to Western imperial pretensions was established, without which many of the options for non-capitalist development open to developing countries today would be out of the question.

Fourth, Soviet primary socialist accumulation had many unintended results. Among these were the economic losses resulting from the uncontrolled style of resource mobilisation (including the speed and methods of farm collectivisation), the associated costs of underestimating inertia and reluctance or resistance down below in the face of higher-level directives and decrees, the multiplication and overburdening of centralised administrative controls on economic life, the hyperactivity of the state security organs and proliferation of purges, the spread of forced labour and widespread alienation of working people (especially peasants) from socialist goals. At each stage governmental coercion, first embraced as a temporary expedient or necessary evil, became permanently institutionalised and hailed as a proper characteristic of socialist construction.

Fifth, these features of Soviet primary socialist accumulation meant that the process proved extremely difficult to complete. Even today some aspects of the primary phase persist. The private sector continues to play an irreducible role in Soviet agriculture and trade. Within the public sector an informal economy based on the use of public assets for private gain persists and cannot be eliminated in spite of decrees and directives. Rapid industrialisation has been successfully carried out, yet many elements of the pre-socialist, pre-industrial economy have been carried over into the Soviet workplace and urban community – labour indiscipline and migrancy, concealed unemployment, archaic controls on information, culture and popular decision-making. Thus the means originally chosen for building a socialist society turn out to have incorporated unexpected limits on the attainment of the original goal.

Sixth, although the Soviet pattern of primary socialist accumulation was not economically predetermined but resulted from political choice, this choice has proved extremely difficult to revise after the event. Right from the start important sections of Soviet society and public opinion, including influential groups at the heart of the Stalinist political system, were ready to have second thoughts and urge a shift to a less coercive path of primary accumulation with more scope for socialist construction and economic development from below. From time to time they were able to secure significant constraints on the actions of Soviet officialdom and, after the death of Stalin these constraints became permanent. But the basic institutions and mechanisms of rule already laid down had meanwhile become strongly entrenched and today remain powerfully resistant to any more fundamental reform.

NOTES

1. The distinction between public and social ownership owes much to the work of Polish economists dating back to the 1950s and 1960s. See, for example, Brus [1975: 18–24].
2. This assessment is more optimistic than that of Gregory [1982: Chapter 5] concerning which the Birmingham authors express reservations.
3. The most famous comment on this phenomenon is found in the use made by Stalin of statistics on grain production and marketings in 1926/7, produced by the economist V. S. Nemchinov, in a speech in April 1928, to argue the case for collectivisation; see Stalin [1940: 208 ('On the Grain Front')].
4. Preobrazhensky's law of primary socialist accumulation, first formulated in 1924, can be found in English translation in Preobrazhensky [1965: Chapter 2 ('The Law of Primitive Socialist Accumulation')].

5.  Filtzer [*1978: 77–8*] has argued that Preobrazhensky recognised this aspect of primary accumulation in terms of the need to overcome the division of labour in society (including managerial hierarchy) through 'proletarian democracy' and the appropriation of knowledge by the working class; Filtzer comments, however, that this aspect of Preobrazhensky's theory 'fought for a platform which effectively "presupposed itself"', in that its prior implementation was an actual condition for its adoption'.

6.  Here and below, Soviet national income is measured according to the Material Product System.

7.  If anything, state policy was still to hold industrial prices down, with consequences analysed by Vyas [*1979: 26–7*]. For more detailed analysis see Harrison [*1984: 76–8*].

8.  Barsov [*1969: 35–50, 125–9*] sets out the methodology for correcting 1928 prices. Objections have been raised on a variety of grounds. Millar [*1974: 752*] objected to the Marxian antecedents of 'labour-adjusted' roubles in the labour theory of value, which Millar interpreted as a welfare theory of claims on output. Millar distinguished between the supposedly 'straightforward empirical measurement' of intersectoral resource flows, and the measurement of their welfare implications, which requires 'choice of a value standard'. This distinction does not seem very satisfactory since even conventional neoclassical economics requires an appropriate value standard for measuring inter-sectoral resource flows – in this case, some indicator of long-run marginal costs obtainable under a perfectly competitive equilibrium. Another criticism is raised by Morrison [*1982: 570–77*] – he claims that Barsov's corrections of 1928 prices both distort the Soviet labour productivity record and amount to a legitimation of wastefully high unit costs in Soviet industry. Again this criticism seems to attach unnecessary moral connotations to a useful heuristic device. Even conventional neoclassical economics recognises the concepts of labour embodied and labour commanded, as definition of the 'double-factoral terms of trade' reveals. (The commodity terms of trade are measured by an index of the price of exports divided by an index of the price of imports. The single-factoral terms of trade are measured by the commodity terms of trade multiplied by an index of labour productivity in the export industries of the exporting country, so that a deterioration in the commodity terms of trade may be offset by a reduction in the labour embodied in the exporting country's exports. The double-factoral terms of trade are measured by the single-factoral terms of trade divided by an index of labour productivity in the export industries of trading partners, so that a deterioration in the single-factoral terms of trade may be offset by an increase in the labour commanded by exports and embodied in imports.)

9.  Ellman [*1975:857*] has argued that, although there was no increase in the net agricultural surplus, the mobilisation of both wage goods marketed by agriculture and of peasant labour was still made possible by farm collectivisation. To this extent collectivisation might still be seen not only as an act of primary accumulation in itself, but also as a necessary condition for the further process of primary accumulation in industry. However Millar [*1984*] has argued that collectivisation itself was not a necessary condition for the mobilisation of basic wage goods or of labour into industry; once collectivisation had done the damage, the procurements system for basic wage goods (and presumably, too, the system of controls over rural labour mobility and recruitment) merely limited the adverse results.

## REFERENCES

Barsov, A. A., 1969, *Balans stoimostnykh obmenov mezhdu gorodom i derevnei*, Moscow: 'Nauka'.

Barsov, A. A., 1974, 'NEP i vyravnivanie ekonomicheskikh otnoshenii mezhdu gorodom i derevnei', in *Novaya ekonomicheskaya politika: voprosy teorii i istorii*, Moscow: 'Nauka'.

Brus, Włodzimierz, 1975, *Socialist Ownership and Political Systems*, London and Boston: Routledge & Kegan Paul.

Bukharin, N. I., 1967, *Put' k sotsializmu v Rossii. Izbrannye proizvedeniya N. I. Bukharina* (ed. Sidney Heitman), New York: Omicron.

Carr, E. H., and R. W. Davies, 1974, *Foundations of a Planned Economy 1926–1929*, Vol. 1, Harmondsworth: Pelican.

Crisp, Olga, 1976, *Studies in the Russian Economy before 1914*, London and Basingstoke: Macmillan.

Cohen, Stephen F., 1975, *Bukharin and the Bolshevik Revolution: A Political Biography 1888–1938*, New York: Vintage.

Danilov, V.P., 1977, *Sovetskaya dokolkhoznaya derevnya: naselenie, zemlepol'zovanie, khozyaistvo*, Moscow: 'Nauka'.

Davies, R.W., 1977, 'The Emergence of the Soviet Economic System 1927–1934', Soviet Industrialisation Project Series No. 9, Centre for Russian and East European Studies, University of Birmingham.

Davies, R.W., 1980, *The Socialist Offensive: The Collectivisation of Soviet Agriculture 1929–1930*, London and Basingstoke: MacMillan.

Davies, R.W., and S.G. Wheatcroft, 1983, 'Soviet National Income Accounts (Balances) for 1928–1930; A Rare Historical Source', Paper presented to the Soviet Industrialisation Project Seminar, Centre for Russian and East European Studies, University of Birmingham. To be published in R.W. Davies and S.G. Wheatcroft, eds., *Materials for the Balance of the Soviet National Economy 1928–1930*, Cambridge: Cambridge University Press (forthcoming).

Ellman, Michael, 1975, 'Did the Agricultural Surplus Provide the Resources for the Increase in Investment in the USSR during the First Five Year Plan?', *Economic Journal*, Vol. 85, December.

Ellman, Michael, 1978, 'On a Mistake of Preobrazhensky and Stalin', *Journal of Development Studies*, Vol. 14, No. 3.

Erlich, Alexander, 1950, 'Preobrazhenski and the Economics of Soviet Industrialization', *Quarterly Journal of Economics*, Vol. LXIV, No. 1.

Filtzer, Donald, 1978, 'Preobrazhensky and the Problem of the Soviet Transition', *Critique*, No. 9.

Gregory, Paul R., 1972, 'Economic Growth and Structural Change in Tsarist Russia: A Case of Modern Economic Growth?', *Soviet Studies*, Vol. XXIII, No. 3.

Gregory, Paul R., 1982, *Russian National Income 1885–1913*, Cambridge: Cambridge University Press.

Harrison, Mark, 1981–82, 'Soviet Primary Accumulation Processes: Some Unresolved Problems', *Science & Society*, Vol. XLV, No. 4.

Harrison, Mark, 1984, 'Why Was NEP Abandoned?', in Robert C. Stuart (ed.), *The Soviet Rural Economy*, Totowa, NJ: Rowman & Allanheld.

Kornai, János, 1980, *The Economics of Shortage*, Vol. A, Amsterdam, New York and Oxford: North Holland.

Lewin, Moshe, 1968, *Russian Peasants and Soviet Power: A Study of Collectivisation*, London: Allen & Unwin.

Millar, James R., 1970, 'Soviet Rapid Development and the Agricultural Surplus Hypothesis', *Soviet Studies*, Vol. XXII, No. 1.

Millar, James R., 1974, 'Mass Collectivization and the Contribution of Soviet Agriculture to the First Five-Year Plan: A Review Article', *Slavic Review*, Vol. 33, No. 4.

Millar, James R., 1976, 'What's Wrong with the "Standard Story" ', *Problems of Communism*, Vol. XXV, No. 4.

Millar, James R., 1978, 'A Note on Primitive Accumulation in Marx and Preobrazhensky', *Soviet Studies*, Vol. XXX, No. 3.

Millar, James R., 1984, 'Views on the Economics of Soviet Collectivization of Agriculture: The State of the Revisionist Debate', in Robert C. Stuart (ed.), *The Soviet Rural Economy*, Totowa, NJ: Rowman & Allanheld.

Morrison, David, 1982, 'A Critical Examination of A.A. Barsov's Empirical Work on the Balance of Value Exchange between the Town and Country', *Soviet Studies*, Vol. XXXIV, No. 4.

Nove, Alec, 1976, 'The "Logic" and Cost of Collectivization', *Problems of Communism*, Vol. XXV, No. 4.

Nove, Alec, 1982, *An Economic History of the USSR*, 3rd revised edn., Harmondsworth: Pelican.

Preobrazhensky, E., 1965, *The New Economics*, Oxford: Oxford University Press.

Rosefielde, Steven, 1980, 'The First "Great Leap Forward" Reconsidered: Lessons of Solzhenitsyn's Gulag Archipelago', *Slavic Review*, Vol. 39, No. 4.

Stalin, Jospeh, 1940, *Leninism*, London: Lawrence & Wishart.

Szamuely, László, 1974, *First Models of the Socialist Economic Systems: Principles and Theories*, Budapest: Akadémiai Kiadó.

Vyas, Arvind, 1978, *Consumption in a Socialist Economy: The Soviet Industrialisation Experience, 1929–37*, New Delhi: People's Publishing House.

Vyas, Arvind, 1979, 'Primary accumulation in the USSR revisited', *Cambridge Journal of Economics*, Vol. 3, No. 2.

Vyas, Arvind, 1985, 'The Contribution of the Soviet Working Class to Industrialisation (1929–1937) and the Question of Historical Alternatives', in R. W. Davies (ed.), *Soviet Investment for Planned Industrialisation, 1929–1937: Policy and Practice*, Oakland, CA: Berkeley Slavic Specialties (forthcoming).

Wheatcroft, S. G., 1984, 'A Reevaluation of Soviet Agricultural Production in the 1920s and 1930s', in Robert C. Stuart (ed.), *The Soviet Rural Economy*, Totowa, NJ: Rowman & Allanheld.

Wheatcroft, S. G., Davies, R. W. and J. M. Cooper, 1982, 'Soviet Industrialisation Reconsidered: Some Preliminary Conclusions about Economic Developments between 1926 and 1941', paper presented to the SSRC Conference on Soviet Economic Development in the 1930s (Third Conference of the International Work-Group on Soviet Interwar Economic History), University of Birmingham. To be published in the *Economic History Reviews* (forthcoming).

Zaleski, Eugène, 1971, *Planning for Economic Growth in the Soviet Union 1918–1932*, Chapel Hill, NC: University of North Carolina Press.

# The Structure and Contradictions of Productive Relations in Socialist Agrarian 'Reform': A Framework for Analysis and The Chinese Case*

## by Marc Blecher

*This article attempts to develop a complex analytical framework for analysing socialist agrarian reform, and to apply it to the case of post-Mao China, perhaps the most sweeping agrarian 'reform' in the history of socialism. The purpose of doing so is to disaggregate the complex changes which have been wrought under the 'responsibility systems' in order to get a more nuanced sense of what has and has not changed, how the various parts fit together, and where the axes of contradiction posed by the 'reform' may lie. This analytical framework may also be of use in comparative analysis of socialist agriculture, though that enterprise is not attempted here. One basic argument of this study is that the 'responsibility systems' of the recent Chinese 'reforms' are neither socialist nor capitalist, but something distinctive, whose potentially heterogeneous elements must be identified, disaggregated, analysed one by one, and then reconstituted, in order to expose their nature, dynamics and contradictions.*

## I. INTRODUCTION

'Reform' has become the order of the day in socialist agriculture throughout the world.[1] It poses difficult analytical and theoretical problems for students of 'actual socialism'.[2] Progress in analysis of these issues has been hampered by the bluntness of the tools at hand, among them the gross concepts of feudalism, capitalism and socialism which keep cropping up. This article attempts to develop a more complex analytical framework for socialist agriculture, and to apply it to the case of post-Mao China, perhaps the most sweeping agrarian 'reform' in the history of socialism. The purpose of doing so is to disaggregate the complex changes which have been wrought under the 'responsibility systems' in order to get a more nuanced sense of what has and has not changed, how the various parts fit together, and where the axes of contradiction posed by the 'reform' may lie. This analytical framework may also be of use in comparative analysis of socialist agriculture, though that enterprise is not attempted here.

* This article was written during a wonderful research leave financed by Oberlin College and hosted by the Institute of Development Studies, University of Sussex (England). I wish to thank them for their material and intellectual support. In particular, I benefited from discussing issues related to those raised here with Gordon White, though I am sure he would not want (nor does he deserve) any of the burden of responsibility for what appears in these pages. The article was presented in draft form at the Institute of Social Studies (The Hague) and the Sinological Institute of the University of Leiden, to both of which I wish to express my gratefulness for sponsoring and hosting enjoyable, stimulating visits; comments of scholars at both institutions were helpful in preparing this revision.

Parenthetically, this exercise may have something to contribute to the thorny and slippery question of 'modes of production'. One of the most serious problems with the debates over this issue has been inadequate conceptualisation of the 'relations of production' — the tendency to reduce them to feudalism, capitalism or socialism. When reality failed to conform to the basic outlines of one of these great 'isms', the response was to begin to speak of combinations of different modes — the great 'articulation' debate.[3] While much progress came from this innovation, it too ran into serious obstacles, the most poignant and damning testimony to which is the fact that so little empirical research has come out of it.[4] The reason for the problem may lie in the fact that the very concept of mode of production, or even its key sub-concept relations of production, is too gross and unwieldy. In any given situation, the real social relations surrounding economic life contain many heterogeneous elements, some of which may have something in common with the great 'isms' and others of which may be hybrids or different species altogether. Indeed, one basic argument of this study will be that the 'responsibility systems' of the recent Chinese 'reforms' are precisely that: neither socialist nor capitalist, but something distinctive. In order to get at this issue, the potentially heterogeneous elements of a given 'relation of production' must be identified, disaggregated, analysed one by one and then reconstituted, thereby exposing the nature, dynamics and contradictions of the whole. That is the methodological approach taken here.

We begin, then, with the following conceptual scheme for unpacking 'relations of production' which, it may be noted, is understood in what Wolpe calls its 'extended' sense in order to capture as many analytical elements as possible.[5] The relations of production in socialist agriculture may be said to be comprised of six elements:

(1) *Ownership* of the forces of production, which in turn has several distinct aspects: *formal* or juridical ownership (as codified in law and legal documents); what I will call *actual* ownership (the capacity to alienate the property or to realise income merely from owning it — by renting it, leasing it, using it as collateral, etc.); and what I will call *practical* ownership or, more simply, *possession* (the capacity to use the property in productive activity unencumbered by competing claims of formal or actual owners, as for example, in Yugoslavian self-managed enterprises).

(2) The relationships and *processes by which labour is mobilised* and applied to the existing natural and capital bases. This includes the *relationship between owners and workers, production of the labour force* (socialisation, training), allocation of the labour force to particular jobs within a division of labour, and *reproduction of the labour force*.

(3) The *productive micro-processes* (determination of the *division of labour*, arrangement of the *labour process, management* of actual production).

(4) *Productive macro-processes* (*planning, investment*).

(5) *Division of the social product* (*distribution* to producers and owners, *appropriation* of the surplus).

(6) The nature and processes of *exchange* (*price* determination, *institutional channels* of exchange, the level of *commodification* of the social product).

With these stipulations in mind, the features of the rural collective relations of production in China in the periods before and after the 1978 'reforms' may now be explicated.

II. HIGH COLLECTIVISM, c. 1965–78

The following generalisations[6] apply to the period starting around 1965 – which brought to an end the various adjustments and readjustments that came in the wake of the formation of the people's communes during the high tide of the Great Leap Forward – and ending around December 1978, when the Third Plenum of the Eleventh Central Committee of the Chinese Communist Party met, a new set of leaders headed by Deng Xiao-ping consolidated their power, and sweeping rural reforms, until then advanced only hesitantly, locally and experimentally, were given official imprimatur. The rural productive relations of this period can be dubbed 'high collectivism'.

*Ownership*

The concept of ownership must be subdivided into its *forms* (formal, actual, practical) as well as its *objects*: land, agricultural capital goods (machinery, animals used for agricultural production [draught animals, fertiliser producers], animals used for consumption or sale, production-related physical plant [for example, pig sties], enterprise capital and consumption goods (housing, personal effects). Let us begin with *land*. With the exception of land on which houses and major through roads were built, almost all agricultural land was *formally* owned by the basic accounting units of the rural collectives – usually the production teams.[7] Turning to *actual ownership*, the teams (or brigades or communes where they were basic units of account) had the power to alienate the land through sale or exchange, although the state set strict limits (for example, land could not be sold to private individuals) and retained a strong role in regulating and even arranging such sales and exchanges. Presumably it also retained a right of eminent domain, although if any unit of the state sought to acquire land from a production team (or brigade or commune), it was required to pay compensation subject to negotiation and value assessment by elaborate formulae. The collective owners of land were also not free to use the land to generate income apart from putting it into production: they could not rent or lease it or put it up for collateral. Here the state retained a small measure of actual ownership through its claim on a share of the land's output as agricultural tax. Finally, *practical ownership* or *possession* – that is, the capacity to use the property in productive activity unencumbered by competing claims – rested with the teams (except for the state's tax claim) for collectively cultivated land, and with households in the form of their private plots. The Chinese term for these is not 'private plots' – which would be *siren di* or *siyou di* – but *ziliu di*, which literally means 'privately (or self-) retained land'. Formal ownership of these plots remained with the teams, which allocated them to peasants for clearly specified periods after which they were taken back for redistribution. Nevertheless, they were a form of private practical ownership or possession since the peasants paid no rent or fees for them, and could keep everything they grew on them free and clear.

*Agricultural capital* can be divided into that owned *in all senses* by the collective units and that owned, also in all senses, by households. Large pieces of agricultural equipment, draught animals and production-related physical plant were formally owned by the collective units, which also could sell, rent, lease or exchange them (although only to other collectives or the state) and reap all the proceeds of their contributions to production. Smaller tools and animals raised for consumption or sale (like pigs or chickens) were generally formally owned by households who could sell, lease, exchange and use them as they wished subject to certain exchange regulations *imposed by the state* (concerning permissible price range, quality [for example, pigs had to reach a certain weight before slaughter], etc.). The major exception was collective ownership of pigs, which was tried in some places, usually with poor results and therefore usually short-lived.

*Formal, actual* and *practical ownership* of *enterprise capital* rested with the collectives. The state exercised a claim against them for income tax, but it could not appropriate them without compensation.

Finally, *consumption goods* like housing and personal effects were usually owned privately, with full rights of alienation and use. The major exception was collective ownership of housing in a few economically advanced places; but even this did not violate the principle of private property (existing private houses were not to be appropriated) so much as obviate or supplement it (by constructing new housing, the occupants of which could either keep their old houses too or dismantle them and sell off the reusable building materials). Of course there were also collectively owned consumer items like television sets, table tennis sets and the like.

## Labour Mobilisation

*Owner–worker relations* in the period of 'high collectivism' can be characterised as akin to co-operative membership. In theory the peasants each owned equal and undivided shares of their collective units. Formally, they had equal political rights in its management, and drew incomes from it as shares of its net distributable income in proportion to the work they did as evaluated by the collective. Their collective incomes were a function, then, both of the collective's economic performance (which determined the value of the work point or labour day) and their own work performance in it (which determined how many work points they drew). It is significant, then, that in ordinary language peasants used the term 'commune members' (*she yuan*) rather than 'employees' to describe each other.

Of course all this applies to their collective work only. Peasants also employed their own labour on a household basis on their private plots and in other household production such as pig and chicken raising. Although often important in helping make ends meet or in generating a surplus for household consumption, these forms of peasant self-employment were generally secondary in terms of total household labour time (excluding housekeeping) and income.

*Production of the labour force* refers to the processes by which people are socialised and trained to fill the economy's needs for labour. In the period of high collectivism, this function was shared among the household, the collective and the state. Specifically, the household communicated values about work and social discipline, and also passed along basic skills. Collectives attempted to foster norms of labour responsibility toward the collective (through formal political education and informal political and social pressure) while also cultivating development of general and specialised technical skills (through schools, formal training programmes and informal processes in the collective work setting). The state too contributed to socialising and training the work force through propaganda as well as political and technical training.

*Allocation of the labour force* was handled by the collective, often quite democratically, for its work processes, and by the household for those it handled. *Reproduction of the labour force* was the primary responsibility of the household, although the collective played a part through its roles in organising and supplying health care, guaranteeing minimum supplies of food and providing welfare subsidies for the very poor.

### Production Micro-Processes

The third category of elements of productive relations is the *micro-processes of production*, including the determination of the *division of labour* and specification and *management* of the actual work processes. Of course, the household handled these micro-processes in the areas of production under its purview. More interesting are the processes of discharging these functions in the collective sector, where they were all handled collectively. Local leaders handled much of this routine work, but there is considerable evidence that: (a) these leaders were elected quite democratically in many places; (b) major criteria in choosing them were their skill and fairness in handling these micro-processes of production; and (c) team members could and often did exercise considerable direct influence over these matters, for example, at meetings to decide how to organise work or how to distribute work points.[8] Moreover, the team members also played a direct role in supervising daily work through social pressure on each other at the work site. They did so at least partly out of economic self-interest: each peasant knew that his or her income depended heavily on the value of the work point, which in turn depended on the economic performance of the team as a whole. Therefore, both in the explicitly political arena of selecting leaders, influencing them, and making collective decisions in directly participatory ways, and in the social-interactive arena of bringing pressure to bear on each other during the work process, peasants were intimately involved in the *collective determination* of their livelihoods.

### Production Macro-Processes

Fourth are the *macro-processes of production*, including *planning* and *investment*. For collective production, these functions were shared by the collectives and the state. In planning, the state set targets and quotas – sometimes for acreage, sometimes for output – for various crops down to the commune level. In theory these were subject to negotiation between the commune and its immediately superordinate level of the state (the county government). While the process has never been studied, subsequent criticisms suggest quite strongly that the communes in fact had little say in the specification of their plans by the state (although they could influence them by indirect means such as failing to meet previous targets). Once the commune targets were set, they were apportioned downward through the remaining layers of the rural collective sector, again in principle (and again, probably much less in practice) through negotiation. The state also regulated the scope of collective production planning and investment through its control over levers of credit, state investment funds, key inputs, technical knowledge and innovations, extension services and so forth. Still, the teams generated much of their own investment capital and made their own decisions about using it, again within legal, political and planning parameters set by the state. In many cases they did so quite democratically.

The state also played an important role in restricting the scope of planning and investment options available to the households in their own productive processes. While in principle peasants could grow anything they wished on their private plots, in practice they could only grow what was either permissible for sale (and profitable within state-determined price structures) or what they could consume themselves. They were expressly forbidden from engaging in certain types of endeavours such as handicraft production, provision of many services on a private basis, commerce or (most certainly!) renting productive resources or labour.

### Division of the Social Product

The fifth aspect, *division of the social product*, has already been touched upon. For collective production, the social product was aggregated for the 'basic accounting unit' (production team, brigade or commune). The state took its share by levying a tax on the basic collectives, and the collectives then took a share – the size of which was determined collectively and often quite democratically, although within parameters set by the state – for reproduction, expanded reproduction and collective consumption. The rest was then divided up among the members, again in a collective decision process which was often highly democratic and participatory, although also within political guidelines emanating from the state (for example, for a time, piece-rate or task-rate payment was permissible though discouraged). The product of the household sector was appropriated and internally distributed directly by the household.

In general, then, while the state and the individual households each played some role in appropriating and influencing the disposition of the social product, the major role was played by the rural collective units.

### Exchange

Once the product was appropriated and distributed, however, it was subject to a process of *exchange valuation* in which the role of the state was crucial through its power to set prices. In a sense, then, *while the collectives played the major role in distributing income, the state*, acting through the price structure, determined how much this income was really worth in terms of the products of the wider economy. Moreover, the state *regulated exchange* directly through its virtual monopoly over commerce. The collectives did have their own supply and marketing cooperatives, which appear to have functioned less as local co-ops than as *de facto* agencies of state commercial enterprises. Some very minor rural markets were permitted, at which, for example, peasants could sell vegetables from their private plots; but these were very tightly circumscribed and regulated by the state.

## Summary

These various features of the rural relations of production are summarised in Table 1. While the collectives played the major role in many areas, state and private forms were also very significant, and in some respects (like commerce) primary. In short, productive relations in the 'high collectivist' period were in fact structured by a complex articulation of state, collective and private forms in which the collectives were often but not always primary.

### III. CONTRACTUAL COLLECTIVISM, 1979 TO THE PRESENT

The changes in the organisation of rural production which have taken place since the Third Plenum are much more than reforms. They amount in many instances to nothing less than a fundamental transformation of many aspects of the relations of production. Before analysis can proceed, a brief summary of the three general categories of responsibility systems is necessary. The first can be called specialised contracting, in which peasants contract with their collectives to do specific tasks, in return for which they receive agreed-upon amounts of work points.[9] The second can be called production contracting (*bao chan*), under which the collective makes a more comprehensive contract with a group of peasants or even with a single household.[10] It allocates land, production expenses, certain inputs and a fixed number of work points to the peasant contractors. It also specifies in the contract a production plan complete with crop targets. In return, the peasants must turn over the targeted outputs to the collective. They receive bonuses or penalties for over- or under-fulfilment. The third form of responsibility system, which has become predominant, is known as 'contracting in a big way' (*da bao gan*). Here individual households contract with the collective to use its land and perhaps certain pieces of agricultural capital. In return, the peasants take responsibility for a share of the collective's tax and grain sales quotas to the state, and also agree to pay to the collective an additional sum which the latter retains for itself. After meeting these obligations, the peasants keep everything they have produced. Should they fail to produce enough to meet their contractual obligations, they must solve the problem themselves by taking on debt or selling off assets.

TABLE 1

SUMMARY OF ELEMENTS OF HIGH COLLECTIVIST AND CONTRACTUAL
COLLECTIVIST RELATIONS OF PRODUCTION

|  | *High Collectivist* | *Contractual Collectivist* |
|---|---|---|
| Ownership |  |  |
| Land |  |  |
| Juridical/formal | Collective | Collective |
| Actual |  |  |
| Alienation | Collective/state | Collective/state |
| Realisation of non- |  |  |
| productive income | State | Collective/state |
| Practical (possession) | Collective(private) | Collective(private?) |
| Agricultural capital |  |  |
| Juridical/formal | Collective(private) | Collective/private |
| Actual |  |  |
| Alienation | Collective(private) | Collective/private |
| Realisation of income | Collective(private) | Collective/private |
| Practical (possession) | Collective(private) | Collective/private |
| Enterprise capital |  |  |
| All senses | Collective | Collective/private |
| Consumption goods |  |  |
| All senses | Private(collective) | Private |
| Labor mobilisation |  |  |
| Employment relations | Collective | Collective/small group/ quasi-tenancy/wage labour |
| Production of work force | State/collective/ private | Private(collective?) |
| Allocation of work | Collective | Collective/private? |
| Reproduction of labour force | Private(collective) | Private |
| Micro-processes of production |  |  |
| Division of labour | Collective | Collective/group/private |
| Management of labour process | Collective | Collective/group/private |
| Macro-processes of production |  |  |
| Planning | State/collective | State/collective/private |
| Investment | State/collective | State/collective/private |
| Division of social product |  |  |
| Surplus appropriation | State/collective | State/collective/private |
| Distribution to producers | Collective | Contractual |
| Exchange |  |  |
| Price determination | State | State/market |
| Institutions | State(collective) | State/market |
| Level of commodification (and |  |  |
| socialisation of production) | Lower | Higher |

Legend:  /  : shared function
        ( )  : minor function

*Ownership*

Under all these categories of responsibility system, *formal ownership of land* remains vested with the basic accounting unit of the collective, which now more than ever is the production team (since accounting at the higher levels of the brigade and commune has come under attack). *Actual ownership of land* resides with the state and the collectives. The previous situation with regard to *alienation* of the land still prevails: only the collectives may do so, under close state regulation. That the Party has of late been issuing warnings to teams not to sell or divide their land for peasant ownership indicates both the strength of the forces which have been set in motion by the 'reforms' and the commitment of the Party to the maintenance of formal and actual ownership at the collective level. (There have been sporadic recent reports of the abolition of production teams altogether, which raises some new questions and possibilities in this and other areas.) In terms of the other aspect of actual ownership − the capacity to realise income directly from mere ownership rather than use in production − whereas under high collectivism only the state could be seen as possessing this aspect of ownership by virtue of its tax collections, now the collectives do as well by appropriating a portion of the social product produced by peasants on land which the team has contracted to allow them to use. Of course the team retained a share of the social product under high collectivism too, but since it was the team which had collectively produced and therefore which owned the product in the first place, this cannot really be conceptualised as appropriation. Even at present, because specialised and production contracting involve renumeration in work points, which ties the interests of the contractors to those of the collective as a whole, it is not strictly correct to see this retention by the collective of a share of the social product as appropriation. But certainly in cases, under 'contracting in a big way', where work points disappear and contracts take the form of an agreement by the collective to allow the peasants to use team land in return for a fixed amount of the output with the peasants absorbing all the residual surplus or loss, we can speak of appropriation.

Here arises one of the major contradictions of *da bao gan* contractual collectivism: *part of the surplus generated by the direct producers is appropriated from them by a collective unit of the associated producers.* This may be conceptualised either as *rent* or as *dues*, depending on other aspects of the productive relations embodied in the collective. To the extent that the collective is relatively autonomous from the members politically and financially (for example, where they were converted into somewhat independent 'companies' [*gongsi*]), this appropriation begins to look quite a bit like rent. To the extent that the collectives (or even 'companies' that succeed them) are more genuinely co-operative in terms of management and distribution, the appropriation would be better conceptualised as association dues.

Finally, there is the question of *practical ownership* or *possession* of land. Under specialized and production contracting, income from the production on the land belongs to the collective, which distributes part of it to its members in accord with the terms of contracts with them to work on the land. So practical ownership still rests with the collective. Yet it is frequently argued that the predominant *da bao gan* system of responsibility, in which households contract to use land (rather than apply labour), amounts in effect to a return to private ownership. The tendency toward long-term contracts has reinforced this view. The retention under *da bao gan* of formal ownership by the collectives is often dismissed tautologically as a *mere* formality. *Da bao gan* can more appropriately be understood as involving an abstract surface right for the peasants to farm an unspecified piece of the collective's land. Long term contracts do make this surface right more concrete by tying it to a particular plot for a long enough period of time to begin potentially to become customary. But even the surface right effected by *da bao gan* is different from practical (not to mention formal or actual) ownership. Peasants who farm land under this responsibility system do so under several serious limitations. First, of course, is the fact that they must pay for it. Second, the state and collectives, through the contracting process, specify to a significant degree what the peasants can grow. Third, upon expiration of the contract, the collective may recall the land for other uses, reallocate it, or set new contractual conditions (that is, raise its charges). Fourth is the possibility of political and policy change in the contracting system itself. Thus, even under *da bao gan* the collectives and the state continue to have many of the prerogatives of practical ownership; that is why the retention of formal land ownership by the collectives is no *mere* formality.[11]

Ownership of *agricultural capital* has changed more markedly. Whereas under high collectivism large pieces of equipment, draught animals and production-related physical plant were collectively owned, and individuals were barred from any aspects of ownership, now peasants may acquire even *formal ownership* of tractors, draught animals and physical plant. Moreover, they may also exercise *actual* ownership by selling or renting it or by hiring labour to work on it.

The fact that the state and collectives retain many aspects of ownership of *land* while the individual peasants are gaining fuller and more extensive ownership of agricultural *capital* creates a potentially serious *structural contradiction* for contractual collectivism. It is likely to present itself with increasing gravity as agricultural development becomes more capital intensive. Peasant owners of key capital inputs may well find themselves in a position to demand stronger ownership forms for themselves in land as well; conversely, the state and the collectives may find it difficult to induce peasants to invest in or to use their own agricultural capital without transferring fuller land ownership to them. Of course, the collectives or the state could counter this by substituting their own agricultural capital for that owned by the peasants. The conditions for them to do so are partly in place, at least in terms of ownership. At present the collectives retain, as under high collectivism, their rights of *formal* ownership of agricultural capital too, and they have, like the peasants, also added new dimensions of ownership by acquiring actual ownership powers which they formerly lacked or had in only the most limited way; specifically, they may now sell or rent out their capital more freely and legitimately than they did in the past. So they are, at least in terms of ownership, in a good position to compete with the individual peasants in the area of agricultural capital. But whether they will be able to do so successfully –

and thereby avoid the possible contradiction between collective land ownership and private capital ownership — depends not only on ownership but also
on their capacity to accumulate financial capital relative to the peasants'
capacity to do so. Here the prospects are harder to predict, since forces exist
in contractual collectivism which would favour both loci of accumulation.

Some of the same tendencies apply to *enterprise capital*. While collective
enterprises still exist and appear to be thriving, peasants are now permitted
— and even encouraged — to open their own private enterprises, either indi-
vidually or jointly by banding together to form joint stock companies. One
particularly interesting development that has received favourable publicity in
the Chinese press has been the formation of joint private–collective enterprises. They may even hire labour to work in these enterprises. Surely some
furious competition between the private and collective sectors (and also
between the private sector and the lower levels of the state sector) is in store;
indeed, the state is hoping that such competition will improve the efficiency
and profitability of collective and local state enterprises. If it goes on for very
long, this competition will surely lead to some social and political contradictions that could be of great moment for Chinese socialism and the Chinese
state. That is, the 'two line struggle' between the 'capitalist and socialist roads'
may rear its head again, this time with the 'capitalist' tendency having a much
firmer material base than it did in the 1960s, when its existence was, perhaps
somewhat dubiously, first identified.

Collective *consumption goods* of the period of high collectivism have now
largely been privatised. Much collective housing has been sold off to individual
households, and public services like collective health insurance plans and
schools have been closed down in many places.

In short, there have been some very significant changes in ownership since
the advent of contractual collectivism. Land remains collectively rather than
privately owned both formally and actually, and the peasants do not appear
to have gained practical ownership or possession of it, although under *da bao
gan*, they have acquired in effect a surface right. If anything, the collectives
have expanded their actual ownership rights in the direction of the capacity
effectively to rent out their land or collect dues for it. In terms of agricultural
capital, enterprise capital and consumption goods, private ownership in
various senses has considerably expanded, sometimes in parallel with and
sometimes even at the expense of, and, more significantly, in potential
contradiction with, collective ownership.

## Mobilisation of Labour

*Employment relations* under the responsibility system are difficult to con-
ceptualise, because they involve contracts between the collectives and the
individual peasants, the latter of whom are in some senses independent of the
collectives (a 'private sector') and in others still *members of the collectives
with which they are contracting.*

In specialised contracting, employment relations differ little from piece-
or task-rate systems of work point allocation which were common during the
period of high collectivism. They are decidedly different from a wage labour

system, since the payment is in work points, which are a claim on a share of the team's distributable income; hence, the peasants still have a strong stake in the overall economic performance of the collective, on which depends the value of their work points. Under 'production contracting' employment relations have something of the character of contractual relationships between private individuals (organised as households or work groups) on the one hand and collectives on the other. But because *remuneration is still made in work points, the contractors are not independent of the collectives with which they are contracting*. The relationship between them cannot, in other words, strictly be seen as one between private and collective sectors. It would be more appropriate to characterise it as one involving *relations between the parts of a collective and the whole collective*. Under *da bao gan* the *identity of interest between the peasants and the collective, which is embodied in the work point, is broken*. In terms of employment relations, the peasant contractors are more fully privatised.

Turning to *production of the labour force*, the role of the collectives and the state has been reduced. Political study in the villages has been cut back or eliminated, and the more individuated work processes of contractual collectivism have reduced the opportunities for members of the collective to instil certain values and patterns of work in each other through social pressure at the actual work sites.

Similarly, the collective has lost some of its role in transmitting and developing skills both off but especially on the job. Under contractual collectivism, socialisation and training of the labour force have fallen more fully under the purview of the households and, to a somewhat lesser extent than before, the state. Despite sharp criticism of 'moral incentives', the recent 'socialist ethics' campaign indicates that the state is still not beneath using moral exhortation and propaganda to try to socialise the labour force into certain values about work in general.

In the high collectivist period, *allocation of work* to specific persons (within a given division of labour) was handled through a process which usually had some significant collective character, albeit to greater or lesser degrees or with more or less explicitness. Now it is made through the *apparently* more individuated, segmented process of contracting. Whether this is just appearance will have to await further research into the micro-politics of the contracting process. Given what is already known about the lively participatory politics that took place in rural China during the high collectivist period over issues of this sort, it may be that a similarly lively political process takes place in the collective over the allocation of contracts. It is also possible that under the new, more segmented divisions of labour, the propensity or capacity of peasants for effective participation in collective affairs may have been eroded. We shall return to this question below.

Finally, while *reproduction of the labour force* even under high collectivism was by and large the responsibility of the household, now the collective's role has shrunk even further, with the decline of collective health services, minimum food guarantees and welfare subsidies for the very poor. As households have gained autonomy, they have presented the state with a major problem of planning population growth.

*Production Micro-Processes*

Under high collectivism, *determination of the division of labour* within the productive unit and *specification and management of the actual work processes* were handled by the collectives, apparently in a rather democratic fashion. To some extent the collectives still discharge these functions, although now less through a collective democratic process and more by arrangement and supervision of contracts. How the collectives now arrive at a division of labour (on the basis of which to let contracts) is also an area for further research, although the general thrust of policies on planning and management would suggest a drift towards technocratic rather than participatory criteria and methods.

Once the division of labour is determined and workers allocated within it, there are still the problems of managing and supervising the work process. Under high collectivism, this was handled by a combination of monitoring by elected local officials, direct mass participatory political processes (at work point meetings, for example), and continuous monitoring by other peasants working on the same job nearby (whose interest in maintaining certain standards of work derived at least partly from the fact that their incomes depended – via the work point – on the economic performance of the collective as a whole). Now, management and supervision of the labour process is the responsibility of the contracting group or household. The peasants have lost control of the capacity to set work standards and monitor work performance for the collective as a whole; hence they have less control over its economic performance. Yet, if they still receive remuneration in work points, their incomes continue to depend on that performance. In this sense, they have been separated from the capacity to control some of the important forces which determine their livelihood. This is a *key contradiction* of the specialised and production contracting responsibility systems, which may have had something to do with their relatively rapid demise and the corresponding rise of 'contracting in a big way' to a predominant position. One major and still unresolved analytical problem revolves around the question of why Chinese peasants, who made high collectivism work satisfactorily for two decades, could abandon it so rapidly and utterly rather than embracing moderate reforms more fully. This analysis suggests that perhaps they preferred depending mainly on themselves to a situation in which they depended on their neighbours but could not control or monitor them.

*Production Macro-Processes*

The state still plays a major role in agricultural *planning*. It is unclear whether the relationship between the lowest level of collective organisation – the team – and its superior units, and among its superior units, in the planning process has changed. Within the team, the method of implementing plans passed down from above now takes the form of regulation by contract with peasant producers. The scope of production planning and regulation has also been reduced, and restrictions on engaging in many sorts of sidelines have been lifted, so that the collectives and peasants have greater latitude to determine the nature of their production activities.

*Investment* decisions and finance, which under high collectivism were undertaken by the state and the collectives, have now been extended to the peasants as well. Individuals, households and groups of peasants may now purchase equipment and use credit to finance productive activities. In agriculture, under the specialised and production contracting types of responsibility system, the collectives provide investment funds and stipulate their use, while under 'contracting in a big way' it is the peasants' own responsibility to invest in the land and the annual crop.

### Division of the Social Product

The state still has the first claim on the social product through taxation. And the collectives still have the next claim for their own accumulation which they exercise either by retaining a share of output before setting aside a distribution fund (under the specialised and production contracting responsibility systems which use work points) or by stipulating rent-like payments in 'contracting in a big way'. Then comes the share for distribution to the peasant producers. Under specialised and production contracting, this share is still subject to collective mediation, since it is allocated in the form of work points which are a claim on a share of the collective distributable income. The use of bonuses and penalties in these systems complicates matters. The most extreme departure from this principle of collective determination occurs under 'contracting in a big way', where peasants' incomes are simply the residual of what they have produced after remitting their taxes and quotas. But in the more moderate forms of responsibility system, it is mistaken to think that collective distribution of income has been abolished. It has not. But there probably has been a marked *attenuation of the extent to which this collective mediation of income is subject to collective determination and control*. Under high collectivism, decisions about income distribution – how much collective income to distribute, what distributive criteria to use and how to apply them – were often subject to lively mass participation. They were based upon and in turn provided the basis for direct mass supervision of the work process. Under contractual collectivism, the contracting process is probably less subject to collective democratic participation, although for now this can only be an hypothesis for future research. Whatever the case may be, where peasants' incomes are, under the specialised and production contract responsibility systems, still subject to collective mediation (through the work point), peasants have lost much of their capacity to control or influence the collective actions through which their incomes are mediated. This may well be another aspect of their major contradiction discussed above: that peasants must depend on each other but have no means of controlling each other.

### Exchange

State determination of almost all prices has now given way to a more variegated pricing structure. For certain basic staples (like grain and cotton), prices remain under close state regulation although they have been adjusted to improve incentives and take greater account of scarcities. For other products, prices have been allowed to seek levels more closely in accord with shadow market prices. For still others, regulations have been removed altogether. At the same time, free markets have been allowed to proliferate and to compete with state commercial agencies, even in key products like grain (although here the state keeps a watchful eye to prevent or to detect speculation). The increased latitude given to prices and markets complements the increased latitude of collectives and peasants to do their own planning and investment; indeed, they are encouraged to look to the market for their signals of what to produce beyond that which they must for state plans and for their own consumption. In fact, the 'reforms' in the area of exchange are intended to undercut the peasants' preoccupation with self-provision, which was reinforced by the planning priorities of the Maoist period. The development of more open and elaborate marketing systems is intended to encourage rural producers to specialise more in accord with their comparative advantage, even to the extent of meeting many of their own consumption needs through purchase rather than their own production. That is, it is expected both to guide their production into profitable areas and to help them concentrate on these areas by relieving them of the need to produce all of their own necessities. Production for exchange is to replace production for use. Socialisation of production is to replace self-reliance. A more fully integrated rural economy is to replace the cellular-like one of the past.[12] All of this is expected to promote quantitative and qualitative development of the productive forces, both in the city and countryside, and both in industry and agriculture.

Here the familiar contradiction of plan and market presents itself. The great plans for increased socialisation of agriculture and rural industry and its tighter articulation with urban industry will, the state has made all too clear, have to take place in China under central planning. Aside from the obvious political motivations of Party leaders and state planners, there are good reasons for this position in terms of China's economic development. To mention just one, markets can probably not be relied upon to make the major infrastructural and human capital investments that the Chinese economy requires or in the relatively balanced form that socialist development demands. Whatever the case may be, as free channels of exchange like open markets and market prices develop, the state will undoubtedly face greater difficulties in realising its agricultural plans through the contracting system. Peasants who face the choice between meeting their contractual responsibilities or producing more profitably for the market can confidently be expected to orient themselves to the latter. And with the general decline of rural collective organs and the explicit separation of local political and economic authority that is accompanying it, the state will find it increasingly difficult to bring meaningful pressures and sanctions to bear on the peasants to make and fulfil contracts on the state's terms. Chinese peasants, like their counterparts in so much of the world, have a genius for avoiding, resisting and, when necessary, defying the power of state authority. To the extent that they can upset the state's plans for them, they can also throw a very large monkey-wrench into its plans for development of the wider economy. The effects of this would reverberate through the cities and the urban-based classes (workers, intellectuals, state salariat) in dangerous and unpredictable ways. Plan and market, therefore, present a very serious contradiction not only to countractual collectivism, but from there to the rest of the Chinese political economy as well.

*Summary*

To what does the change from high collectivism to contractual collectivism amount to? What manner of beast is this new set of productive relations? Let us first say what it is *not,* in order to clear the air of simplistic analyses which have been advanced in various quarters. Contractual collectivism is *not capitalist*: it has not created unadulterated or primary private ownership (although it has expanded it within continuing collective ownership), and it has not separated the producers from the means of production. *Nor does it spell the end of collectivism.* It is *not a return either to feudalism or to a private economy of independent smallholders.* Rather, it forms a complex articulation of collective and private elements under reduced but still continuing state regulation.

The analytical problem is to sort out the relationships among these collective, private and state elements. Quantitatively, there has clearly been a devolution of various powers downward from the state to the collectives and from the collectives to the private sphere (organised as groups of peasants, households or even single individuals). More interesting and difficult is the qualitative specification of their relationships. They are defined by contract, but how are these contracts to be understood? What sort of mediation between collective and private do they constitute? And how does it differ from the collective/private relationship under high collectivism?

Clearly there is a greater *separation* now between the collective and the private spheres. Under high collectivism, the private sphere was enmeshed almost completely in, and depended almost completely on, collective units and productive relations. The major exceptions were the private plot and the household pig. Now, peasants have acquired private property in agricultural and enterprise capital, and greater independence in *using* the land (although they are still debarred from *owning* it in any meaningful way, including *possessing* it as defined here). They also play greater roles than before in defining the division of labour, managing the labour process, engaging in planning and investment, and participating in the wider economy through exchange. Although allocation of income to them is still collectively mediated in specialised and production contracting (via distribution in work points), segmentation of the contract process and the division of labour along with the use of bonuses and penalties have undercut the scope and importance of this. Moreover, in 'contracting in a big way', the collective mediation of income has effectively been broken. Yet, it is also clear that the collectives (as well as the state) continue to play major roles in various aspects of ownership, labour mobilisation, the macro- and micro-processes and production, division of the social product, and exchange. So the separation of private and collective forms is only partial at best.

We are brought back, then, to the question of the nature of the continuing ties that bind. They are contractual, but not in the sense of agreement between fully independent parties. Peasants are still members of their collectives, and as long as collectives continue to exercise various functions in the productive relations (such as ownership, division of social product, labour mobilisation, and perhaps even the contracting process itself), this is no mere juridical formalism. *Responsibility system contracts define relationships between the collective and its parts in a setting in which the parts have a particular interest but in some instances also a general interest in the whole.* It is this continuing link between private and collective interest which defines their distinctive character. They must be understood, therefore, as embodying a productive relationship which is neither fully collective nor fully private, but instead something of a *hybrid*: a *distinctive* species which derives some of its characteristics from each of its parents but which is irreducible to either of them and in that sense is something new under the sun.

IV. CONCLUSION: THE CONTRADICTIONS OF CONTRACTUAL COLLECTIVISM

With these structural features of contractual collectivism in mind, we can now proceed to analyse some of its contradictions. A number of these, which have already been discussed, can be termed *structural contradictions* because they represent tensions among aspects of contractual collectivism itself. One is that between the predominantly collective character of land ownership and the increasingly private character of ownership of agricultural capital. This will grow more serious as the latter continues to gain importance in rural economic development. Another is the contradiction between the continuing role, at least under the specialised and production contract systems, of the collectives in determining the incomes of individual peasants on the one hand and, on the other, the diminished capacities of those same peasants to influence that collective process, either through direct supervision of fellow peasants on the job or at collective meetings where income-related matters are decided. A third is the tension between state planning (implemented through the contracts) and the expansion of private, free markets (which attracts peasants to extra-contractual production). A fourth is the contradiction between the expansion of private ownership of enterprise capital and the development of local collective and state-run enterprises; this too will become more serious as local enterprises loom larger and larger in the more diversified rural economy envisioned by Chinese planners. Some of these contradictions may help explain changes which the responsibility systems have undergone as they have developed over the past few years. For example, that between collective income determination and declining collective social and political relations may, as argued above, have had something to do with the unexpectedly[13] rapid movement toward the highly individualistic 'contracting in a big way' after two decades of reasonably successful high collectivism. For the future, they suggest that contractual collectivism is less stable a 'reform' than is implied by the great enthusiasm for it expressed by Chinese leaders and by so many outside observers.

Contractual collectivism also stands in contradiction with other elements of China's socialist political economy, some of these quite fundamental. The first of these has to do with the commitment of any socialist country to basic economic *equality*, albeit within parameters set by the need to provide economic incentives to workers and administrators so as to promote the development of the productive forces (another fundamental goal of socialism, to which we shall return). This commitment is summed up in the phrase 'pay according to work', the basic principle of socialist distribution. This seemingly simple phrase is, of course, quite ambiguous in practice, where it raises complex problems. Partly it means the absence of distribution according to ownership − distribution according to work *and only work*. But contractual collectivism contradicts this in permitting peasants to earn income by renting out their private capital, hiring labour to work on it and engaging in commerce for profit (unless the labour expended in trade is seen as productive work, a not altogether fanciful notion). Partly, 'pay according to work' means distributing the social product to the producers in accordance with the amount of socially necessary labour time they put into producing it − that is, in accordance with the law of value. But this can only be made operative to the extent that the transformation problem − the conversion of values into prices − is solved, an achievement which has eluded China as it has other economies. Vegetable farmers in the Shanghai suburbs do not owe their very high incomes to harder work than, or to the fact that they employ more dead labour than, their poor cousins growing low yield staple crops in Guizhou. Partly, 'pay according to work' means the use of more refined, precise and direct measures linking work to remuneration. The incentive value of such measures has been a major justification for the responsibility systems. Yet underneath the loud and so oft-repeated claims that contractual collectivism is needed to boost labour incentives, only the scantiest evidence and argument has actually been adduced to the effect that labour incentives failed under high collectivism − in other words, that peasants were goofing off − or that finer ones could not be erected in a more fully collectivist institutional setting.[14] While a more definitive conclusion would require a more detailed analysis, for now it can be said that, contrary to much of the propaganda and official justifications of contractual collectivism, which by and large have been accepted at their face value among so many outside observers, there is no *prima facie* reason to suppose that contractual collectivism comes any closer than high collectivism to realising the socialist principle of 'pay according to work'. Due partly (but not exclusively) to this, economic inequality in rural China is definitely on the rise. Far from evincing any concern about this, the Dengists applaud it, asserting that inequality is a good incentive, and that in any event it poses no threat of new class formations because of the absence of private property. But since private property is not at all absent, there is cause for serious concern. There is no reason to think that China will be able to avoid facing in some form the problems that uneven development and growing inequality and class stratification have presented in many other countries, including serious imbalances in demand structures, rising social tensions, and the politicisation of discontent arising therefrom.

Second, contractual collectivism contradicts the socialist commitment to *democratic control* by producers over the means of production, the conditions of work and other aspects of social life. The division of the collective into small social and economic segments and the concomitantly reduced scope of collective economic and political functions or purpose has severely undercut the social-interactive and interest bases for collective participatory politics − peasants are less in contact with each other and have less to be in contact with each other about. The political life of the production teams is, it can be hypothesised, far less lively, democratic or popular than it was in the past, and those decisions which the teams still have to make are probably decided in a much more elitist, administrative and technocratic manner.[15] The result is that in some very fundamental ways the peasants may have lost what ability they had secured under high collectivism to influence their conditions of work. It is implied in much official publicity that one advantage of the responsibility systems is that the peasants can now work more free of the oppresive authority of local officials. Indeed, it is now the peasant household which controls the micro-processes of daily production, such as arranging its division of labour and managing the actual work process. But in present social conditions this undoubtedly means greater authority not for all 'the peasants', but mainly for the male household heads. It therefore stands in contradiction to the goal of reducing patriarchy, to which we shall return below. But this aside, households still have not gained any significant influence over the state planning process, over investment decisions (beyond those small ones they make themselves), or over the larger division of labour within which their own contractual tasks are embedded. In short, they have gained some control over who in the household will do what, and to some extent what the household will do as a whole in the area of extra-contractual production. But they have not gained, and perhaps have even lost, influence over what they will be producing for the state and the collective. They have probably lost influence too over what they will be doing for the state or the collectives in other areas, such as military recruitment or selection of local leaders and functionaries. Finally, they have probably lost influence over the distribution of valued resources from the state, such as financial assistance, material supplies or educational opportunities.

Third, contractual collectivism has been accompanied by reduced provision of basic *social welfare* and services. To be sure, these changes have as much to do with policy as with the structural nature of contractual collectivism itself. That is, it would certainly be possible for the collectives or the state to undertake leadership in these areas – such as providing basic medical care, food rations for the needy, and minimal guarantees for the elderly (the old 'five guarantees' of high collectivism) – within the context of contractual collectivism. But to the extent that contractual collectivism undercuts the unity and solidarity of the collectives in political, ideological, social and material terms, it reduces their capacity to take a leading role in these areas, and also helps to undercut any propensity of the peasants to see their collective interests and responsibilities in addition to their private ones.

Fourth, and related to the previous point, contractual collectivism undercuts the capacity of the collectives and, through them, of the state, to promote *social modernisation*, such as the abolition of 'wasteful' consumption on feasts, the attack on superstition and aspects of religion, control of population growth, and so forth. The Dengist leadership, which has identified the source of many of the difficulties of China's rural socialist development (and indeed in its politics and state structures at large) in the continuing 'feudal' character of the country (and particularly the countryside), clearly regards the promotion of social modernisation as a key goal. One of the main purposes it has set for contractual collectivism is the elimination of the material base of the feudal economy – that is, the preoccupation of the peasants (and, it is alleged, their collectives) with self-provision and subsistence – and its replacement with patterns of production and consumption more articulated to the wider economy. Beyond the material level, the state leadership is also attacking 'feudal' culture directly through its campaigns for 'socialist morality' and against 'spiritual pollution'. Yet, the responsibility systems reduce this same leadership's capacity to reach the peasantry with its modern message. In the past, the collective units had been important grassroots organs in campaigns to control population, attack superstition and promote social change in other ways. Now that these local centres of political mobilisation have been transformed into mere units of economic administration, the capacity of the state leadership to pursue its social goals for the peasantry is more circumscribed.

A fifth contradiction – actually, an aspect of the previous one – is the effect of contractual collectivism on the socialist commitment to improving *equality between men and women*. By assigning greater autonomy and an increased role in production to the male-dominated household, the position of women is in myriad ways put at greater threat compared with high collectivist days. Women will now likely become subject to husbands and fathers in the sphere of production in ways which were far more muted under high collective forms of production. Even more serious is the reappearance of female infanticide, the pious condemnations of which in the Chinese press ring somewhat hollow when it is recalled that this particularly hideous recrudescence has something to do with the rural 'reforms' promoted by this very same leadership.[16]

Finally, there is the possible and, it can be argued, rather likely contradiction between contractual collectivism and the *development of the productive forces*, a basic goal of socialism and certainly one stressed most highly by the Dengist leadership. Indeed, the main reason offered for promoting the responsibility system is that it is the productive relationship most appropriate to the present stage of development of the forces of production, and that it can promote their further development. 'Development' here has two meanings: raising the *level* of productive forces (economic growth, production of more modern, sophisticated products) and increasing their level of *socialisation* and diversity (specialisation, commodification, integration, commercialisation).

It is probably too soon to evaluate the effects of contractual collectivism on production with much definitiveness. Grain production has risen unevenly since 1979, for reasons too complex and uncertain to summarise easily here. Cash and luxury crops have done much better, as planning has been readjusted and peasants have been given latitude to respond to the demands of the market. Whether these changes prove to be of a one-shot nature – allowing peasants to take up excess or underutilised capacity in labour, land and capital – or whether they provide a basis for continuing growth based on ever-greater intensity of production and continuing peasant entrepreneurship is impossible to say. Chinese economists and planners have identified low labour productivity as a major problem and have sought to raise it primarily by shedding labour from agriculture. Beyond this measure, increased labour productivity will require structural changes in farming, such as mechanisation, farmland reconstruction and infrastructure development, which could be impeded by the resuscitation of small plots and contractual collectivist institutions.

The expansion of cash crop production mentioned above attests to the effectiveness of the 'reforms' in advancing the level of socialisation of production based on specialisation of the productive forces. One Chinese account trumpeted triumphantly the fact that already 100 million peasants have dropped out of grain production.[17] Yet again the question arises of whether the reorganisation into small farm plots and the division of labour on a household or small group basis sets real limits to the development of more specialised, sophisticated kinds of production in the long or even medium run. Moreover, it is not at all clear that such specialisation could not have been undertaken on the basis of high collectivist productive relations. Chinese accounts do not make this any clearer, since they identify a main source of the predominance of self-reliant production as misguided planners and political leaders as well as the basic features of the high collectivist relations and structures of production.

In short, then, there are real questions about the argument that contractual collectivism is more appropriate than high collectivism to the present level of productive forces and to their future development. Nicholas Lardy has recently argued in a major study that the key obstacles to China's agricultural development, both historically and at present, lie not in the realm of productive relations but rather in macro-policies such as pricing, crop planning and marketing.[18] 'Much current analysis within China seems flawed ... in its belief that decollectivization can provide the basis for sustained growth of agriculture.'[19] His argument – and mine – is not that contractual collectivism will necessarily hurt agricultural growth in the long run, but that it may not help it either, and that the policy changes which can provide sustained growth do not require contractual collectivism or some other form of decollectivisation.

NOTES

1. Christine Pelzer White and Gordon White, 'Editorial', in Christine Pelzer White and Gordon White (eds.), 'Agriculture, The Peasantry and Socialist Development', *IDS Bulletin*, Vol. XIII, No. 4 (Sept. 1982), p. 2 and *passim*.
2. This infelicitous but now widely current phrase traces its provenance to Rudolf Bahro, *The Alternative in Eastern Europe* (London: New Left Books, 1978). Bahro speaks, in translation, of 'actually existing socialism'. The phrase refers to socialism as it has appeared in various countries, rather than as an ideal or ideological concept.
3. The literature here is far too extensive to attempt comprehensive bibliographic reference. Two of the most prominent summaries of the major viewpoints and issues are: Aidan Foster-Carter, 'The Modes of Production Controversy', *New Left Review*, No. 107 (Jan./Feb. 1978), pp. 47–77; and Harold Wolpe, ed., *The Articulation of Modes of Production* (London: Routledge & Kegan Paul, 1980).
4. This point is made in Foster-Carter, op. cit.
5. Wolpe, op. cit., pp. 34–43.
6. Of course this exercise involves much generalisation over time and space, in the process doing violence to the myriad variations of which those who have done detailed research on rural China (among which I count myself) are painfully aware. I will spare the reader any further apologies or self-exculpations on this point.
7. Very small plots were used by higher levels of the collectives – usually the brigades and communes – for experimentation or for the officials of these units to engage in their own productive labour. For the purposes of this analysis they can be regarded as insignificant.

8. Marc Blecher, 'Leader-Mass Relations in Rural Chinese Communities: Local Politics in a Revolutionary Society', Ph.D. dissertation, University of Chicago, 1978; 'Consensual Politics in Small Rural Chinese Communities', *Modern China*, Vol. V, No. 1 (Jan. 1979); John Burns, 'The Election of Production Team Cadres in Rural China, 1958–74', *China Quarterly* 74 (June 1978); Marc Blecher, 'The Mass Line and Leader-Mass Relations and Communications in Basic-Level Rural Communities', in Godwin Chu and Francis Hsu (eds.), *China's New Fabric* (London: Routledge & Kegan Paul International, 1983), pp. 63–86.
9. This is the system of 'contract work for specialised tasks, calculating reward by linking it to yield' (*zhuanye chengbao, lianchan jichou*).
10. Among others, the systems of 'unified management, linking output quota to the individual' (*tongyi jingying, lianchan daolao*), 'production contracted to the group, compensation linked to output' (*baochan daozu, lianchan jichou*), 'production contracted to households' (*baochan daohu*), and 'small-lot contracts, fixed compensation' (*xiaoduan baogong, dinge jichou*).
11. Perhaps one exception will help illustrate the point. Peasants have come closer to acquiring practical ownership over wasteland which they have cleared: they are given free and clear rights for up to several decades to farm this land as they wish and keep all the proceeds.
12. The term 'cellular' derives from Audrey Donnithorne, 'China's Cellular Economy: Some Economic Trends Since the Cultural Revolution', *China Quarterly*, Vol. 52 (Oct.–Dec. 1972), pp. 605–19.
13. That the pace of the 'reform' as implemented by the peasants surprised even the most reform-minded Chinese leaders and planners is a point made by Andrew Watson, 'Agriculture Looks for "Shoes that Fit": The Production Responsibility System and Its Implications', *World Development*, Vol. XI, No. 8 (Aug. 1983), pp. 705–30.
14. Some very interesting theoretical work on this topic has been done by Louis Putterman, 'A Modified Collective Agriculture in Rural Growth-with-Equity: Reconsidering the Private, Unimodal Solution', *World Development*, Vol. XI, No. 2 (Feb. 1983), pp. 77–100.
15. This is certainly an area meriting much further empirical research than has been possible to date.
16. To be sure, the main cause of female infanticide today is the continuing preference of peasants for boys in the context of the draconian one-child policy and persistent patriolocalism. But one can hypothesise that if peasants did not have to depend on their offspring for old-age support, they would be less distraught at the birth of a baby girl. Chinese rural collectives did not solve the problem of comfortable old-age support, although they did make some modest attempts – for example, the 'five guarantees' (of housing, food, shelter, clothing and burial) for elderly people with no (male) offspring to support them. With the rise of contractual collectivism, even this slight achievement has been eroded, and the possibility of further progress seriously threatened.
17. 'Fewer Grain Growers in Rural Areas', *Beijing Review*, Vol. XXVI, No. 13 (28 March 1983), p. 5.
18. Nicholas Lardy, *Agriculture in China's Modern Economic Development* (Cambridge: Cambridge University Press, 1983).
19. Ibid., p. 220.

REFERENCES

Bahro, Rudolf, 1978, *The Alternative in Eastern Europe*, London: New Left Books.
*Beijing Review*, 'Fewer Grain Growers in Rural Areas', Vol. 26, No. 13.
Blecher, Marc, 1978, *Leader-Mass Relations in Rural Chinese Communities: Local Politics in a Revolutionary Society*, Ph.D. dissertation, University of Chicago.
Blecher, Marc, 1979, 'Consensual Politics in Small Rural Chinese Communities', *Modern China*, Vol. 5, No. 1, pp. 105–126.
Blecher, Marc, 1983, 'The Mass Line and Leader-Mass Relations and Communications in Basic-Level Rural Communities', in Godwin C. Chu and Francis L. K. Hsu (eds.), *China's New Social Fabric*, London: Routledge & Kegan Paul International.
Burns, John, 1978, 'The Election of Production Team Cadres in Rural China', *China Quarterly*, No. 74, June, pp. 273–96.
Donnithorne, Audrey, 1972, 'China's Cellular Economy: Some Economic Trends Since the Cultural Revolution', *China Quarterly*, No. 52, Oct.–Dec., pp. 605–619.

Foster-Carter, Aidan, 1978, 'The Modes of Production Controversy', *New Left Review*, No.107, Jan.–Feb., pp.47–77.

Lardy, Nicholas, 1983, *Agriculture in China's Modern Economic Development*, Cambridge: Cambridge University Press.

Putterman, Louis, 1983, 'A Modified Collective Agriculture in Rural Growth-with-Equity: Reconsidering the Private, Unimodal Solution', *World Development*, Vol.11, No.2, pp.77–100.

Watson, Andrew, 1983, 'Agriculture Looks for "Shoes That Fit": The Production Responsibility System and Its Implications', *World Development*, Vol.11, No.8, pp.705–30.

White, Christine Pelzer and Gordon White (eds.), 1982, 'Agriculture, The Peasantry and Socialist Development', *IDS Bulletin*, Vol.13, No.4.

Wolpé, Harold (ed.), 1980, *The Articulation of Modes of Production*, London: Routledge & Kegan Paul.

# Transforming Feudal Agriculture:
# Agrarian Change in Ethiopia since 1974

*by Ajit Kumar Ghose\**

*This article seeks to examine the nature and consequences of agrarian change in Ethiopia since the revolution of 1974. It argues that while the reforms implemented since 1975 have effectively destroyed the age-old feudal framework of agriculture, they have not yet created a coherent new framework. Even though the government's proclaimed objective is to develop a co-operative framework, not much progress in that direction has so far been made. In fact, state policies in the past few years were dictated by the need to cope with short-term problems arising from a decline in production and marketed surplus of food in the immediate aftermath of the reforms. The analysis in this article shows that the basic problem of peasant agriculture is that it currently produces only a meagre economic surplus. At this stage, therefore, agricultural growth is to be achieved primarily through the promotion of labour-investment. This is the principal argument for co-operativisation. This view suggests state policies which are quite different from those pursued in the past few years.*

## I. INTRODUCTION

Prior to 1974, agrarian economy in Ethiopia was feudal in the classical sense of the term. Peasants had usufructuary rights in land, no significant category of landless labourers existed and agricultural surplus[1] was extracted by a small group of overlords, composed of military-bureaucratic and ecclesiastical elites, in the form of tributes. For historical reasons, the system of share-cropping came to dominate in the south and a direct tribute system operated in the north of the country. These aspects have been well studied and we need not go into the details here.[2] We need only note that a large surplus was being extracted from a low-productivity agriculture. This, on the one hand, kept the peasantry desperately impoverished and, on the other, preserved primitive cultivation practices. The surplus itself was frittered away in wasteful consumption of the elite.

Following the revolution of 1974, a series of radical land reform measures were implemented. The age-old feudal order was overthrown, land was

---

\* The author is a Senior Research Economist at the International Labour Office, Geneva. This article is based on a larger study undertaken for the World Employment Programme of the ILO. Thanks are due to Dharam Ghai, Samir Radwan and Ashwani Saith for helpful comments and suggestions. Neither the above-mentioned individuals nor the ILO should, however, be held responsible for the views expressed.

nationalised and usufructuary rights were redistributed on a massive scale. Use of hired labour by peasant households and transfer of land through sale, lease or mortgage were prohibited. The result was the emergence of a peasant economy system. The few pre-existing private commercial farms were transformed into state farms.

But the land reforms, by abolishing landlordism, also abolished the established modes of surplus extraction. Peasants, freed from obligations to pay rent and tributes, naturally increased self-consumption. Agricultural output, moreover, declined quite sharply in the immediate aftermath of the land reforms. The result was that marketed output of food declined sharply and this had disastrous consequences for urban income distribution. There was an urgent need to increase the marketed output of food, but at the same time consumption of the peasants could not be squeezed further, for this would have defeated the very purpose of the land reforms. It was in response to this situation that the state farm sector was expanded very rapidly during 1979−81, primarily by bringing fallow land into cultivation. Meanwhile, efforts were also made, with some success, to develop co-operatives in the peasant sector.

Through these processes, the agrarian economy came to acquire a characteristic typical of transitional situations: co-existence of several modes of production. Even though peasant farms presently constitute the dominant type of production unit in agriculture, co-operative and state sectors are in fact expanding. Besides, the state sector, although small, plays a vital role in Ethiopian economy. And the government's stated objective is to transform the entire peasant sector into a co-operative sector.

This last is a delicate and difficult task, but it is also a necessity. The basic constraint on development in Ethiopia is that agriculture presently produces little economic surplus.[3] It is only at the cost of poverty for the peasantry that a surplus is extracted from agriculture today. Yet, in the foreseeable future, agriculture must bear the burden of providing the investible resources for national development. In other words, not only must agriculture finance its own growth, it must also finance industrialisation of the country. The problem, therefore, is one of generating agricultural growth without further squeezing the consumption of the peasantry. This requires mobilisation of labour − an investible resource which is available − on a significant scale for capital construction in agriculture so that a part of the consumption of the peasantry is transformed into investment. In other words, the feasible form of investment at this juncture is labour-investment. Experience tells us that labour-investment is best promoted within a co-operative framework.

Given this context, this study will focus on three specific aspects: present state of agriculture, economic logic of co-operativisation and a growth path consistent with co-operativisation strategy.[4] Co-operativisation, of course, cannot but be a process stretched over time. Meanwhile, agricultural growth must also occur. What is necessary, therefore, is to devise a strategy of agricultural development which, while promoting growth, also encourages (or at least does not hinder) co-operativisation. This is the central problem of the transitional economy.

The empirical materials used in preparing this study were derived either from official sources or from small-scale surveys carried out by the author in mid-1982. Data are scarce in Ethiopia and, even when available, are not always reliable. Caution is necessary, therefore, in interpreting the data. In view of this, this study does not aim to be empirical in the strict sense of the term and uses carefully selected data mainly for illustrative purposes.

The article is organised as follows. In the second section, the structural changes that have already occurred since 1974, the transitional forms which have emerged as a result of the changes and the growth experience of this period, are discussed. In the third section, the economic logic of transition to a collective agriculture is examined. In the fourth section, the government's programme of co-operativisation is outlined and its major weaknesses are highlighted. In the fifth section, the problem of integrating a growth strategy with a strategy of institutional transformation is addressed.

## II. AGRARIAN ECONOMY IN TRANSITION: A BRIEF SKETCH

### Structure of Landholding

The land reform measures implemented since 1975 have brought into existence a transitional agrarian structure whose basic features can be briefly outlined as follows.[5] All rural land is owned by the state and cultivating households can only have usufructuary rights in land. Any household willing to employ family labour for cultivation can have access to land sufficient for its maintenance, subject to a maximum of ten hectares. In principle, use of hired labour is prohibited, as is the transfer of land through sale, lease, mortgage or similar arrangements.

Around 5.5 million (66 per cent) of Ethiopia's estimated 8.3 million peasant households are now organised into about 20,000 peasant associations. Indeed, in most areas, households can have access to land if and only if they are members of particular peasant associations. A peasant association is, in principle, organised on an area of about 800 hectares, and all the heads of the households residing in the area are entitled to its membership. The functions of peasant associations include periodic redistribution of land in accordance with changes in the size and composition of membership; administration of public property, promotion of producers' co-operatives; establishment of service co-operatives, undertaking of villagisation programmes; establishment of Judicial Tribunals (that is, autonomous rural courts) for dealing with disputes among peasants and establishment of defence squads for maintaining law and order at local levels. A few peasant associations have already established producers' co-operatives, although not always with the participation of all the members. Within a single peasant association, therefore, a producers' co-operative may co-exist with independent peasant farms. Attempts to establish service co-operatives have been more successful; by 1984, there were 3,903 service co-operatives with a total membership of about 4.5 million households (54 per cent of all peasant households).

Prior to the revolution of 1974, there already existed a small number of state farms which were developed either as settlement schemes or as schemes to attract foreign capital. Besides, there also existed a small number of larger private farms which engaged in the production of commercial crops with modern technology. These two types of farms were reorganised to constitute the state sector in agriculture after 1975.[6] Subsequently (particularly between 1979 and 1981), many new state farms were established, mostly on hitherto uncultivated land but sometimes by displacing peasant households. The state farms are highly mechanised large units (mostly between 4,000 and 10,000 hectares) which are run by the government through a highly centralised and hierarchical management structure.[7] The workers on them cannot really be placed in the same category as peasants; they are skilled or semi-skilled and usually have an urban background. Indeed, they are organised into trade unions rather than into peasant associations. Nevertheless, the state farms are engaged in the production of crops and have to be treated together with other production units in agriculture.

There are, then, three types of production units in agriculture at present: peasant farms, producers' co-operatives and state farms. Their relative importance can be gauged from the data presented in Table 1. The peasant farms are of overwhelming importance; they account for around 95 per cent of the cultivated area. The producers' co-operatives account for less than two per cent of the area and just over one per cent of the country's peasant families. The state farms currently account for less than four per cent of cultivated area. A set of slightly different estimates, presented in Table 2, gives us some idea of the changes in the relative importance of the three types of production units during the period 1975/76−1982/83. It can be seen that both producers' co-operatives and state farms have grown in importance while the weight of the peasant sector has declined. The pace of change, however, has been very slow.

Within the private peasant sector, land distribution remains unequal.[8] The degree of inequality, however, is low and can be attributed to three factors. First, inter-regional differences in the land/man ratio are considerable. Second, peasant households traditionally engaged in the production of permanent crops (for example, *enset*) have been allowed to retain relatively large farms. Third, land has tended to be allocated on a per capita basis so that variations in farm size reflect variations in family size to an extent.

The producers' co-operatives vary a great deal in terms of land area and membership. But a large majority of them have a land area of up to 60 hectares and a membership of up to 100 households. Data in Table 1 would seem to suggest that land area per peasant household is higher in the co-operative sector than in the peasant sector, but in fact the existence of a few relatively well-off co-operatives introduces an upward bias in the average for the sector. A sample of 837 producers' co-operatives for which somewhat detailed data are available, shows an average land area of 57 hectares and an average membership of 80 households per co-operative.[9] This implies an average landholding of 0.7 hectares per peasant household in the co-operative sector compared to 0.8 hectares in the private peasant sector (excluding coffee farms). In fact, it is known that, in general, it is the poorer peasants who have joined the producers' co-operatives.

Superimposed on the private peasant and collectie sectors are the service co-operatives. Each service co-operative covers several (usually between five and ten) peasant associations and draws its membership from among the members of these associations. Initial capital consists of contributions by the

TABLE 1

DISTRIBUTION OF LAND AREA AND RURAL FAMILIES
BY TYPES OF PRODUCTION UNIT, 1982/83

| Item | Peasant Holdings | Producers' Co-operatives | State Farms |
|---|---|---|---|
| Area under annual crops (th. hectares) | 5,546 (94.5) | 114 (1.9) | 213 (3.6) |
| Peasant families engaged in the production of annual crops (th.) | 7,106 (98.7) | 94 (1.3) | - |
| Worker families permanently employed in the production of annual crops (th.) | - | - | 18 |
| Area under coffee (th. hectares) | 441 | - | 9 |
| Peasant families engaged in coffee production (th.) | 1,100 | - | - |
| Workers' families permanently employed in coffee production (th.) | - | - | 0.7 |
| Total area under crops (th. hectares) | 5,987 (94.7) | 114 (1.8) | 222 (3.5) |
| Total number of peasant households (th.) | 8,206 (98.9) | 94 (1.1) | - |

*Notes*:  In estimating area under state farms, we have left out of account the land operated by Horticulture Development Corporation, Animal and Fish Development Corporation, and Ethiopian Seed Enterprise. These and Agricultural Equipment and Technical Service Corporation employ a considerable number of workers and are administered by the Ministry of State Farms Development. Relief and Rehabilitation Commission administers settlement schemes whereby some fallow land has been brought under cultivation, and land under sugar cane is administered by the Ethiopian Sugar Corporation, and these have also been excluded from the above estimates. Consequently, the estimate of total cultivated area is a slight underestimate.

No estimates of the number of worker families permanently employed by the coffee-producing state farms were available. The estimate in Table 1 is the author's and is based on the estimated average number of workers per hectare on state farms producing annual crops.

The figures in parentheses indicate percentages.

All the estimates should be regarded as approximate.

*Source*:  Information supplied by the Ministries of Agriculture, State Farms Development, and Coffee and Tea Development.

constituent peasant associations and membership fees paid by the individual members. This initial capital is used to develop small-scale processing and service industries whose profits can be used for further investment. The service co-operatives also act as agents of the state-owned Agricultural Marketing Corporation (AMC) – selling farm inputs and basic consumer goods to peasants and purchasing agricultural products from them – and have the responsibility for developing basic welfare services (schools, clinics, etc.)

TABLE 2

RELATIVE IMPORTANCE OF THE THREE TYPES
OF PRODUCTION UNITS, 1976/77–1982/83
(Percentages)

| Crops | Period | Peasant Farms | | Producers' Co-operatives | | State Farms | |
|---|---|---|---|---|---|---|---|
| | | Area | Output | Area | Output | Area | Output |
| Major | 1975/76 | 98.4 | 97.9 | 1.0 | 0.8 | 0.6 | 1.3 |
| Foodgrains | 1976/77 | 98.9 | 98.8 | 0.8 | 0.5 | 0.3 | 0.7 |
| | 1977/78 | 98.9 | 98.0 | 0.8 | 0.6 | 0.3 | 1.4 |
| | 1978/79 | 98.7 | 97.5 | 0.7 | 0.7 | 0.6 | 1.8 |
| | 1979/80 | 96.0 | 96.1 | 2.4 | 1.5 | 1.6 | 2.4 |
| | 1980/81 | 95.9 | 95.1 | 1.5 | 1.0 | 2.6 | 3.9 |
| | 1981/82 | 94.3 | 94.2 | 2.2 | 1.2 | 3.5 | 4.6 |
| | 1982/83 | 95.1 | 95.3 | 1.9 | 1.3 | 3.0 | 3.4 |
| All crops | 1975/76 | 97.9 | 96.9 | 1.1 | 0.8 | 1.0 | 2.3 |
| excluding | 1976/77 | 98.3 | 97.5 | 0.8 | 0.5 | 0.9 | 2.0 |
| coffee | 1977/78 | 98.2 | 96.4 | 0.8 | 0.7 | 1.0 | 2.9 |
| | 1978/79 | 98.1 | 96.1 | 0.8 | 0.7 | 1.1 | 3.2 |
| | 1979/80 | 95.2 | 95.1 | 2.4 | 1.5 | 2.4 | 3.4 |
| | 1980/81 | 94.6 | 93.9 | 1.5 | 1.1 | 3.9 | 5.0 |
| | 1981/82 | 93.6 | 92.7 | 2.2 | 1.3 | 4.2 | 6.0 |
| | 1982/83 | 94.4 | 94.3 | 2.0 | 1.2 | 3.6 | 4.5 |

*Sources*: Ministry of Agriculture, Ministry of State Farms and Central Statistical Office.

## Labour in Peasant Agriculture

According to available estimates, about 89 per cent of the country's population lives in rural areas.[10] A recent survey showed the rural participation rate to be about 63 per cent.[11] The participation rate in urban areas is reported to be about 45 per cent.[12] On this basis, the proportion of the labour force in rural areas works out to be about 92 per cent. Since only about two per cent of the rural workers are reported to be engaged in non-agricultural activities, the share of agriculture in the total labour force appears to be just over 90 per cent. Even by the standards of developing countries, this is a very high proportion. And, as the data in Table 1 suggest, virtually the whole of this labour force is in the private peasant sector.

There is little statistical evidence on the pattern of labour use in peasant agricultue. In most areas, however, the cropping season extends from June to January, and this implies a slack period of four months. Some allowances must be made for the usual slack season activities. On the other hand, seasonality of labour requirements in crop production means that labour is not fully employed even during the cropping season. The rate of underemployment, therefore, could be anywhere between 25 and 40 per cent.

To this observation can be added some estimates on the basis of the results of a survey conducted in Arssi region in 1981. These show that, given the typical cropping pattern, a two-hectare farm requires 197 days of human labour (see Table 3). A large proportion of the holdings in the country are

TABLE 3

LABOUR REQUIREMENTS OF CROP PRODUCTION
ON A TWO HECTARE FARM IN ARSSI, 1981

| Crop | Labour-days Per Ha | Cropping Pattern (Ha/Crop) | Required Labour-days |
|------|------|------|------|
| Wheat | 102 | 0.38 | 39 |
| Barley | 102 | 0.54 | 55 |
| Teff | 102 | 0.29 | 30 |
| Maize | 102 | 0.33 | 34 |
| Horsebeans | 72 | 0.19 | 14 |
| Field peas | 72 | 0.07 | 5 |
| Others | 102 | 0.20 | 20 |
| Total | | 2.0 | 197 |

*Sources*: Arssi Rural Development Unit [*1982*]; Central Statistical Office [*1980*]

actually below two hectares in size.[13] In fact, the data in Table 1 suggest than an average peasant holding is only 0.8 hectares in size. Since land per worker would be even less than this, the degree of underemployment is obviously high, although it would be misleading to suggest any particular numerical magnitude.

Underemployment, of course, is not a new phenomenon; it is a legacy of the past. If anything, underemployment has probably declined in the post-reform period since the expansion of the state farm sector has created new opportunities for seasonal employment of peasant labour. The important point to note is that underemployment is linked to the low productivity in agriculture; in large part, it is due to technological backwardness. Both the yield rates and the intensity of cropping, for example, are very low and underemployment would decline if they could be raised. On the other hand, currently underemployed labour could be utilised to create technological conditions for its own fuller employment. For example, minor irrigation works, drainage and various other land improvement activities could be undertaken by labour and these could lead to higher cropping intensities and yields. Indeed, in Ethiopia, even such activities as building fair-weather rural roads would improve government delivery systems and facilitate the work of extension agencies; these would, in turn, lead to technological change.

## Growth of Production

Growth of agricultural output as well as of food output was quite impressive during the four-year period 1977/78 – 1982/83 as Table 4 shows. Agricultural output grew at an annual rate of 10.3 per cent and food output grew at an annual rate of 10.5 per cent. Both these rates were higher than the rate of growth of population which is estimated to have been around three per cent. However, to an extent, this high growth reflected a recovery rather than a trend; 1977/78 was a bad crop year and agricultural output had declined quite

TABLE 4

GROWTH OF AGRICULTURAL OUTPUT

| | 1977/78–1982/83 | | 1975/76–1982/83 | |
| | Production | Area | Production | Area |
|---|---|---|---|---|
| All crops (excluding coffee) | 10.3 | 2.1 | 5.2 | 1.1 |
| Peasant Farms | 9.8 | 1.3 | 4.7 | 0.6 |
| Producers' co-operatives | 24.7 | 21.5 | 11.3 | 9.1 |
| State farms | 20.4 | 31.1 | 15.9 | 21.3 |
| All food crops | 10.5 | 2.0 | 5.5 | 1.4 |
| Peasant farms | 9.9 | 1.1 | 4.9 | 0.9 |
| Producers' co-operatives | 25.9 | 21.1 | 11.7 | 11.4 |
| State farms | 33.2 | 63.7 | 20.9 | 28.3 |

*Sources*: Ministry of Agriculture; Ministry of State Farms; and Central Statistical Office.

sharply during the two preceding years partly because of the disruptions caused by the land reforms. Growth during the seven-year period 1975/76–1982/83 was lower: 5.2 per cent per annum for total agricultural output and 5.5 per cent for foodgrains output. Thus, the growth performance remains impressive even after the effect of recovery is eliminated.

The data presented in Table 4 also reveal some underlying features of the process of growth. For the agricultural sector as a whole, the major source of growth was the growth in yield rates; the expansion in cultivated area was modest. However, improvement in yield rates was in fact confined to the peasant sector alone; yield rates remained unchanged in the co-operative sector and declined quite sharply in the state farm sector. This in spite of the fact that the pattern of resource allocation was heavily biased in favour of the state farm sector. For example, the state farms, with just over four per cent of the cultivated area, were allocated 76 per cent of the available chemical fertilisers and 95 per cent of the improved seeds in 1981/82 (see Table 5). Nearly all of the modern farm machinery were also concentrated on the state farms. In other words, state investment in agriculture was directed almost exclusively to the state farm sector.

Second, since the cultivated area expanded in all sectors, it seems clear that although the co-operative and state farm sectors grew in importance within the agrarian economy, they developed largely outside the domain of the private peasant economy. New state farms, it is known, were established mostly on previously uncultivated land. But what seems remarkable is that the growth of the co-operative sector was not accompanied by a corresponding decline of the peasant sector. This suggests that efforts to persuade the peasantry to form producers' co-operatives have not met with a great deal of success and that most of the new co-operatives probably grew out of settlement schemes. Third, it can be seen from the data in Table 4 that the private peasants and the co-operatives (outside the coffee sectors) hardly engage in the production of commercial crops. The major commercial crop (other than coffee) in Ethiopia is cotton which is produced exclusively by state farms. A noticeable

TABLE 5

DISTRIBUTION OF CHEMICAL FERTILIZERS AND IMPROVED SEEDS
(Percentages)

| User | Chemical Fertilizers 1981/82 | Improved Seeds 1981/82 | 1982/83 |
|------|:---:|:---:|:---:|
| Peasants and Producers' co-op. | 23.58 | 4.1 | 12.3 |
| State farms | 76.42 | 94.8 | 80.9 |
| Settlements | - | 1.1 | 6.8 |

*Note*: Estimates for improved seeds refer to the following crops: wheat, barley, maize, teff and sorghum.

*Sources*: Agricultural Marketing Corporation [*1982*] and Ethiopian Seed Corporation [*1984*].

aspect of the growth performance of the state farms is that the output of food crops increased at a much faster rate than that of cotton. During the period 1975/76–1981/82, the output of cotton grew at a rate of 2.6 per cent per annum.[14] Thus it is clear that most of the new state farms established between 1978/79 and 1981/82 engaged in the production of food crops. Evidently, the rapid expansion of the state farm sector was an emergency measure designed to overcome the food crisis experienced during 1975/76–1977/78. The attempt to rapidly increase food production by expanding the state farm sector, however, proved costly. The new state farms often were established on infertile, marginal land. Considerable technological and management problems were also encountered and we shall come back to this point.

Coffee, the most important export crop of Ethiopia (accounting for more than 60 per cent of total export earnings), has so far been left out of account. For the purpose of this study, a detailed analysis of the coffee economy is unnecessary and a few brief observations will suffice. Data presented in Table 1 clearly indicate that both private peasants and state farms are engaged in coffee production, but private peasants account for the bulk of the area and output. The available evidence suggests that the annual output of coffee has grown at a steady rate of around two per cent per annum throughout the period 1974/75–1981/82, and that the growth performance of private peasant farms and state farms has been similar to that of the state farms.[15]

A final aspect of the growth process which is worth noting is the growth of regional inequalities. Traditionally, regional inequalities have been considerable in Ethiopia because of wide differences in resource-population balance, variations in weather conditions and extreme lack of market integration (these aspects will be discussed in greater detail in the following section). These conditions have remained virtually unchanged, but the government's efforts to increase food production in the short run have tended to exacerbate the inequalities. For example, whatever modern inputs such as chemical fertilisers were distributed to private peasants went almost exclusively to the peasants in Arssi, Shoa, Gojjam and Gondar regions, that is, precisely the regions which have traditionally been producers of food surpluses.[16]

In sum, the disruptions caused by the land reforms, it seems, adversely affected only the production of food crops; production of cotton and coffee continued to grow at trend rates. The reason lies in the fact that redistribution of usufructuary rights in land occurred mostly in areas growing food crops. Even before the reforms, cotton was grown either by state farms or by private commercial farms; reforms involved a straightforward conversion of the private commercial farms into state farms. In coffee-growing regions, land-lordism was abolished but no significant restructuring of peasant holdings occurred. Output of foodcrops recovered rather rapidly but, unfortunately, the process of recovery involved a hurried expansion of the state farm sector and growing regional inequalities.

It would seem inappropriate to conclude this discussion of the growth process in agriculture without making any reference to the present famine. The trends discussed so far provide no indication at all of an impending famine and this may appear surprising. But it should be borne in mind that, in a country like Ethiopia, even one bad crop in one region can produce a disastrous famine; the reasons will be clear from the observations in the following section. Unfortunately, we have no data for the agricultural years of 1983/84 and 1984/85. But it cannot be doubted that food output declined quite drastically in some parts of the country in these years.

### Marketed Output of Food and its Control

Although no estimates of marketed output of food for pre-reform periods are available, there are good reasons to believe that it constituted quite a high proportion of total food output. About 40 per cent of the foodcrop area was under crop-sharing tenancy and rent constituted around 50 per cent of the output of tenanted area.[17] On this account alone, therefore, about 20 per cent of agricultural output accrued to a small class of landlords. Furthermore, peasants paid various forms of tribute to their landlords, particularly in the north of the country. For obvious reasons, the bulk of the landlords' share of the food output was destined for the market. Moreover, the peasants, owners and tenants alike, needed to market a part of their output in order to pay taxes and to buy essential consumer goods. On the whole, therefore, it would seem that marketed output must have constituted at least 25 per cent of gross output of foodcrops.[18]

The land reforms freed the peasantry from obligations to pay rent and tributes. Given their low level of consumption, it was natural for the peasants to increase their own consumption. Under the circumstances the self-consumption ratio for agriculture increased and the marketed output of food declined quite sharply as a consequence. According to one available estimate, only 11.2 per cent of the peasant sector's output was marketed in 1977/78.[19] And output itself was lower than that of 1975/76 by about 13 per cent.

The result of a sharp decline in the marketed output was a severe compression of food consumption of the urban population effected through a sharp rise in food prices in relation to urban incomes. A system of partial rationing, introduced by the government, moderated the redistributive effects of this process; but there is little doubt that a significant redistribution of food consumption in favour of the urban rich did take place and urban poverty increased sharply.[20] An urgent problem faced by the government, therefore, was that of increasing the volume of marketed output as rapidly as possible. The most direct method of doing this was a rapid expansion of the state farm sector since almost the entire output of this sector was marketable. As noted earlier, this inded was the method chosen by the government.

The government, furthermore, sought to acquire direct control of a part of the marketed output so as to be in a position to determine its distribution among the various segments of the non-agricultural population. The state-owned trading organisation – the AMC – expanded the scale of its operations at a rapid rate during the period 1977/78 – 1981/82. The state farms and the producers' co-operatives were obliged by law to sell their marketable output to the AMC. The service co-operatives, acting as agents of the AMC, purchased a growing proportion of the peasant sector's marketed output. Private traders were required to sell a part of their stocks, purchased from the peasants, to the AMC at negotiated prices. Through these methods, the AMC came to control about 40 per cent of the total marketed output of foodgrains by 1982.

The results of these measures can be seen from the data presented in Table 6. First, marketed output of foodgrains increased at a very rapid pace between 1977/78 and 1981/82; the proportions reported in Table 4 imply an average annual growth rate of 21.9 per cent against a growth rate of foodgrains output of 8.0 per cent. Second, even though the rapid expansion of the state farm sector clearly played a role in augmenting the marketed output, the role of the peasant sector was of crucial importance. The marketed output of the peasant sector grew at an annual rate of 18.5 per cent while the output grew at an annual rate of 6.9 per cent. In 1981/82, the peasant sector still accounted for 84.1 per cent of the total marketed output of foodgrains.[21]

TABLE 6

MARKETED OUTPUT OF FOODGRAINS, 1977/78–1981/82

|  | 1977/78 | 1981/82 |
|---|---|---|
| Marketed output of foodgrains as per cent of foodgrains output: | | |
| All sectors | 11.7 | 19.0 |
| Private peasant sector | 11.2 | 17.0 |
| Percentage share in total marketed foodgrains of: | | |
| Private peasant sector | 92.8 | 84.1 |
| Producers' co-operatives | - | 0.7 |
| State farms | 7.2 | 15.2 |

Note:　In estimating these parameters, Eritrea and Tigrai have been left out of account. For 1977/78, it has been assumed that the state farms sold 55 per cent of their foodgrains output to the AMC (i.e., the self-consumption ratio was 0.45), a percentage actually observed for 1981/82. For 1981/82, it is assumed that the AMC controlled 40 per cent of the total marketed output of foodgrains.

Sources:　Ministry of Agriculture; Ministry of State Farms; and Agricultural Marketing Corporation.

Two important points emerge from the above facts. First, in spite of the government's policy of concentrating resources on the state farms, the urban economy remained nearly as dependent on the peasant sector for its food supply as it was in 1977/78. Second, food consumption of the peasants could not have improved much. This raises the question as to why the peasants increased their sales at such a high rate rather than increase their own consumption. The answer seems to lie in the growing regional inequalities which characterised the process of growth. Although the peasantry as a whole does not seem to have benefited from growth, a class of prosperous peasants seems to have emerged in certain parts of the country. This, in fact, is clearly suggested by the data presented in Table 7; only four regions – Gojjam, Shoa, Arssi and Gondar – accounted for nearly 86 per cent of the AMC's purchases from peasants in 1981/82.

TABLE 7

PERCENTAGE DISTRIBUTION OF AMC PURCHASES OF
AGRICULTURAL PRODUCTS BY REGION, 1981–82
(From Sources other than State Farms)

|            | Foodgrains | Total  |
|------------|------------|--------|
| Gojjam     | 31.60      | 33.02  |
| Shoa       | 21.81      | 20.38  |
| Arssi      | 23.22      | 21.37  |
| Gondar     | 10.25      | 10.86  |
| Wollo      | 6.68       | 5.64   |
| Wollega    | 1.22       | 4.01   |
| Bale       | 3.38       | 3.16   |
| Kaffa      | 1.39       | 1.19   |
| Sidamo     | 0.33       | 0.28   |
| Illubabor  | 0.12       | 0.09   |
| Total      | 100.00     | 100.00 |

*Note*:   No purchases were made in the other regions. For purposes of these estimates, coffee, cotton and sugarcane were excluded.

*Source*:  Agricultural Marketing Corporation [*1982*].

*The State and the Peasantry: New Methods of Surplus Extraction from Agriculture*

The land reforms, by abolishing landlordism, brought the peasantry into direct relationship with the state on the one hand and abolished rent and tributes as modes of extraction of agricultural surplus on the other. Subsequently, the state, as the new landowner, devised its own methods of extraction. Three such methods can be identified in today's Ethiopia: direct taxation of peasant agriculture; control of pricing and marketing of agricultural products; and expansion of the state farm sector. The last two of these measures, it will be argued below, involve implicit taxation of peasant agriculture.

Two types of taxes are collected from peasant households: a land use fee and an agricultural income tax. The land use fee is a fixed rate (10 birr) per peasant household and makes no allowances for inequalities in size of land-holding or for differences in soil fertility. The agricultural income tax has an elaborate structure. The peasant households having an income of up to 600 birr per annum are required to pay a fixed sum of 10 birr per annum. Incomes in excess of 600 birr are to be taxed, in principle, at progressively higher rates. In practice, however, it is very difficult to determine the level of income of private peasant households, and few of them report their incomes to be above 600 birr. Crude estimates show that the two taxes together presently constitute only three per cent to four per cent of gross output value of the peasant sector.

As noted earlier, the government has attempted to control the prices of major agricultural products, particularly foodgrains, through direct intervention in marketing. It also has a monopoly of distribution of ferti-lisers and thus is able to control its price directly. The AMC purchases and distributes a proportion of the marketed output of the peasants and supplies fertilisers to them – all at officially determined prices. However, the AMC's control over the private peasants' marketed output of foodgrains is not as yet very significant; this can be seen from the data presented in Table 8.

TABLE 8

PERCENTAGE DISTRIBUTION OF AMC PURCHASES OF
AGRICULTURAL PRODUCTS BY SOURCES OF SUPPLY,
1981/82

| Sources of Supply | Foodgrains | Total |
|---|---|---|
| Peasants | 3.44 | 3.23 |
| Merchants | 37.63 | 41.17 |
| Service co-operatives | 18.18 | 18.96 |
| Producers' co-operatives | 1.78 | 1.79 |
| State farms | 37.28 | 33.26 |
| Other state agencies | 1.69 | 1.59 |
| Total | 100.00 | 100.00 |

Note:  For purposes of these estimates, coffee, cotton and sugarcane were excluded.

Source: Agricultural Marketing Corporation [1982].

In fact, its purchases from private peasants (including purchases channelled through the service co-operatives) amounted to only ten per cent of their marketed output in 1981/82. The amount of fertilisers used by the peasants is also quite small at present; in 1981/82, for example, only 944 tonnes were used by them.

That price control measures serve as methods of surplus extraction is indicated by the data presented in Table 9. Three points in particular should be noted. First, the official prices sometimes imply labour-values (column 5) which are lower than even the minimum daily wage (1.92 birr) fixed by the government. Second, official prices clearly imply a general undervaluation of peasant labour (compare columns 5 and 7). Third, peasants clearly stand to lose if the AMC sells them fertiliser only on condition that they sell their

TABLE 9

COST OF PRODUCTION, PRICES AND TERMS OF TRADE, ARSSI 1981

| Crop | (1) | (2) | (3) | (4) | (5) | (6) | (7) | (8) | (9) |
|------|-----|-----|-----|-----|-----|-----|-----|-----|-----|
| Wheat | 11.47 | 31.0 | 19.53 | 7.5 | 2.60 | 40.0 | 3.80 | 3.5 | 2.7 |
| Barley | 11.06 | 27.0 | 15.94 | 8.1 | 1.97 | 32.0 | 2.59 | 4.0 | 3.4 |
| Teff | 9.56 | 36.0 | 26.44 | 10.2 | 2.59 | 55.0 | 4.45 | 3.0 | 2.0 |
| Maize | 3.53 | 17.0 | 13.47 | 7.2 | 1.87 | 26.0 | 3.12 | 6.4 | 4.2 |
| Sorghum | 2.94 | 20.0 | 17.06 | 3.4 | 5.02 | 35.0 | 9.43 | 5.4 | 3.1 |
| Horsebeans | 11.16 | 25.0 | 13.84 | 14.44 | 0.96 | 33.0 | 1.52 | 4.3 | 3.3 |
| Field peas | 11.04 | 34.0 | 22.96 | 8.3 | 2.77 | 40.0 | 3.49 | 3.2 | 2.7 |

*Notes*: (1) Material costs of production: birr per 100 kg.
        (2) Purchase prices offered by the AMC: birr per 100 kg.
        (3) Difference between (1) and (2).
        (4) Labour days required per 100 kg.
        (5) Value of a labour-day implicit in AMC prices: birr ($= (3)/(4)$).
        (6) Prices at local markets: birr per 100 kg.
        (7) Value of a labour-day implicit in market prices: birr.
        (8) Ratio of fertiliser to crop prices fixed by the AMC.
        (9) Ratio of fertiliser to crop prices prevailing in local markets.

*Source*: Computed from data provided in Arssi Rural Development Unit [*1982*].

crops to the AMC (compare columns 8 and 9). It is not clear to what extent one can generalise from this evidence. But the tentative conclusion must be that the price control measures do operate as mechanisms of surplus extraction from the peasantry, although the surplus presently extracted through these mechanisms cannot be large.

That the state farms are instruments of surplus extraction from the peasant sector can be seen from the following facts. First, the resources allocated to the state farms could have been allocated to the peasant sector. In that case, production in the peasant sector would be higher than it is at present. But so would be the per capita consumption in rural areas in the absence of a matching increase in taxes. Given the low levels per capita production and consumption, the elasticity of marketed output with respect to total output is unlikely to be high. By allocating resources to the state farms, therefore, the government essentially avoids having to tax the peasant sector more heavily than at present. To put it in another way, allocation of resources to state farms involves indirect taxation of the peasant sector.[22]

Second, it can be argued that the state farms are engaged in the exploitation of peasant labour. The permanent labour force employed by the state farms is small and highly paid. For much of their production activities, the state farms in fact depend on hired casual labour which is supplied by peasants in search of cash incomes. Casual labourers are usually paid a daily wage equal to the statutory minimum daily wage of 1.92 birr. In general, average labour productivity on state farms is much above this while the implicit wage rate of permanent workers is much above the average labour productivity.[23]

III. NATURE OF THE AGRARIAN PROBLEM

At the present stage, the fundamental problem of development of agriculture in Ethiopia is that the peasant sector produces only a meagre economic surplus. Indeed, agricultural output is barely adequate for sustaining and reproducing the labour force in the peasant sector. Nevertheless, as we saw above, a surplus is currently extracted through the mechanisms of taxation, market intervention and diversion of resources to state farms. This surplus is not large, but it none the less imposes on the peasantry a heavier burden than it can bear with ease.

The proposition that in the peasant sector there is no residual surplus either to be accumulated internally or to be extracted by external agents is supported by the following observations. More than 96 per cent of the peasant sector's output (excluding coffee) is accounted for by foodgrains. Even so, foodgrains output and consumption are extremely low in per capita terms. The data presented in Table 10 illustrate the point.

TABLE 10

FOODGRAINS PRODUCTION AND CONSUMPTION, 1977/78

| Item | Estimates |
|---|---|
| Total foodgrain production in peasant sector (excluding Eritrea and Tigrai) (th. tonnes) | 3908.2 |
| Marketed surplus (th. tonnes) | 429.9 |
| Losses (th. tonnes) | 195.4 |
| Seed requirements (th. tonnes) | 273.4 |
| Rural consumption (th. tonnes) | 3009.5 |
| Rural population (excluding Eritrea and Tigrai) (th.) | 22,142 |
| Production per head of rural population (kg) | 177 |
| Consumption per head of rural population (kg) | 136 |

*Note*: The first four estimates are based on the findings reported in Ministry of Agriculture [*1978*].

The figure for per capita consumption excludes livestock products and *enset* which are important substitutes for grains in some regions. On the other hand, it makes no allowance for carry-over stocks. More importantly, it is now known that the population was seriously underestimated in the past.[24] On the whole, there can be little doubt that per capita consumption, at 136 kg., was very low (a per capita grain consumption of 200 kg. is generally accepted as the minimum norm). This estimate pertains to 1977/78 which was a particularly bad crop year. There was an appreciable increase in foodgrains production during the period 1977/78–1981/82; per capita output is estimated to have been around 209 kg. in 1981/82 (about 18 per cent higher than in 1977/78). However, marketed output increased at a much faster rate than total output so that per capita consumption in rural areas was, on rough estimates, 148 kg. in 1981/82, that is, about nine per cent higher than that in 1977/78.[25] And this estimate, too, is an overestimate because rural population was underestimated.[26]

In itself, it is curious that, with output growing at a rapid rate, consumption in rural areas should increase so much less rapidly in a situation where the initial level of consumption was so low. As suggested earlier, the phenomenon can be explained in terms of regional inequalities and lack of market integration. The extent of regional inequalities is indicated by the data presented in Table 11;

TABLE 11

PEASANT SECTOR'S OUTPUT OF FOODGRAINS PER CAPITA
OF RURAL POPULATION BY REGION, 1978/79

| Region | Output in Kg |
|---|---|
| Arssi | 580 |
| Bale | 218 |
| Gondar | 300 |
| Gamu Goffa | 46 |
| Gojjam | 201 |
| Hararghe | 60 |
| Illubabor | 211 |
| Kaffa | 215 |
| Shoa | 242 |
| Sidamo | 53 |
| Wollega | 134 |
| Wollo | 86 |

Note:    Population estimates were underestimates, but the estimation bias was randomly distributed across regions.

Sources:  Production estimates were taken from Ministry of Agriculture [1979] and population estimates were taken from Central Statistical Office [1978].

in 1978/79, foodgrains output per capita of rural population varied from a meagre 46 kg. in Gamu Goffa to an impressive 580 kg. in Arssi. It should be pointed out that *enset* is a major crop in Gamu Goffa and that Hararghe, Sidamo and Wollo have sizeable nomadic populations (who rely more on livestock products than on grains). Nevertheless, the fact remains that regional inequalities were high and, as noted earlier, very probably grew in the subsequent periods.

Even so, if markets were developed, food consumption might have been better distributed than production across regions. Unfortunately, transport and communications are very undeveloped in Ethiopia and the degree of monetisation of the rural economy is also very low in most regions. Consequently, movement of food across regions is very limited, particularly so for rural areas. This is clearly reflected in the extreme variation in prices of foodgrains across regions observed in Ethiopia.[27] The result is that, whatever the level of foodgrains production for the country as a whole, rural people in some regions live perpetually on the verge of starvation.

Not only is per capita production low, but it also is unstable. Almost the entire cultivated area in the peasant sector lacks irrigation. Production, therefore, fluctuates a great deal with fluctuations in rainfall. The problem is particularly serious in some regions of the country which are drought-prone. These happen to be the same regions where foodgrains production per capita of rural population is extremely low even in normal years. The spectre of famine is thus ever present.[28] These facts suggest two important conclusions. First, the overall economic surplus, meagre as it is, is not stable. Second, a part of this surplus, ideally, ought to be kept aside as an insurance against bad crop years. The difficulties of transport impose the further condition that grains must be stored locally if disastrous famines are to be avoided.

Clearly, the essence of the agrarian problem in Ethiopia today is the absence of an economic surplus and the task is to generate a process of investment which, on the one hand, does not necessitate an additional squeeze on the consumption of the peasantry and, on the other hand, promotes self-reliance. The major form of such investment is labour-investment. It may be recalled that the peasant sector, at present, is a reservoir of unutilised labour power. What is needed is a mobilisation of seasonally idle labour for capital construction so that a part of the actual consumption of the peasantry is in effect transformed into investment. There are activities which require simple tools and much labour, and which can increase agricultural production very significantly. Examples are minor irrigation works, drainage, land clearing, construction of storage facilities and rural roads, etc. It is only when an economic surplus has been generated through the accumulated effects of such activities that a different pattern of accumulation (involving surplus extraction at an increasing rate by the state) can be usefully contemplated. It is this fact which underlines the relevance of co-operative agriculture; for, only within the framework of a co-operative agriculture can the full potential of labour-investment be realised.

IV. THE GOVERNMENT'S PROGRAMME OF CO-OPERATIVISATION: A CRITIQUE

The objectives and processes of institutional development envisioned by the government for Ethiopia's agrarian economy are stated, in a scattered fashion, in a number of policy documents.[27] The objectives include creation of conditions for planned development, consolidation of the small and fragmented peasant holdings with a view to promoting the use of modern technology and the elevation of traditional crafts to the level of small-scale industry. As for the process of transition, three stages of co-operative development are envisaged. An elementary producers' co-operative or a *malba* is one:

1. where farmland, except for up to one-fifth of a hectare per household left for private cultivation, is collectively operated;
2. where the members allow the use of their implements and draught animals for co-operative production; and

3. where distribution of income is according to:
   (a) labour supplied by the members; and
   (b) implements and draught animals contributed towards co-operative production.

An advanced producers' co-operative or a *welba* is one:

1. where all land is made collective property (but up to one-tenth of a hectare is left for household use);
2. where all implements and draught animals become collective property; and
3. where distribution is in accordance with the amount of labour contributed by members.

A high-level co-operative or a *weland* is one:

1. where land and means of production of several *welbas* are pulled together; and
2. the members of each *welba* are converted into members of a *habre* (roughly a production brigade) of the *weland*.

A *weland* is the highest form of co-operative envisaged. The planned process of institutional transformation involves, sequentially, peasant associations transforming themselves into *malbas*, *malbas* transforming themselves into *welbas*, and groups of *welbas* merging together to form *welands*. Roughly speaking, a peasant association of today is seen as a *habre* of the future and a service co-operative of today is seen as a *weland* of the future.

From the above description, it seems clear that co-operativisation has been viewed essentially as a method of promoting large-scale production with modern technology rather than as a method of promoting accumulation in peasant agriculture. The basic rationale of co-operativisation in the Ethiopian context — promotion of labour-investment in a situation where no real economic surplus exists — does not seem to have been recognised by the policy-planners. As a consequence, differences between a state farm-oriented development strategy and a collective farm-oriented development strategy have not been clearly perceived; both have in effect been visualised as being dependent on state investment and imported imputs, and hence as alternatives.

This basic flaw in the co-operativisation strategy perhaps explains certain features of the process of agrarian change over the past years. In the first place, the progress in co-operativisation has been quite disappointing. No *weland* has so far been formed, nor have many peasant associations transformed themselves fully into *malbas* or *welbas*. In most cases, only some members of a peasant association have joined together to form a *malba* or a *welba*; consequently, the existing *malbas* and *welbas* are quite small in size. More significantly, between 1977/78 and 1982/83, most of the new *malbas* or *welbas* apparently evolved out of new settlement schemes.[30]

This disappointing progress in co-operativisation is only partly explained by the fact that the government chose to accord priority to expanding the state farm sector during this period in view of the urgent need to increase food supplies in urban areas. For, there is no real contradiction between expansion of the state farm sector and that of the co-operative sector unless it is supposed that they compete for state investment and imported goods, that is, unless it is supposed that they both involve the development of capital- and technology-intensive large-scale farming. Unfortunately, such a supposition seems to have been made in formulating state policy over the past years. This is even indicated by certain characteristics displayed by the existing producers' co-operatives.[31] There is no evidence to suggest that the co-operatives have made efforts to promote labour-investment. On the other hand, many of them have attempted to mechanise, thus incurring huge debts and making themselves dependent on imported fuel, machinery and spare parts, as also on outsiders for repair and maintenance services. Given this general orientation, co-operativisation has involved considerable state investment. And yet, the co-operatives have performed no better than peasant farms in terms of production; nor have they been able to improve the living standards of their members to any significant extent. Hence there is no real incentive for the peasants to opt for co-operative farming in preference to family farming.

   In short, a basic shortcoming of the government's programme of co-operativisation is that it is premised on a supposed superiority of large-scale over small-scale farming, a supposition whose validity is by no means established. In Ethiopian conditions, co-operative farming can be regarded as superior to peasant farming, not because the former is larger in scale than the latter, but because the former provides a more effective framework for mobilising surplus labour for capital construction in agriculture than the latter. Unless the realisation of this potential is made the central objective, co-operativisation is unlikely to develop on an enduring basis.

V. AGRICULTURAL GROWTH AND INSTITUTIONAL TRANSFORMATION:
SOME CONCLUDING OBSERVATIONS

Rural economy in Ethiopia is at crucial crossroads. The post-1974 agrarian reforms have created the necessary conditions for transformation but have not defined its precise path; this will be determined by policies pursued at this juncture. For this reason, future policies need to be based on a clear understanding of the nature of inter-relationships between agricultural growth and institutional change so that short-run exigencies do not undermine long-run goals. Growth is badly needed in Ethiopia. Food supply per capita of rural population is extremely low, and population is expected to grow at a rate of around three per cent per annum in the foreseeable future. A rate of growth in food production of at least three per cent seems absolutely essential, and faster rates would obviously be desirable. It is tempting to make agricultural growth the overriding objective of development policy.

   Yet, a strategy of high growth may be neither feasible nor desirable at this stage. Such a strategy will almost certainly require a rapid expansion in cultivated area. It is true that there is a great deal of scope for expanding the cultivated area and no doubt this should be exploited in the long run. However, a rapid expansion of cultivated area in the short run will require careful planning, substantial investment and a good deal of mechanisation so that, in the Ethiopian context, a rapid expansion of the state farm sector will be necessary. Given the present conditions in the state farm sector, this will be inefficient in the first place. Second, such a strategy will call for a substantial flow of resources into agriculture. Since Ethiopia's industrial sector is too weak to be able to provide the resources, substantial inflow of foreign aid over a considerable period will be necessary. Agriculture, moreover, will become increasingly dependent on imported inputs and hence increasingly vulnerable to fluctuations in trade and aid flows. Even the skills requirements of a steady expansion of mechanised cultivation will be difficult to meet.

These are some of the lessons that can be usefully drawn from the experience of the recent past. Between 1977/78 and 1982/83, the bulk of the state investment went to the state farm sector, but the return to investment in terms of increased output was dismally low. While the sector expanded rapidly in terms of cultivated area, yield rates of crops declined very sharply. Most state farms today make financial losses so that they are incapable of expanding on the basis of their own resources. While this may partly be due to inappropriate structure of administered prices, there are reasons to believe that the state farms are inefficient users of resources.[32] First, seed rates are high and yield-responses to fertilisers are low so that current unit costs of production are unusually high. Second, the utilisation rate of machinery is extremely low. This reflects itself in the unduly high value of depreciation. This state of affairs results partly from the fact that in single crop agriculture, heavy farm machinery (for example, tractors or combines) cannot but be underutilised and partly from bad maintenance, lack of adequate repair facilities and irregular availability of spare parts. Third, while the bulk of the productive work is done by temporary workers, hired at a daily wage equivalent to the minimum wage set by the government, the state farms maintain an elite work force on a permanent basis. These workers are skilled or semi-skilled, are drawn from urban areas and are paid relatively high wages. They are also entitled to welfare services which are unavailable to the rest of the rural population. Unit costs of labour supplied by the permanent workers are in fact generally above the average labour productivity.

In short, high investment requirements, low returns to investment, the prospect of growing dependence on imports and foreign aid and labour problems combine together to make a state farm-oriented development strategy difficult to contemplate. Perhaps even more importantly, such a strategy, even if feasible, does not really address the fundamental problem of development of Ethiopia's agriculture, that is, the lack of an investible surplus. It is the need to overcome this problem, and not the supposed advantages of large-scale over small-scale production, which emphasises the desirability of a co-operativisation strategy. For co-operative farming provides the most appropriate framework for promoting labour accumulation. The key aspect of labour process in co-operative farming is the valuation of labour in terms of work points. The value of a work point is indeterminate *ex ante* because it depends on the overall production performance of a co-operative unit and this is known only at the end of a production cycle. The practice facilitates labour accumulation because addition of work points merely lowers the value of a work point and this allows increases in employment without corresponding increases or decreases in the 'wage bill'; it also means that the burden of accumulation is distributed in equal proportion among all workers.

It should be evident that a co-operativisation strategy entails promotion of intensive cultivation. It emphasises local efforts rather than state investment, efficient use of labour rather than mechanisation and peasant consumption rather than surplus extraction from peasant agriculture. Agricultural growth, therefore, can be relatively independent of imports and foreign aid, and state investment can be devoted to developing infrastructural facilities, research and extension services.

It has to be recognised, however, that co-operativisation is by nature a slow process while the need for agricultural growth is immediate. It is thus necessary to use the service co-operatives for the purpose of promoting labour accumulation in the transitional period. The problem is that a service co-operative has no direct control over the labour power of its members. The only way it can promote labour accumulation is by collecting a tax from its members and by then employing labour for capital construction on wages (thus effectively transferring the tax revenue back to the taxpayers). Apart from being a cumbersome process, this method has a major disadvantage: the existence of private peasants renders it difficult to distribute the costs and benefits equitably. Nevertheless, efforts in this direction are worthwhile not merely because they will help achieve growth in the short run but also because they will encourage co-operativisation.

The question remains: can an adequate growth of agricultural production be achieved through these methods? In principle, the answer is in the affirmative. Yield rates in agriculture in Ethiopia are very low and marginal returns to efforts towards raising yields and increasing cropping intensity are likely to be high. Measures to improve yield rates and efficiency of input use on the existing state farms, to promote labour accumulation and thus encourage co-operativisation in the peasant sector, and to develop rural infrastructure through state investment should ensure at least the minimum necessary growth rate in the short run. Higher growth rates will become feasible once co-operativisation makes significant internal accumulation possible and the state farms are able to expand on the basis of their own profits.

NOTES

1. Throughout this article the term 'agricultural surplus' is used to mean that portion of the peasant sector's output which is appropriated without compensation either by feudal overlords (as in pre-revolution Ethiopia) or by the state (as in present-day Ethiopia).
2. For discussions and bibliography, see Abate and Kiros [1983]. A good journalistic account is available in Halliday and Molyneux [1981].
3. Throughout this article, the term 'economic surplus' refers to the excess of agricultural output over and above the cost of reproduction of labour power in agriculture (or, in other words, the subsistence requirements of the agricultural population).
4. The term 'co-operativisation' is preferable to the term 'collectivisation' because we wish to refer exclusively to the process of development of producers' co-operatives. Collectivisation is a wider term; it refers to the process of development of both co-operatives and state farms.
5. For details of the reform measures implemented since 1975, see Abate and Kiros [1983], Rahmato [1982] and Kiros [1982]. For an evaluation of the reform process, see Rahmato [1984].

6. For details, see Abegaz [*1982*].
7. The state farms producing coffee are managed by the Ministry of Coffee and Tea Development and those producing sugarcane are managed by the Ethiopian Sugar Corporation.
   All the other state farms are managed by the Ministry of State Farms Development.
8. For a detailed discussion, see Ghose [*1985*].
9. The detailed data are presented in Ghose [*1985*].
10. Cf. Office of the Population and Housing Census Commission [*1984*]. The estimate per-
    tains to the year 1984.
11. Cf. Ministry of Agriculture [*1977*]. The estimate pertains to the year 1976.
12. Central Statistical Office [*1978*]. The estimate pertains to the year 1978.
13. For details, see Ghose [*1985*].
14. During the same period, the area under cotton increased at an annual rate of around five
    per cent. The yield rate of cotton, therefore, also declined, though much less sharply than
    in the case of food crops. The estimates are based on data supplied by the Ministry of State
    Farms.
15. These observations are based on data supplied by the Ministry of Coffee and Tea Development.
16. For evidence on the pattern of distribution of chemical fertilizers, see Agricultural Marketing
    Corporation [*1982*].
17. Cf. Abate and Kiros [*1983*].
18. Major foodcrops in Ethiopia are teff, barley, wheat, maize, millet, pulses and oilseeds. Leaving
    aside the coffee-growing regions, these crops account for nearly 97 per cent of the peasant
    sector's output.
19. See Ministry of Agriculture [*1978*]. The survey from which this estimate was derived did not
    cover Eritrea and Tigrai.
20. See Saith [*1982*] for a detailed analysis of this aspect.
21. Note that these estimates refer to the period 1977/78–1981/82 and not to the period 1977/78–
    1982/83 as in the case of Table 4.
22. This scenario, of course, is based on the assumption that resources would be allocated evenly
    across regions and groups of peasantry. If resources are concentrated either in selected regions
    or at the hands of particular groups of peasantry, the elasticity may well be high, as indeed
    was the case in Ethiopia during 1977/78–1981/82.
23. For some evidence, see Ghose [*1985*].
24. The first population census in the country was conducted in 1984. The rural population,
    according to the census, was 32.8 million (excluding Eritrea and Tigrai). Assuming a rate
    of growth of population of three per cent per annum and unchanged rural-urban distribution,
    the implied rural population in 1978 should have been about 27.5 million or about 24 per
    cent higher than the estimate used in Table 10.
25. The two estimates are comparable. In both cases, the methodology applied is the same and
    two regions – Tigrai and Eritrea – are left out of account.
26. Results of the 1984 census suggest a rural population of 30.9 million for 1982 while the figure
    used to estimate per capita production and consumption for 1981/82 was 24.7 million.
27. See Saith [*1982*] for an analysis of price variations across regions.
28. The present famine, at the cost of thousands of lives, has again highlighted the fundamental
    weaknesses of the agrarian economy.
29. For details, see Kiros [*1982*].
30. Even so, there were only 1,489 producers' co-operatives with a total membership of 94,376
    peasant households by the end of 1984. For further details, see Ghose [*1985*].
31. The observations which follow are based on the author's general impressions in the course
    of field visits and his detailed study of two producers' co-operatives. For details, see Ghose
    [*1985*].
32. The observations which follow are based on the author's field observations and his detailed
    study of two state farms. See Ghose [*1985*].

REFERENCES

Abate, Alula and Kiros, Fassil G., 1983, 'Agrarian reform, structural changes and rural develop-
    ment in Ethiopia' in A. K. Ghose (ed.), *Agrarian Reform in Contemporary Developing
    Countries*, London: Croom Helm.

Abegaz, H. Y., 1982, *The Organisation of State Farms in Ethiopia After the Land Reform of 1974*, Saarbrücken: Verlag.

Ghose, A. K., 1985, 'The Agrarian Problem in Ethiopia', Geneva: ILO, [*forthcoming*].

Government of Ethiopia, Agricultural Marketing Corporation, 1982, *Annual Report*, Addis Ababa.

Government of Ethiopia, Arssi Rural Development Unit, 1982, *Cost of Production of Major Crops and Grain Selling Prices*, Assella.

Government of Ethiopia, Central Statistical Office, 1978, *National Sample Survey, Second Round, 1969/77*, Addis Ababa.

Government of Ethiopia, Central Statistical Office, 1980, *Agricultural Sample Survey, 1979/80*, Vol. V, Addis Ababa.

Government of Ethiopia, Ethiopian Seed Corporation, 1984, *Annual Report*, Addis Ababa.

Government of Ethiopia, Office of the Population and Housing Census Commission, 1984, *Population and Housing Census, Preliminary Report*, Addis Ababa.

Government of Ethiopia, Ministry of Agriculture, 1977, *Rural Population and Employment in Agriculture*, Addis Ababa.

Government of Ethiopia, Ministry of Agriculture, 1978, *Area Production, Yield, Use of Fertilizers and Marketed Production of Major Crops*, Addis Ababa.

Government of Ethiopia, Ministry of Agriculture, 1979, *Area Production and Yield of Major Crops for the Whole Country and by Region in 1974/75–1978/79*, Addis Ababa.

Halliday, Fred and Molyneux, Maxine, 1981, *The Ethiopian Revolution*, London: Verso.

Kiros, Fassil G., 1982, 'Mobilising the Peasantry for Rural Development', paper presented at the 7th International Conference of Ethiopian Studies, Lund, Sweden (mimeo).

Rahmato, Dessalegn, 1982, 'Agrarian Reform in Ethiopia: A Brief Assessment', paper presented at the 7th International Conference of Ethiopian Studies, Lund, Sweden (mimeo).

Rahmato, Dessalegn, 1984, *Agrarian Reform in Ethiopia*, Uppsala: Scandinavian Institute of African Studies.

Saith, Ashwani, 1982, 'The Distributional Dimensions of Revolutionary Change: The Case of Ethiopia', Working Paper, The Hague: The Institute of Social Studies.

# The Distributional Dimensions of Revolutionary Transition: Ethiopia

*by Ashwani Saith\**

*This study attempts to investigate some of the distributional costs that have attended upon the process of revolutionary transition in Ethiopia, focusing on the crucial role of the rural sector in this regard. The central variable through which this sector influenced national economic performance was the marketed proportion of output. The study deals with this linkage and with the macroeconomic distributional outcomes of the growth process for the rural and urban sectors. The probable distributional implications of the Ten Year Plan are elicited, and the sobering findings provide the motivational force behind a few strategic policy considerations that are briefly outlined. It is argued that the national economic growth process was seriously imbalanced, and the sluggishness of agriculture meant that the growth was financed through an inflationary process which passed on the costs of accumulation substantially on to the poorer sections of the population.*

## I. INTRODUCTION

In this article we will investigate some of the distributional costs that have attended upon the process of revolutionary transition in Ethiopia. It is inherent in the nature of such transitions that they are marked by internal upheavals and external disturbances, and Ethiopia has had more than her share of these since 1974. Our concern is more with the manner in which such growth impinged upon the distributional dimension than with the precise influence of these exogenous events on the growth or distributional performance. We begin with some observations in section II on the redistributive aspects of the rural institutional transformation. The crucial variable through which this sector influences national economic performance is the marketed proportion of agricultural output. This linkage and the macroeconomic distributional outcomes of the growth process are analysed in section III. The disastrous distributional implications of this process for large sections of the urban sector are then summarised in section IV, where some estimates of the incidence of urban poverty are reported. If a significant proportion of the urben population lost out, some sections have gained. Section V identifies the winners and losers in the distributional balance-sheet for the period. The final section considers

*This article is a shortened but otherwise unrevised version of a research report completed in Ethiopia in August 1983. The subsequent famine in rural Ethiopia makes the analysis and the policy implications of this article more rather than less relevant. Although I am grateful to several colleagues, notably Keith Griffith, Shyam Nigam, Vali Jamal, Ajit Ghose and Justin Maeda for helpful discussions, I alone am responsible for the views expressed in this article.

probable distributional outcomes of the Draft Ten Year Plan as it stood at end-1983. The somewhat sobering findings of this and the earlier sections provide the motive force behind the few strategic policy considerations that are briefly outlined.

## II. RURAL REDISTRIBUTION

Prior to the Revolution, there were two prime sources of rural poverty and inequality. The first was the extreme inequality in land access and ownership; the second was and remains the fragile dependence of various regions on the vagaries of the weather. Post-Revolution policies have attacked both primarily through institutional means.

At a stroke, which was frequently violent, the Land Reform removed the class of landlords from the countryside. Ownership was vested in the state; and peasants were entitled to usufructuary rights, land allocations to households depended on total land availability in the newly-formed *kebele* and the number of households in it; and the allocation to households depended on their size and labour force. The maximum limit on a holding was set at ten hectares. The immediate result of this has been to provide a basic floor to rural consumption and has guaranteed that no household would starve due to a lack of access to land. The substantial direct impact on the reduction of rural poverty as well as inequality should be self-evident. Using extremely approximate orders of magnitude, assume that 30 per cent of the rural output was directed to a numerically negligible class of landlords constituting, say, five per cent of the rural population; that the tenants formed 65 per cent of the population and retained 40 per cent of the net output; and that the remaining 30 per cent of the output and population were in the 'independent' category. Assume also that in net terms, this last group breaks even in the Land Reform and that all the landlords' rents are shared between the reformed ex-landlord and the tenant and landless population. The effect would be to raise the ex-tenant incomes to the average level or, on the above assumptions, by approximately 50 per cent. All households covered with incomes up to one-third below the poverty line would be lifted over it.

But this simple view might overstate the redistributive effects of the reform. First, some benefits, say, about five per cent, have been taxed away. Second, the reform was of the 'ceiling' type, where the redistribution applied strictly only to the holdings greater than ten hectares in size. Hence, in land areas, where the mean land availability was under ten hectares, say, two to four hectares, and even where the initial land distribution was quite skewed — as in most areas — not much land would become available for redistribution. Third, some perverse cases are possible, and not entirely improbable. Consider the situation where many holdings are under ten hectares in size, but where there is a high incidence of tenancy in this size class. It is possible then that following the banning of tenancy, small landlords would evict their tenants and cultivate larger holdings than before, although still under the official ten-hectare limit. Hence, the forced decline in rents could result paradoxically in a net loss to the tenants. Fourth, the Ethiopian Land Reform cannot simply be assumed not to have suffered the problems encountered in such ceiling-type reforms elsewhere, namely, that the above-ceiling landowners give up the inferior plots of land for redistribution. This can have a considerable effect in perpetuating income inequalities. Fifth, while land was so transferred, other means of production, for example, draught animals, were not. Again, the experience of other countries shows that such a partial reform would not make a proportionate impact on incomes. This is emphasised by the high sensitivity of crop yields to the time of ploughing and sowing, a condition which characterises most of rural Ethiopia due to the lack of controlled irrigation. Sixth, the land reform would have bypassed – in large measure – those scattered subsistence, non-monetised agriculturists which form significant numbers in several provinces.

Some of these factors limiting redistribution are countered by specific responses to them. Thus, in areas of land scarcity, the effective limit of the size of a holding is well below ten hectares, although, in general, the larger owners retain holdings which are substantially larger than those of the poor peasant. Further, the tax is rather loosely collected, although in view of its nominal progressivity, this laxness would benefit the richer peasants more. However, the poor peasants, especially where they form a co-operative, often side-step taxes also by the under-reporting of areas newly brought under cultivation. This would compensate for any real tax incidence, a result which is assisted through the present inability and unwillingness of the state to enforce land tax measurements and collections strictly.

However, the other four factors limiting the redistributive effects of the reform still hold some force, and it would appear, therefore, that in aggregate terms, the one-off redistributive gains for the poorer sections are unlikely to have been anywhere near the 50 per cent figure first adopted. No doubt a substantial number gained significantly; yet the reform must also have by-passed, or improved only marginally, the incomes of an equally large number. In general, it could be stated that the benefits would be greater where the land ownership and operational distributions diverged most, *and* where high proportions of the owned holdings belonged to size classes greater than ten hectares. In so far as this reduction in inequality occurred, localised poverty would no doubt be eradicated. Yet it must be remembered that rural poverty in many parts of Ethiopian is not a localised but a general phenomenon. The scattered cultivation pattern in many parts is in itself an indication of the absence of any real economic surplus. In such areas, the reduction of poverty cannot depend on such a redistribution; it has to rely upon the dynamic growth advantages of the new institutional structure in conjunction with other state policies designed to achieve this goal.

Let us turn now to the second source of rural poverty, namely, that arising from major agricultural fluctuations. This source has strong regional contours; indeed, it is arguable that apart from the intra-unit inequalities which prevail, the major form that inequality and poverty take is regional in character. Such disparities are widely marked in Ethiopia, as can be seen from any regional profile of relevant agricultural variables. There is clear evidence of a powerful concentration of resources, outputs, marketed surplus and incomes in a few provinces, such as Gojjam, Gondar, Arssi and Shoa. In turn, the cycle of causation is reproduced through the high allocation of yield-raising inputs in the same regions. Further, some of these areas, especially Shoa, form the industrial backbone of Ethiopia. This is due, of course, to Addis Ababa and its strong gravitational pull on new industries. The danger with such extreme concentrations is that they tend to soak up a wide range of scarce resources. Indeed, from a short run point of view, allocational choices could further exacerbate the position. The availability of a reliable and relatively efficient infrastructure would no doubt invite planners to place important new industrial enterprises in this heartland, just as the need to extract a high marketed proportion from incremental agricultural output would further divert scarce chemical fertilisers to the already developed and high income agricultural regions. And inexorably small-scale industries also prosper in these developed areas. Thus, of the total number 1,485 private manufacturing establishments, 1,164 are located in Addis Ababa, Shoa and Eritrea; these account for 82 per cent of the 15200 persons employed. It is also clear that some agriculturally prosperous regions score well on certain nutritional indicators, while highly industrialised ones do better than most on other indicators which are dependent on urban services. Those which are neither fare poorly. These data also point out the abysmally low general levels of these indicators across the board (see Saith [*1983: Tables 2, 3*]).

One major source of regional disparities lies in the variations in geo-natural conditions. Areas with variable weather are not conducive to agricultural or local industrial growth. The scattered and semi-nomadic populations of Wollo, Hararghe and Sidamo are thus subjected to frequent disasters through droughts which decimate both people and livestock.

It has been argued in the case of Wollo and Hararghe that the famines of 1974/5 were due to exchange entitlement failures (see Sen [*1981: Chapter 7*]). While the stricken population certainly lost most of its purchasing power, this should not hide the fundamentally fragmented nature of the Ethiopian regional economy. This implies a lack of market integration of an extreme kind. Very considerable grain movements would be required in normal times to compensate for the wide regional variations in the degree of self-sufficiency in foodgrains [*Ghose, this volume: Table 1*]. In theory, the flow of such movements would be governed by regional price variations which would invite food inflows up to a point where the disposition of supplies would equilibrate prices after adjusting for transport costs. Reality appears to follow a rather different course. Tables 1 and 2 reveal remarkably high price differentials across the board. The average quotations are taken from important markets at *awraja* or *woreda* levels in October 1981, and hence can be used as an index of market integration. Gojjam displays the lowest variability in intra-regional prices for most crops, while Tigrai, Wollo, Gamo Goffa and Bale seem highly volatile. The food deficit areas expectedly show higher prices, but the differentials are remarkably high, as a comparison of Hararghe and Tigrai with Gojjam and Gondar reveals. The variability is generally greater in the case of the four inferior crops on which the poorer population depends. Thus, teff and wheat have the lowest coefficients of variation, and sorghum the highest. Relative prices of the different crops also alter ranks frequently. Detailed data indicate a remarkably dissimilar price structure and growth rates even between contiguous, well-connected *awrajas* of the same province, with

TABLE 1

INTRA-REGIONAL PRICE SPREADS BY CROPS, OCTOBER 1981

1. Average Quotations in (birr/quintal), Local Markets

| | Arssi | Bale | Gemu-Goffa | Gojjam | Gondar | Harerghe | Keffa | Shoa | Sidamo | Tigrai | Wollo |
|---|---|---|---|---|---|---|---|---|---|---|---|
| Teff | 55.50 | 62.30 | 64.72 | 36.85 | 42.73 | 128.30 | 69.50 | 70.80 | 76.78 | 90.43 | 57.86 |
| Wheat | 58.62 | 51.78 | nq | 39.33 | 38.17 | 91.00 | 78.00 | 69.00 | 65.70 | 66.08 | 61.81 |
| Maize | 35.00 | 40.60 | 27.33 | 20.50 | 20.00 | 69.67 | nq | 41.17 | 33.80 | 50.00 | 33.67 |
| Barley | 33.70 | 32.39 | 47.08 | 22.50 | 29.00 | nq | 40.00 | 49.58 | 42.65 | 43.38 | 39.18 |
| Sorghum | nq | nq | 34.00 | 22.83 | 27.38 | 101.70 | 39.50 | 48.21 | nq | 65.35 | 46.20 |
| Millets | nq | nq | nq | 22.56 | 26.60 | nq | nq | nq | nq | 100.00 | nq |

2. Coefficients of Variations (%)

| | Arssi | Bale | Gemu-Goffa | Gojjam | Gondar | Harerghe | Keffa | Shoa | Sidamo | Tigrai | Wollo |
|---|---|---|---|---|---|---|---|---|---|---|---|
| Teff | 12.87 | 17.28 | 20.64 | 6.11 | 16.82 | nc | nc | 15.85 | 9.38 | 19.91 | 18.19 |
| Wheat | 13.09 | 24.31 | nc | 13.35 | 14.22 | nc | nc | 17.54 | 16.46 | 25.84 | 19.70 |
| Maize | nc | 36.49 | 31.11 | 13.89 | nc | nc | nc | 18.09 | 22.82 | nc | 32.02 |
| Barley | 31.09 | 5.58 | 12.99 | 14.36 | 9.65 | nc | nc | 18.32 | 18.44 | 52.08 | 19.70 |
| Sorghum | nc | nc | 50.02 | 9.26 | 25.22 | nc | nc | 27.01 | nc | 28.78 | 21.89 |
| Millets | nc | nc | nc | 15.37 | 8.10 | nc | nc | nc | nc | nc | nc |

Sources: (1) Food Supply System: *Meher Synoptic Report, 1981*, Early Warning and Planning Service, RRC, March.
(2) Market Dependent Food Supply System: *Food Supply Status and Forecast by Administrative Region*, EW and PS, RRC, March 1982.

Notes: nq = not quoted; nc = not computed because of small number of quotations.

TABLE 2

INTER-REGIONAL PRICE SPREADS BY CROPS, OCTOBER 1981*

| Crop | Number of price quotations for crop | Maximum regional average/ price birr/quintal | Minimum regional average/ price birr/quintal | Average of regional averages birr/quintal | Coefficient of variation of regional averages (%) |
|------|------|------|------|------|------|
| Teff | 11 | 128.3 | 36.9 | 68.7 | 34.4 |
| Wheat | 10 | 91.0 | 38.2 | 62.0 | 24.9 |
| Maize | 10 | 69.7 | 20.0 | 37.2 | 37.5 |
| Barley | 10 | 49.6 | 22.5 | 38.0 | 21.1 |
| Sorghum | 8 | 101.7 | 22.8 | 48.2 | 49.3 |
| Millets | 3 | 100.0 | 22.6 | 49.7 | 71.6 |

*Source:* As for Table 1.

*Note:*    *This table uses the average prices given in Table 1.

*prices doubling over the year in one awraja* market while dropping significantly in a neighbouring one. All the evidence points to a highly fragmented market structure with very imperfect flows of grain and information between them. This has important implications for ensuring food security to the vulnerable areas and populations beyond providing them with exchange entitlements (say, through food-for-work schemes) and letting induced market flows do the rest. Against this background, we need to bear in mind the significant intensity and frequency of sharp fluctuations in sown areas, yields and production of major crops even at the national level.

The response of the state to this problem has been substantial, although symptomatic. It has attempted to monitor and forecast food insecurities and shortages through the Early Warning and Planning Services Unit of the Relief and Rehabilitation Commission (RRC). Against this background the enormity of the RRC's efforts in moving drought- (and war-) affected people into relief settlements is quite impressive. Apart from these relief settlements, the RRC also develops regular settlements for drought-affected populations, nomadic people, unemployed persons, and overcrowded farmers. Such settlements are sometimes rather expensive, since they are heavily dependent upon comprehensive support from the state for several years during which they make their tentative transition into self-sufficiency. They frequently suffer also from an over-centralised control process which makes the settlement unit too dependent with regard to both input allocations and production decisions. Settlements, like state farms, cannot keep their own financial accounts, and this damages the efficiency of their resource use. Further, it is necessary to initiate the political participation of the settlers in the production and general decision-making processes. At present, there is a real danger of developing a multi-layered structure from the settler to the international donor agencies, with each lower layer overly dependent on successively higher ones.

Another major way by which the settlement programme reduces rural poverty as well as inter-retional inequality is through the villagisation of scattered peasant holdings. This programme has made some headway, especially in Bale, where it is anticipated that the entire rural population will soon inhabit specially set-up settlements. This will permit not only the state service and delivery systems to incorporate this population into their network but, as importantly, will provide some necessary preconditions for the emergence of collective units which can internalise the wide range of production and social externalities not reaped by individual peasants. With regard to the wider strategic issues concerning regional disparities, it has to be admitted that any headlong or dramatic attempt to 'solve' this historical problem is likely to prove an expensive failure. However, the policy framework developed in this article has inherent in it processes which would diminish the disparities through development at the periphery. Thus, in view of a high degree of economic fragmentation, a special if not overriding priority would have to be assigned to rural infrastructure based on four complimentary activities. First, through labour accumulation facilitated by the co-operative structure, rural roads should be developed linking co-operatives to feeder roads, and these to the main gravel highways. Second, local storage capacity for foodgrains should be constructed at critical supply points, widely dispersed. Over a period, these silos should begin to serve as the grain banks of the co-operatives of the region. Third, local rural industries located at the service-co-operative level should be initiated, at first on the basis of the demand of the members for simple consumer goods and farm implements, and subsequently for a wider range of products, including industrial ancillaries, and consumer goods for a wider market. Such industries, as also the infrastructural creation activities could have a strong seasonal dimension in the present phase of development. Lastly, and perhaps most significantly, concerted efforts should be made to harness the considerable small-scale irrigation potential of the country, but again through the institutional device of the producers' or service co-operatives. The great advantage of the former would be that such activities would be self-financed, and would be non-inflationary in the short run, and strongly anti-inflationary in the long run when their benefits come on stream. The objective should be through such schemes to integrate the economy, to develop rural diversification, and to provide food security. The key to achieving these is the extension of the area of stable grain yields through irrigation. Once again, the objectives of growth and equity appear to be harmonious within a 'boot-strap' strategy of local, self-financed, labour accumulation generated and organised within the emergent rural collective institutions. But critical to the success of these measures is the rapid expansion of the co-operative mode of organisation. In this respect, the experience thus far is extremely disappointing [*Ghose, this volume*].

## III. THE INFLATIONARY PROCESS

Thus far, we have focused on the rural institutional transformation. We will consider now the distributional costs of this difficult transition. The analysis is based in general on the benchmark data for the end years, 1974/5 and 1979/80. This period is characterised in the main by economic stagnation when the performance is considered in per capita terms. The benchmark analysis hides very substantial year-to-year fluctuations in most national aggregates but shows up quite starkly the staggering and steady erosion of real private consumption per capita. This decline is accompanied by an increase in the incidence and intensity of poverty in the urban areas, and an erosion of the gains of the redistributive land reforms in the rural sector. In short, the story is one of impoverishment without growth. No doubt, there are powerful, even overwhelming, exogenous forces which provide one part of the explanation. A prime factor might be the armed conflicts in the north and south. These conflicts have occurred primarily within the borders of the country and, apart from shutting off important production areas, have generated a fearsome flow of displaced persons. To this burden has been added that created by a series of droughts, making it necessary to re-settle a population virtually of the size of Addis Ababa. Third, the revolutionary transition in the country-side was far from peaceful in several important agricultural regions, and the dust did not settle on the class struggles till 1978/79 in some areas. To top it all, international economic trends have been adverse, with coffee prices dropping in the latter half of the period and petroleum prices rising substantially in the first. Notwithstanding this awesome list of 'disturbances', it will be attempted here to find an economic explanation of the recent experience. Needless to say, these are not incompatible: the exogenous factors could provide some of the 'givens' of the economic explanation, which then proceeds to analyse how what happened did happen. The exercise has more than mere academic interest. It is hoped that it will provide an analytical framework within which the Draft Ten Year Investment Plan (DTYP) could be vetted for determining its possible and probable distributional outcomes. And perhaps beyond the provision of a simple framework, it might also offer a few insights some fundamental constraints to available egalitarian growth strategies.

It should be mentioned at the outset that the extreme paucity of reliable statistical information frequently forces assumptions which might not be acceptable in most other circumstances. The reader is therefore cautioned that the story which follows frequently relies on statistics which are 'guestimates'. A second problem arises, however, from our methodology. It would be immediately apparent that the national economy is in a fluid state. Yet in our analysis we are implicitly stating it as being in equilibrium in the years 1974/75 and 1979/80, which form the end-years of the period under study. Further, a quick check would reveal that even this short period is marked by two sub-periods, the first of decline, up to 1977/78, and the second of subsequent recovery. However, adopting such short periods would make a self-contained analysis of each even more hazardous.

By taking a five-year period it is hoped that the analysis will capture the averaged effects of lagged processes. Furthermore, it is arguable that the 'up-turn' in the economy is deduced from rather thin evidence. If one focuses, in Table 3, one 1977/78, it is easy to regard it as the base of the upturn. But the performance of that year was dominated by the exogenous factors listed. The cheerful manufacturing growth rate of 23.8 per cent in 1978/79 has more to do with the coming-on-line of Asmara industry once again, a one-off recovery boost. On the other hand, both 1978/79 and 1979/80 have been good harvest years and the absence of growth is discouraging. It is to be doubted if the upturn could withstand even one indifferent crop season. On the other hand, it would be valid to expect production to respond to the increased institutional stability, but this factor does not appear to have transformed the economic performance of the recent past sufficiently for one to place great faith in the 'upturn'.

The story starts with agricultural performance since 1974/75. In aggregate terms, the sector grew by 8.4 per cent over the period, but still lost some of its gains from the land reform. There are several reasons for this. The first concerns the relatively high rate of growth of population. We assume that population grew at 2.8 per cent per year over this period. This is higher than the officially firm, but unofficially dubious, rate of 2.5 per cent. This itself would more than offset the real growth, and imply a per capita *decline* in agricultural GDP by 5.1 per cent. This decline is reduced by the very high rural out-migration rate, which reduces the growth rate of the rural population to 2.2 per cent, and of (rural) per capita agricultural GDP to $-2.8$ per cent over the period. Thus, agriculture exports some of its deterioration to the urban sector. Second, agricultural taxes have withdrawn approximately five per cent of agricultural incomes, and this is not accounted for in the above figures. Third, the growth rates of state farms and settlements have been much in excess of the above rates, implying a lower growth rate for peasant and co-operative agriculture. The combined effect of these three factors could imply a decline of about eight per cent in the per capita income of the peasant and co-operative sectors. On the other hand, it might have gained somewhat through an improvement in the terms of trade. This is difficult to establish or quantify since it turns on the rate of increase of prices paid by merchants for purchases from this sector. The relative price of food to non-food items increased in Addis Ababa by 27.7 per cent but peasants sell to merchants and to the Agricultural Marketing Corporation (AMC), not to Addis consumers. AMC buying prices have been held constant since 1979, since when non-food prices have risen by over ten per cent. Since one-eighth of the sales of the peasant sector (= peasants, producer co-operatives and service co-operatives) go to the AMC at fixed prices, and the rest to merchants, the price offered by the latter would have had to rise by more than 25 per cent to prevent any terms of trade loss, on the assumption that the price of inputs sold to agriculture also rose at ten per cent. Considering that the overall 'Food' open-market price index itself rose by about ten per cent over the period, and that the 'Cereals' index actually fell by two per cent, it would be fair to assume that the terms of trade did *not* move in favour of grain producers.

There remains the question concerning coffee performance. Here, despite the fact that the state intercepts the vast proportion of revenues, the terms of trade were in favour of coffee producers when we make 1974/75 the base year. Should the base be shifted to 1975/76, the producer price of coffee drops by 6.5 per cent; over the 1975/76–1979/80 period Addis Ababa non-food prices rise by ten times that figure. Thus, it would appear that after a post-Revolution bonanaza in 1974/75 coffee incomes have suffered a persistent hangover. For our purposes, we should also note that coffee production and exports rose over this period by 13.5 per cent and 70.2 per cent respectively. This would imply a further though marginal reduction in the growth rate of

TABLE 3

ANNUAL PER CAPITA* GROWTH RATES OF GDP BY INDUSTRIAL ORIGIN AT CONSTANT 1960/61 FACTOR COST

| Sector | Base year weight | 1975/76 | 1976/77 | 1977/78 | 1978/79 | 1979/80 | 1980/81 | 1974/74 to 1980/81 | End year weight |
|---|---|---|---|---|---|---|---|---|---|
| Agriculture | 0.483 | 0.0 | −2.7 | −4.3 | −0.4 | 1.9 | −0.3 | −5.3 | 0.459 |
| Handicraft & Small-Scale Industry | 0.048 | −2.5 | −1.6 | −4.6 | 1.2 | −0.2 | −0.4 | −7.3 | 0.045 |
| Manufacturing | 0.043 | −1.9 | −0.5 | −6.5 | 23.8 | 7.5 | 2.7 | 25.4 | 0.055 |
| Building & Construction | 0.054 | −20.5 | 3.5 | −7.1 | 4.8 | 13.4 | 0.1 | −8.6 | 0.073 |
| Transport & Communications | 0.065 | 0.6 | 1.0 | −0.5 | 5.5 | 3.8 | 5.1 | 11.4 | 0.049 |
| Trade & Other Services | 0.294 | 0.0 | −0.6 | −1.1 | 2.7 | 1.6 | 0.4 | 3.8 | 0.306 |
| GDP | 1.000 | −1.4 | −1.4 | −3.6 | 2.4 | 2.7 | 0.4 | −0.4 | 1.000 |

Source: National Accounts Division, NRDC and CPSC Secretariat.

Note: *The rate of growth of population is assumed to be 2.8 per cent per year.

the non-coffee sector. In sum then the evidence suggests a marginal erosion to the tune of five to ten per cent of the post-land reform per capita incomes of the peasant sector. What are the implications of this for the other sectors of the economy? In order to explore this issue, we must unavoidably speculate about the behaviour of the agricultural marketed surplus, the single most important factor through which agricultural performance impinges upon the national economy.

There are no statistics available on recent trends or levels of the marketed surplus of agriculture with the exception of 1977/78, and we have to rely on very rough estimates. Let us assume that in 1974/75, 30 per cent of the net output was extracted by a small class of landlords which consumed only one-quarter of it and marketed the rest. This implies a marketed percentage of 22.5. For the following, first full crop year after the Revolution, it is being assumed that of the 30 per cent previously accruing to the landlords, one-half would be marketed. Both the increase in peasant income, as well as the uncertainties of the time would encourage greater retentions while urban people would also be increasing their demand for security reasons. Thus, it is following the best recent growth performance that food prices shot up by 41 per cent. The estimates are presented in Table 4 which shows 1978 as the lowest year for the marketed percentage, although urban availabilities were probably lower in earlier years. From 1979/80, with flows from the state farms coming on-line, and an increasing intervention by the AMC, the urban position begins to improve steadily, although paradoxically per capita gross availability was probably lower in 1981/82 than in 1975/76. The major feature is a sharp decline rural areas, and high rises in foodgrain prices.

The price rise of 1976 seems to have more to do with the reduction in urban supplies than with any substantial demand-side increase in exchange entitlements in the immediately preceding years, when gross domestic expenditure on private consumption rose by about six per cent per year at current prices. The rise of 17.3 per cent in 1975–76 is more the result than the cause of that early price rise. Yet it would be misleading and incorrect to view the inflationary process predominantly as a supply-side problem.

Let us follow the flow of marketed surplus into the urban sector. Here, the behaviour of the different non-agricultural sectors is interesting. While Industry, Building, Construction (since 1975/77), Transport & Communications, and Trade show positive period growth rates, Handicrafts & Small-Scale Industry (HSSI) stays in steady decline (Table 3). Thus the two consumption and, in particular, necessities-oriented sectors fare poorly, their GDP in per capita terms falling by 5.3 per cent (in agriculture) and by 7.3 per cent (in HSSI). Yet, despite this constraint posed by the supply of necessities, namely, commodities consumed by the majority of the population, real GDP per capita stayed nearly level in per capita terms ( = −1.0 per cent) during a period of relatively high population growth. No doubt this hides the dampening effect of the high rate of immigration into urban areas which raises the urban population growth rate above 5 per cent per year. At a national level, however, it is necessary to explore how this 'development' in a relative sense, of near-zero GDP growth was financed in the face of a 5.1 per cent fall in the real GDP from Agriculture.

## TABLE 4

### MARKETED SURPLUS OF FOODGRAINS: SOME ESTIMATES

| Year | Estimated marketings as percentage of output | Total output of food grains ('000 quintals) | Quantity marketed per urban person in quintals | Quantity retained per rural person in quintals | Rate of growth of food price index in Addis Ababa |
|---|---|---|---|---|---|
| 1975/75 1975 | 22.5 | 42,991 | 3.28 | 1.40 | 4.5 |
| 1975/76 1976 | 15.0 | 51,600 | 2.45 | 1.80 | 41.9 |
| 1976/77 1977 | | 49,946 | | | 16.8 |
| 1977/78 1978 | 11.8* | 45,005 | 1.47 | 1.56 | 17.0 |
| 1978/79 1979 | 11.8 | 45,505 | 1.40 | 1.55 | 18.0 |
| 1979/80 1980 | 16.4** | 51,493 | 2.06 | 1.62 | 5.2 |
| 1980/81 | | | | | 4.7 |
| 1981/82 | 17.9** | 57,776 | 2.37 | 1.75 | |

Notes:  * Agricultural Sample Survey data, CSC.
\*\*Estimated from AMC statistics and other sources.

TABLE 5

SOME STATISTICS ON ECONOMIC PERFORMANCE AND PLAN TARGETS

| Variable | Actuals 1974/75 to 1979/80 (period growth rates) | DTYP targets (annual growth rates) |
|---|---|---|
| 1. Real GDP (1960–61 fc) growth | 13.1 | 7.5 |
| 2. Population growth | 14.2 | 3.0 |
| 3. Real GDP growth per capita | − 1.0 | 4.4 |
| 4. Real Private Consumer Expenditure | − 16.0 | 6.6 |
| 5. RPCE per capita | − 26.4 | 3.5 |
| 6. Real Agri. GDP growth | 8.4 | 4.5 |
| 7. Real Agri. GDP growth per capita | − 5.1 | 1.5 |
| 8. Coffee Exports growth | | 10.0 |
| 9. Domestic Crop Production growth | | 3.5 |
| 10. Food Price Index | 139.9 | |
| 11. General AA CPI | 109.8 | |
| 12. Food/non-food relative price index | 27.7 | |
| 13. Real wages of low paid worker | − 32.2 | |
| 14. Real wages of high paid worker | − 52.3 | |
| 15. GDP deflator | 35.4 | |

Source: Official Statistics; various reports; Draft Ten Year Plan.

Most of the answers to this question are to be had in the numbers provided in Table 5. Before going to the statistics, however, it might be useful to make some simple a priori observations. Let us consider an economy which has set itself the target of growth without a reduction in the standard of living of the poor. For a targeted growth rate of income of y and a population growth rate of p, the per capita growth of income would be approximately, $y - p$. If the income elasticity of demand for necessities is e, then we obtain the following relationship:

$$n = p + e(y - p) \qquad (1)$$

where n represents the required rate of growth of the supply of necessities. Should this relationship hold, there would be no inflationary pressures on the price of necessities. Or, for any given n, there is a maximum warranted rate of growth of income, $y^*$. If $y > y^*$, then the prices of necessities would be bid up and the real rate of growth of consumption reduced. This assumes that the growth rate of the supply of necessities is inelastic. If we adopt a positive supply elasticity with respect to price, then to that extent some real loss in growth of consumption is reduced. However, short-run supply elasticities for foodgrains in developing countries facing structural problems are negligible, and Ethiopia is probably no exception.

Indeed the facts suggest that agricultural output was quite insensitive to price increases in the short term. In our equation, the new equilibrium is arrived at then through a reduction in the value of e. This value reflects a weighted mean of class-specific elasticities, and a decline in it is achieved through a reduction in the real incomes of the poorer classes with higher e values.

The instrument of this income transfer is food price inflation, which has a stronger negative real income effect on the poor than on the richer classes. The distribution of income therefore worsens, and the higher-than-warranted aggregate income growth rate is financed through forced savings in the form of lower consumption by the poor.

Let us consider the growth figures for 1974/75 to 1979/80, assuming a value for e = 0.6, not too unrealistic at Ethiopia's very low level of living. Using (1), it is possible to derive the warranted, or equilibrium values for each of y, n and e. (It is assumed that the population growth rate is fixed.) These equilibrium values are represented in Table 6 by y*, n* and e* respectively, and stand for period growth rates. Equation (1) shows that the warranted growth rate for GDP growth, given the levels of other variables, was 4.5 per cent, while the actual rate of 8.4 per cent was much in excess. This emphasises at once the *relative* nature of the constraint posed by n on y. It is obviously possible for y to exceed y*. What is not possible then is to meet the objective of egalitarian growth. Conversely, equation (2) reveals that for the observed level of y = 13.1 per cent to be in equilibrium, the necessary value of n was 13.5 per cent, again much higher than the actual 8.4 per cent. The third relation focusing on e brings up the question of adjustment mechanisms. If n, p and y refer to actual values, and if e = 0.6 does not equilibrate the values, then through some mechanism, e must have the flexibility to adjust. Where the

TABLE 6

WARRANTED AND ACTUAL GROWTH RATES OF INCOME AND NECESSITIES
1974/75–1979/80

| Equation | Actual Values | | | | Warranted Values | | |
|---|---|---|---|---|---|---|---|
| | p | e | y | n | e* | y* | n* |
| 1 | 14.2 | 0.6 | (13.1) | 8.4 | | 4.5 | |
| 2 | 14.2 | 0.6 | 13.1 | (8.4) | | | 13.5 |
| 3 | 14.2 | (0.6) | 13.1 | 8.4 | 5.3 | | |

*Notes:* (1) Each warranted value is derived from equation (1) in text by using actual values of the other relevant variables, and may be compared with its own actual value given in parentheses.
(2) For explanation of value of e*, see text.

warranted growth rates are exceeded, two possibilities exist. First, the entire distributional profile could be depressed (or controlled) so as to achieve the required balance between the excessive demand and available supply of necessities. Such an effect could be obtained through comprehensive controls over the pricing and distribution of necessities. Hence the loss of consumption would be shared by all. Secondly, and more generally, the rising price of foodgrains would act as an inequitable rationing device, transfering real incomes and food consumption from the poor to the rich. Thus, the value of e would be adjusted to its warranted level via income redistribution from the poor to the rich. A comment on the odd value of e* ( = 5.3) is necessary.

The value is generated in the context of negative income growth rates, and hence implies that with a one per cent drop in incomes, the drop in foodgrains consumption would have to be 5.3 per cent instead of the 'plausible' value of 0.6 initially assigned to e. In order to be meaningful, the proportion of income going to the consumption of necessities would have to be equal to, or less than 1/e, or, in this case, about 19 per cent of the budget. In other words, foodgrains would have to acquire the status of a luxury commodity!

That the implied massive redistribution as well as a wide impoverishing effect did occur is directly confirmed by the evidence in Table 5. Real private consumer expenditure declined by 16.0 per cent in aggregate, and by a crushing 26.4 per cent in per capita terms. The decline was clearly achieved primarily through the negative redistributive impact of the rising price of food, the index value of which rose to 240 over its 1974/75 level. The price of food relative to non-food items in the Addis Ababa index appreciated by 27.7 per cent. In the meantime, the real wage of the low paid industrial workers, to use one distributional proxy, fell by a third, and that of the better paid one, to half its base-year real value. In this context, it should be noted that such inequality measures as the gini coenefficient lose meaning; when wide social classes are thus impoverished, the level of inequality so measured could be seen to be declining, an effect more grotesque than comforting.

Two other points might be noted. We are concerned with a period during which incomes and foodgrain availabilities declined in per capita terms. One might ask: how would it have helped to have restricted the actual level of y to its warranted rate of 4.5 per cent when in doing so it would in fact have lowered the per capita growth of GDP by another 8.6 per cent points below zero? Would this not have intensified poverty through higher unemployment? The answer could be that the additional employment generated by the 13.1 per cent rate, produced goods which were not consumed by the employed, and that the real wages of the additionally employed were in reality drawn from the wages of the already employed. Further, such intense inflationary processes invariably have a way of reducing the economically weaker sections into utter destitution. Ultimately, it could be argued that the additional GDP produced would contribute to the process of economic construction of the country. This might be undeniably true; yet it would still raise the question as to whether such a socially costly process of financing this construction was unavoidable.

This introduces the second argument: would it not be better to finance the development through generating an external resource gap? To some extent this effect did also supplement the inflationary financing of development. The deficit on the balance of trade rose sharply in the years to 1977/78, mirroring an opposite trend of similar magnitude in domestic savings. However, the impact of this on the availability of foodgrains was marginal. The share of foodgrains in total imports rose from 2.7 per cent to 4.2 per cent, implying an increase in availability of 0.7 per cent in per capita terms over the entire period. The share of food in total exports also declined, but this was of negligible magnitude. In net terms, therefore, the trade gap would have helped to lift y above y*, without directly raising n. And to the extent that these resource inflows were imported, they would not have had to be generated in the first place through inflationary financing. In subsequent rounds of the operation of the multiplier, however, the effects would be similar on the whole to those obtaining from domestically financed investment.

Perhaps a brief mention should be made of the probable operation of a negative multiplier as well. The decline in the Handicrafts & Small Scale Industrial sector can partly be attributed to the uncertainties and restrictions imposed upon the private sector by the Revolution, but it could certainly also be attributed in part to the decline in demand that the inflationary process would have caused, as higher proportions of family budgets were being diverted to those producing and/or trading in foodstuffs.

Finally, our analysis based on n and y runs in terms of national aggregates, although clearly the model underlying it is one involving inter-sectoral transfers of marketed surplus from agriculture to non-agriculture. This aggregation conceals some important aspects of the process. First, it ignores the possibility of non-inflationary productive investments based on rural labour accumulation, and thereby exaggerates the strategic necessity of extracting and transferring rural surplus product. Second, it ignores the fact that the rural sector is largely insulated from the urban food market, since it has the first claim to foodgrain consumption. The implication follows that the urban areas are thus rendered even more vulnerable to variations in agricultural output and marketed product. This fact was starkly highlighted by the recent Ethiopian experience, and the extreme consequences for the urban population form the subject matter of the following section which documents the impoverishment of an increasing proportion of urban households.

IV. ASPECTS OF URBAN POVERTY

First, there appears to be some reason to believe that urban income inequality has been reduced by the post-1975 economic trends. The 1978 Lorenz curve for the Addis Ababa income distribution keeps within that for the 1976 one. The perverse explanation lies essentially in the relatively higher rate of the erosion of the real incomes of the higher income earners who are covered by the wage freeze on the one hand, and who tend to buy a higher proportion of the food basket from the open market (where prices have risen at a faster rate than in the *kebele* shops), on the other.

Second, data reveal a very high proportion of the urban population living in poverty, defined in a conventional manner (Table 7). While these data are subject to the usual cautions, they also do suggest an increase in this proportion in the post-1976 period. This conclusion is corroborated by independent information on the trend in real wages and employment and hence has to be taken seriously as reflecting probable real trends.

Third, while the unemployed fall almost entirely within those in poverty, it has to be noted that the majority of the poor comprise own account or family workers in the informal sector, and even those in regular employment. Thus, a regular job is not a guarantee of keeping a household out of poverty in the present economic conditions in urban Ethiopia.

TABLE 7

INCIDENCE OF POVERTY, VARIOUS YEARS

|  | Food Poverty | Total Poverty | 1.3 Poverty |
|---|---|---|---|
| (1) Addis Ababa, 1976 | 32.6 | 51.2 | 57.2 |
| (2) Addis Ababa, 1978 | 34.3 | 56.2 | 64.1 |
| (3) Urban Areas, 1978 | 35.4 | 59.5 | 65.4 |
| (4) Industrial Employees, 1979/1980 | 31.3 | 51.6 | 58.0 |

*Sources*: (1)–(3) Jamal, V., unpublished paper.
              (4) From CSO, *Results of the Survey of Manufacturing Industry*, 1979/80, April 1982.
*Note:* For details, see Saith [*1983*].


V. SOME ELEMENTS OF A DISTRIBUTIONAL BALANCE SHEET

In Section II it was argued that since 1974/75, the peasantry had probably had up to ten per cent of their gains from the land reform eroded in per capita terms. In Section IV, we had evidence of a startling fall in the real income of the working class in the urban areas: by up to one-third of its 1974/75 level for low paid workers, and by up to one-half for the higher paid ones. This contrast between the two groups is explicable in terms of the analysis of the inflationary process in Section III. Unlike the workers, the peasants were largely insulated from the inflation. Indeed, it is a measure of their institutionalised separation that during a period of such dramatic increases in food prices, including a relative price increase of nearly 30 per cent against non-food items, they still found their real incomes declining to some extent. Seeing that aggregate GDP per capita was nearly steady over the period somebody must have gained. In Section III, the inflation was explained in terms of imbalanced growth but, at that level, no specification was made about the production relations or market structure for foodgrains. The task of preparing a comprehensive balance sheet of gains and losses is too vast, and perhaps impossible to fulfil given the data available. In this section, we will provide some indicative evidence to suggest where the surpluses generated through inflation might have lodged.

Consider first the urban working and salaried class. It started the post-Revolutionary period well, with a reduction in rents of approximately 50 per cent. If rent payments constituted about 30 per cent of the household income in 1974/75, the gain was 15 per cent. But this real increase disappeared the following year through the erosion of wages by the rise in prices. And in the same year, the high income earner had his wage level frozen if the wage or salary was 450 birr or more per month. This group would have lost much more, since a higher proportion of them might have owned a house and, therefore, not benefited from the rent adjustment. Using the detailed guidelines of the wage freeze, a comparison between the incomes of the 'through' worker (who started with wage level in 1974/75 such that he never suffered from the freeze in any year) and the 'blocked' worker (whose wages were frozen from the outset), is made in Table 8. The blocked worker's real wage is reduced to 46 per cent of its original level in a seven-year period, and that of the through worker to 60 per cent. However, of the 72,113 permanent employees in manufacturing industry in 1979/80, less than five per cent had wages or salaries in excess of 450 birr/month. Even here, the freeze could have been sidestepped through promotions, or through a 'redefinition' of jobs, or through the provision of benefits in kind. And the freeze could have been avoided in the case of new job entrants, or by new enterprises. Turning to the lower end, we should note that the monthly minimum wage was pegged throughout the period at 50 birr, and was not raised to account for inflation. New workers in this category (which covers perhaps 20–25 per cent of all industrial workers in manufacturing) could therefore still be employed at 50 birr till the end of the period. Given the high rates of rural–urban migration over the period, we can expect the emergence of labour crowding at the bottom end. Some confirmation comes from the fact that between 1978/79 and 1979/80, the percentage of employees earning less than 100 birr rose by one per cent while the money wage rate could have increased by about seven per cent even within the official wage guidelines. Hence, it is likely that while low paid employees were getting squeezed, the higher paid ones were escaping the net. The overall effect was that the real labour income of the average industrial employees declined by about one-third over the 1974/75–1979/80 period.

The other vital event for the poorer sections was the increase in the relative importance of the grain purchasable from the *kebele* shops at controlled prices. During 1981/82 these shops supplied 44.7 kgs of foodgrains per household per month in Addis Ababa as against the nominal ration level of 65 kgs per month. For the remaining one-third, the household would have had to rely on the open market where, prices, on average, were 50–60 per cent higher in 1981/82. While the AMC's supplies clearly perform a vital role, a few qualifications need to be made. First, the coverage of urban areas other than Addis Ababa is very restricted but, since price data are not available for cities other than Addis, it is difficult to form any idea of the relative difference. However, it is probable that open market prices are lower in the smaller towns, and the net effect might be less than would be implied by the Addis differentials indicated in Table 9. The second point concerns the movement in the relative prices of the 'poor' and the 'rich' cereals baskets at the *kebele* shop. *Kebele* prices of the superior cereals dropped in 1979/80–1981/82 by about four per cent, while the inferior ones have risen by nine per cent. The open market prices also show a similar disparity with the former group registering an increase of 11.6 per cent as against one of 26.6 per cent for the latter group. While in times of inflation and real income decline, the open market movements can be explained by a part of the population switching to the consumption of inferior grains, the *kebele* price movements could also possibly be an indication of misguided policy. Third, the decline in the prices of teff at the *kebele* is matched by a rise of ten-fold in the quantity of teff handled by the AMC. The evidence certainly argues that while the increases in the coverage of the AMC will have helped the poorer sections, the change in relative prices has moderated, although clearly not obliterated, that gain. In general, the relative price movement went against the 'poor' cereals basket by 13.4 per cent in two

TABLE 8

NOMINAL AND REAL WAGES OF 'THROUGH' AND 'BLOCKED' EMPLOYEES, 1974/75 TO 1981/82

| Year | Maximum 'through' nominal wage (birr/month) | Minimum 'blocked' nominal wage (birr/month) | Addis Ababa cost of living index 1974/5 = 100 | Real 'through' wage (birr/month) | Real 'blocked' wage (birr/month) |
|---|---|---|---|---|---|
| 1974/75 | 316.5 | 450.0 | 100.0 | 316.5 | 450.0 |
| 1975/76 | 363.9 | 450.0 | 128.6 | 283.0 | 349.9 |
| 1976/77 | 389.4 | 450.0 | 150.0 | 259.6 | 300.0 |
| 1977/78 | 420.6 | 450.0 | 171.4 | 245.4 | 262.5 |
| 1978/79 | 420.6 | 450.0 | 198.9 | 211.5 | 226.2 |
| 1979/80 | 450.0 | 450.0 | 207.8 | 216.6 | 216.6 |
| 1980/81 | 450.0 | 450.0 | 220.6 | 204.0 | 204.0 |
| 1981/82 | 481.5 | 481.5 | 231.6 | 207.9 | 207.9 |

Source: Based on Statistics on Nominal Wages from ILO-JASPA Ethiopia Report, [1983: Chapter 9].
The index for 1975 is placed against 1974/75, and so on.

TABLE 9

RELATIVE PRICES OF 'RICH' AND 'POOR' FOODGRAINS BASKETS IN ADDIS ABABA

| | AMC Price | | Open Market Price | | Composite Price | |
|---|---|---|---|---|---|---|
| | *1979/80* | *1981/82* | *1979/80* | *1981/82* | *1979/80* | *1981/82* |
| *Rich Basket* | | | | | | |
| birr/quintal | 58.52 | 56.23 | 82.58 | 92.19 | 66.46 | 68.09 |
| Index | 100.00 | 96.09 | 100.00 | 111.64 | 100.00 | 101.22 |
| *Poor Basket* | | | | | | |
| birr/quintal | 44.21 | 48.17 | 58.00 | 73.42 | 48.76 | 56.50 |
| Index | 100.00 | 108.96 | 100.00 | 126.59 | 100.00 | 114.77 |
| *Poor/Rich Relative Price Index* | 100.00 | 113.39 | 100.00 | 113.39 | 100.00 | 113.39 |

*Source*: *AMC Annual Report*, 1981/82.

*Notes*: The composite price is calculated giving a weight of two-thirds of the AMC price and one-third to the open market price. The 'rich' basket comprises teff (grades 1 and 2), white, and mixed wheat; the 'poor' basket comprises teff (grade 3), maize and barley. The weighting pattern reflects that of the purchase pattern in the AMC's operations for Addis Ababa in 1974. For details, see Saith [*1983: Table 25*].

years. But whatever the gains through the extension of the coverage, section IV showed up a high level and rising trend of poverty in urban areas.

Did the capitalist class, such as remains after the Revolution, gain? The evidence is insufficient to sketch any comparisons over the period, but Table 10 provides some clues. In all manufacturing enterprises employing ten or more workers and using power-driven machines, the share of the private sector in the total gross value of production was 5.8 per cent, and for the year 1978/79 (when private investment rose at current prices for the first time since 1974/75), its performance and profitability indicators do not show it up as being a great money spinner. Indeed, it could be argued that, in the context of declining real wage rates throughout public and private industry, the more profitable public enterprises have treated their workers no differently from the private sector. It should be noted, though, that both sectors had to operate within the same official wage guidelines. Clearly, the public sector gained from the urban wage squeeze in terms of high operating surpluses. The other interesting feture in Table 10 is that the food and drink industries were more profitable than average which is consistent with the argument developed in section III.

Let us turn briefly to the rural sector. The overall trends have been mentioned in section II. Here we need only note a few additional points. First, agricultural taxes rose from about 0.8 per cent of agricultural GDP to 2.5 per cent over the period. Second, the period saw a 133 per cent increase in the producer price of coffee, while world prices for Jimma Coffee rose by 250 per cent. The difference between the two prices was 87 per cent in 1974/75 and, applying that as the maximum margin, coffee producers were losing 2,600 birr/ton in intercepted profits, or about 250 million birr in 1979/80. This represents one-eighth of the total agricultural GDP for that year. Here it should

TABLE 10

SELECTED STATISTICS OF PUBLIC AND PRIVATE SECTOR MANUFACTURING INDUSTRY,
1978/79

| | Sectoral Share in gross value of Production | Share of labour cost in value added at factor cost | Mark-up on cost | Rate of profit on book value of assets | Labour cost/ employee |
|---|---|---|---|---|---|
| | % | % | % | % | birr/month |
| Food Manufacturing | | | | | |
| 1. Public | 25.8 | 19 | 42 | 113 | 168 |
| 2. Private | 34.5 | 60 | 8 | 30 | 118 |
| Beverages and Tobacco | | | | | |
| 1. Public | 15.6 | 21 | 31 | 107 | 227 |
| 2. Private | 10.6 | 64 | 5 | 38 | 200 |
| All Industries | | | | | |
| 1. Public | 100.0 | 63 | 24 | 92 | 173 |
| 2. Private | 100.0 | 32 | 11 | 35 | 141 |
| Public/Total % | 94.2 | | | | |

Source: CSO, Survey of Manufacturing Industries, 1978/79.

be noted that while agricultural GDP per capita fell by 5.1 per cent over the reference period, and GDP per capita by one per cent, the real GDP generated by 'Public Administration and Defence' rose by 22.5 per cent in per capita terms. This sector improved its share in GDP from 6.97 per cent in 1974/75 to 8.61 per cent in 1979/80. Some of the reasons for this are readily understandable, yet it does tell us something about how some of the surplus generated was utilised.

Finally, let us examine the structure of agricultural prices. This is summarised in Table 11. The corresponding data on purchases are provided by Ghose [this volume, p. 137: Table 6] where the caution is sounded that the aggregate figure is an estimated one. The price differentials are staggering even if we allow for exceptionally high handling costs. Thus, for maize, the Addis Ababa open market price is 264 per cent more than the price which the peasant receives. Even the differentials for AMC buying and selling prices are very high indeed. There appears to be prima facie evidence to hypothesise that the intermediaries are gaining an undue share of the profits. Let us compare the relative position of merchants and the AMC. Of the total 8.8 million quintals that are marketed, the direct share of the AMC is 12.5 per cent. But it buys another 21.5 per cent through the merchants. The merchants are required to sell one-half of their purchase to the AMC, but our estimates suggest that they actually hand over one-half of that, that is, 24.5 per cent. The AMC receives, in addition, another 1.52 million quintals from the state farms. Hence, its share of the total marketed surplus from all sellers becomes 44 per cent, with merchants still holding the majority share of 56 per cent apart from the 18 per cent of the gross total they sell to the AMC. Let us attempt to form some idea of the magnitude of trade profits, howsoever approximate. In 1981/82 the AMC paid out 110.7 million birr for its purchases, against which the value

TABLE 11

PRICES OF SOME MAJOR FOOD COMMODITIES: AMC PRICES

| | Peasant associations | Merchants producers/service co-operatives | AMC retail price | Addis Ababa free market retail price birr/quintal |
|---|---|---|---|---|
| *Teff Gr. I* | | | | |
| 1979 | 35 | 40 | 71.75 | 96 |
| 1980 | 35 | 40 | 69.45 | 99 |
| 1981 | 41 | 46 | 63.79 | 110 |
| *White* Wheat | | | | |
| 1979 | 34 | 39 | 57.05 | 89 |
| 1980 | 34 | 39 | 59.97 | 80 |
| 1981 | 34 | 39 | 56.16 | 88 |
| *Maize* | | | | |
| 1979 | 17 | 21 | 35.45 | 41 |
| 1980 | 17 | 21 | 45.83 | 49 |
| 1981 | 17 | 21 | 43.76 | 62 |
| *Sorghum* | | | | |
| 1979 | 23 | 27 | 50.34 | 76 |
| 1980 | 23 | 27 | 53.90 | 67 |
| 1981 | 23 | 27 | 52.88 | 77 |

*Source*: Official statistics; various reports.

of the grain basket sold was 165.1 million. This implies a gross mark-up of nearly 50 per cent. The charge of 54.4 million birr is roughly accounted for as follows:

| | *(in million birr)* |
|---|---|
| Costs of impurities and storage losses | 20.3 |
| Containers and bags | 7.1 |
| Transport (estimated) | 12.5 |
| Trade costs (estimated) | 10.0 |
| Total handling costs | 49.9 |

This implies a mark-up of 4.5 million birr or 4.1 per cent. Clearly, the storage losses make a big dent and, here, state farm grain cost 8.2 birr/quintal while that purchased from farmers and merchants cost 4.8 birr/quintal. Therefore, as things stand, the AMC could not be said to be making profits from the poor, although it could do better by the poor by controlling its costs more effectively.

The story about the merchants is different. The AMC basket of sales, if evaluated at Addis Ababa open market prices, would sell at 265 million birr, that is, an extra 100 million. Thus, while the AMC's average price is 54 birr/quintal, for the same basket, the merchants price is 86.5 birr or 32.5 birr/quintal above what can be characterised as a 'fair' profit price if we allow grain loss for merchants to be lower since they do not procure any grain from state farms. If this differential is applied to the figure of 5.8 million quintals of grain purchased by merchants, we can derive an estimate of 188.5 million birr for the extra-normal profits earned by them during 1981/82. This could be as much as five per cent of the total agricultural GDP. Or, put in a more pejorative manner, the annual extra-normal profits of Ethiopia's grain merchants could support about 225,000 families at the food poverty line or about 125,000 at the poverty line including non-food articles as well. If, for illustrative purposes, we consider the estimated incidence of poverty in Addis Ababa and consider only the likely *shortfall* of the poor families from the poverty line, it would be possible for Addis poverty to be removed altogether from these extra normal profits. Of course, it is possible that traders have higher costs than the AMC, since they are likely to be operating in more scattered markets and the Addis Ababa open market prices are also unlikely to prevail in most other towns. Yet, even if we allow for an exceptionally wide margin, our deduction might still hold good.

In conclusion, we may say that in a period of negative per capita growth, the successful attempt to keep the level of GDP growth rate higher than its warranted level generated a vicious inflationary process which transferred some of the surplus into real increases in 'public administration and defence' noticeably, but most dramatically into the pockets of private traders.

There are two strategic points to elicit. First, that the role of the AMC should be extended with great vigour. This also brings into sharp relief the crucial role that well-functioning state farms can perform. Second, that while some real growth can be captured by inflationary financing, there are enormous leakages and these are all from the pockets of the poor.

## VI. POLICY PERSPECTIVES ON THE DRAFT TEN YEAR PLAN

Thus far, we have been concerned primarily with analysing the recent developmental experience of the country. In this section we will offer some comments, first, on the Draft Ten Year Plan (DTYP) and, in the light of these, provide some policy suggestions of a strategic nature.

The basic growth targets of the DTYP are set out in Table 5. Clearly, they are remarkably ambitious; our question is: are they consistent with the broad distributional objectives of the development strategy? Before attempting this, it should be mentioned that distributional policies, in general, have not been integrated into the analytical or policy framework of the DTYP. This would apply to inter-class, inter-sectoral as well as to inter-regional issues. This treatment of distributional variables is no different from that adopted in the development plans in most developing countries which carry out detailed national planning exercises. There, as in Ethiopia, the plan is confined to the core production and investment processes and neither income distribution nor employment profiles are endogenised. These crucial factors are meant to be tackled independently through specific policy instruments. The exclusion of the distributional dimension also infringes the internal demand–supply balances of the plan, since the distributional profiles that it generates might neither throw up, say, adequate savings, nor provide a final demand profile which matches the output mix generated by the plan. However, given the present state of the country's statistical and economic system, such exercises are impracticable, and we will therefore focus on the wider distributional features of teh DTYP. Also excluded is any discussion or test of the feasibility fo the DTYP targets in narrow technical terms.

In keeping with our mild scepticism over the officially adopted population growth rates, we will assume a growth rate of population of 3.0 per cent per year over the period. This does not alter any of our arguments in a significant fashion. One other statistic has been altered: the growth rate for agriculture. In the DTYP, this is pegged at 4.5 per cent per annum. However, this includes the rapidly expanding export sector which carries a base-year weight of about 12 per cent, and which has a target growth rate of ten per cent per annum. This implies a growth rate of 3.5 per cent for the non-export domestic agricultural sector, and we will utilise this rate in our calculations. Let us return then to the simple analytical device used in our discussion of the inflationary process and compute the 'warranted' levels, $y^*$, $n^*$ and $e^*$, and compare these with the targets for $y$, $n$ and $e$. This is done in Table 12 which offers some strategic insights into the possible distributional dilemmas and implications of the DTYP. With $n = 3.5$ per cent, $y^* = 3.8$ per cent, implying a warranted per capita GDP growth of under one per cent per annum, in contrast to the targeted 4.5 per cent or more. If we set $y = 7.5$ per cent, then $n^* = 5.7$ per cent.

TABLE 12

WARRANTED AND TARGET GROWTH RATES FOR GDP AND AGRICULTURE IN DTYP

| Equation | Target Values | | | | Warranted Values | | |
|---|---|---|---|---|---|---|---|
| | $p$ | $e$ | $y$ | $n$ | $e^*$ | $y^*$ | $n^*$ |
| 1 | 3.0 | 0.6 | (7.5) | 3.5 | | 3.8 | |
| 2 | 3.0 | 0.6 | 7.5 | (3.5) | | | 5.7 |
| 3 | 3.0 | (0.6) | 7.5 | 3.5 | 0.125 | | |

*Note:* Each warranted value is derived from equation (1) in text by using the target values of the other relevant variables, and may be compared with its own target value given in parentheses.

With serious doubts being cast on the feasibility of the target of $n = 3.5$ per cent, this enhanced rate warranted by the 7.5 per cent GDP target must be ruled out as quite unrealistic. Yet, that is what the DTYP demands. Or else, we can attempt again to ignore the constraint posed by $n$, and allow the elasticity of demand, that is, the income distribution, to adjust in a manner which generates $y = 7.5$ per cent with $n = 3.5$. The low value of $e^* = 0.125$ and its sharp drop from 0.6 indicates the massive dimension of the distributional changes required. Seen in another way, it provides a measure of the scale of resource mobilisation or control over incremental consumption necessary. This could be achieved either through the means of a comprehensive public control over the procurement and distribution of foodgrains or, as in the past, it could be left to market forces to redistribute incomes as before, with its unavoidable inequitous outcome. The major point to elicit is that the targets as set, do not appear to meet the very rough requirements for being non-inflationary. Especially in view of the earlier destructive experience of the inflationary process, it is vital that some further consideration be given to alternative investment strategies which do not suck the economy into another inflationary whirlpool.

Both in the elementary model used, as well as in the one implicit in the DTYP, a prime determinant of the rate of non-inflationary (and hence, egalitarian, given the present foodgrain market structures) growth of GDP would be the availability of marketed surplus. This should not imply, however, that no superior growth strategy is possible, superiority being judged here in terms of the simultaneous achievement of preferred growth and distributional outcomes. Let us outline three alternative cases.

## Case A: The DTYP

This is the present strategy as enshrined in the DTYP. It assumes further that the institutional transformation both in rural and urban areas will be steady but slow, with the result that the DTYP will be implemented and its outlays attempted to be disbursed within only a partially socialised economy. This option arouses great pessimism with regard to its ability to meet its growth or distributional objectives. The worst scenario envisaged is one in which the heavily import and aid dependent industrial sector flounders due to foreseeable absorptive bottlenecks, where agricultural growth also suffers due to its crucial dependence on centrally provided industrial inputs, where the rationing system is only partial, and where urban unemployment is high and rising. This is a recipe for disaster. Of course, the worst fears might not be realised, but there is something to be said for avoiding a strategy which has no floor if it goes wrong.

## Case B: DTYP Plus Food-Consumption Floor

This is identical to Case A except that it adds the necessary floor through the extension of the AMC to all major grain markets still controlled by private merchants on the one hand, and the rapid expansion of the state farm sector on the other. Jointly, these would allow a full-cover public distribution system in all urban areas. Therefore, if found socially acceptable, the effective rate of growth of consumption or real wage could be lowered directly to finance the gap between the targeted and the warranted GDP growth rates. In contrast to Case A, this reduction would not occur through the market mechanism of income transfers and, therefore, would prevent a high rate of inflation of foodgrains on the one hand, and a serious deterioration in the degree of inequality on the other. This bears some resemblance to the present plan strategy, in so far as one has actually crystallised at all. While this does cater to the distributional issues, it is still subject to several weaknesses. First, it is dependent on the flow of marketed surplus to an extent which could distort the institutional priorities in the countryside. Second, it suffers from all the reservations listed about the import and aid dependent industrial package. Third, its implications for regional concentration are bound to be unfavourable. Especially in view of the absorptive capacity problem, most important enterprises are bound to gravitate towards the big cities and the need for marketed surplus beyond that obtainable from the state farms would reinforce the already existent pattern of extreme concentration of modern inputs in the few agriculturally developed regions of the country. Fourth, it is unlikely to generate the order of urban employment that is required over the plan period. This failure has various ramifications. For one, unemployment would probably become increasingly worse in the smaller towns or else, the migration into the prime cities from other smaller urban centres would increase without, of course, affecting the overall employment outcome. For another, this would mean an exacerbatian of the social costs of such urbanisation, manifest in the forms of an expanding urban lumpenproletariat, prostitution, and begging. Clearly, none of these phenomena should have an extended life in a socialist system. Furthermore, such unemployment would undermine the utility of the rationing system which would fail to reach this needy class on account of their exchange entitlement failure. To meet the distributional objectives, therefore, it would become necessary to rely increasingly on institutional devices of income sharing as a strategic rather than purely tactical option.

## Case C: An Alternative

This offers an alternative strategic framework for a revised DTYP. The central principle underlying this concerns what is adopted as a trinity of objectives, namely, growth, distributional equity, and grassroots participating institutions.

The earlier cases are crucially dependent upon an extended circular flow of investible resources extracted from agriculture and invested in industry and related sectors in the form of large projects. This involves little direct participation on the part of the savers and investments occur largely outside the units or sectors from which resources are extracted. Inevitably, aggregate domestic investments would depend upon the open and hidden contributions of peasant agriculture which would also remain a net contributor or loser in resource terms. It is arguable that this type of investment process is unsuited to an economy like Ethiopia where the level of available investible surplus is low and scattered in small denominations, where the degree of economic fragmentation is extreme, and where even the relatively well-developed centre is unlikely to be able to bear the burden imposed upon it. In addition, this strategy is unmindful of harnessing for productive purposes those investible rural resources which are not extractable and therefore not useable through the centralised and dichotomous investment process mentioned above.

The collective framework, that is, Case C, takes the relative emphasis away from major industrial investments and places it on investments within the rural sector. The industrial shift involves the locational, size, product and technology dimensions, making the sector less import-intensive and more labour-intensive. Thus, even if the scale of investment was to be lowered, there might be few net losses (in GDP terms) to output, and perhaps even a net gain in terms of intermediate-level skill creation, as well as in direct and indirect employment generated. This would ease the urban poverty problems to some extent while achieving a better dovetailing between the industrial needs of the rural investment programmes and the output-mix of the industrial ones.

However, the central plank of the argument in Case C is the re-designing of the investment strategy for the rural sector and involves breaking away from the logic underlying the postulated dependence of y* on n. If this link could be broken, it might become possible to retain relatively high aggregate growth targets in any revised plan without jeopardising the self-imposed distributional constraints. Here it should be emphasised that in reality, agriculture supply bottlenecks are seldom absolutely rigid. However, this margin of supply response is already built into the target, n. But, in the case of the DTYP, it has been argued that n does not include the resource-generating effects of the monetisation − of hitherto self-sufficient, autarkic sub-systems in the rural sector − released through the device of inflationary deficit financing. This seems to have lent some respectability to an otherwise thoroughly discredited ruling-class instrument of financing development from the incomes of the poor. Especially in such an economically fragmented economy as Ethiopia, this dangerous option is more likely to result merely in higher inflation. Indeed, to the extent that the price elasticity of n is low (and it would rarely exceed 0.2−0.4 even in the long run), the scheme would be relying more on forced savings than on increased supplies.

The method by which the link between y* and n is broken in Case C is more fundamental. No doubt urban industrialisation would still need grain. Here, a truncated relationship between the two sectors would still operate, mediated by the preponderance of the AMC and *kebele* ration shops in the grain supply system. The treatment and premises concerning the rural sector, however, are quite different. Here, a strategy which uses the rural consumption fund as a source of investment through the utilisation of surplus labour for rural infrastructure creation would free y* from n.

Our de-linking of y* and n is thus more structural in nature. The various elements of such a programme, which would be executed through producer cooperatives within the framework of service co-operatives, need to be mentioned. Briefly, these would cover rural road construction and maintenance; land improvement projects including afforestation, water conservancy and control (wells, small-scale irrigation projects); construction of dispersed grain storage facilities, villagisation projects, and other similar works which depend primarily on seasonal labour and local resources. Apart from this infrastructural range, a second group would relate to rural industries catering, at first, to local demand for village-based traditional products, for example, textiles, pottery goods, metal work products, wood work, straw and bamboo articles, etc. Another prime area for local investment effort is in the setting up of local workshops at the service-co-operative level for the production, repair, and improvement of local farm implements. Dairy farms, bee-keeping, grain milling, coffee-processing, and some service activities (such as a canteen) would all qualify as candidates. The fundamental advantage of this approach is that investible resources are ploughed back within the same unit. This also provides a powerful way of initiating development at the periphery, thus contibuting to the objective of regional equalisation as well. This would have considerable advantages, too, for the spread of producer co-operatives. In addition, while bypassing the obstacle posed by economic fragmentation, such investments would nevertheless be attacking it, thus raising the degree of economic integration. No doubt, these investments would require industrial inputs at a higher level than before and the financing of this might imply that the planners have to give up some of the surplus extracted from the agricultural sector for use by it within its boundaries. In our opinion, this approach provides the basis for achieving high growth targets in the medium term without compromising on the distributional front at the class, sector, or regional levels.

Two qualifications need to be registered. First, this does not imply that the DTYP target of $y = 7.5$ per cent per annum becomes feasible in this strategy. Even in Case A, the argument was only partly that it was probably not achievable; rather, that achieving it with $n = 3.5$ per cent would almost certainly lead to a vicious inflationary spiral, thereby worsening income distribution. In Case B, the burden of financing would be shared in an egalitarian manner through the rationing system but its average level would not be any different. What is being argued is that, first, for any given n, $y^*$ (C) › $y^*$ (A, B), and second, the rate of growth of n would be substantially greater over time in Case C than in Case A or B. Thus, Case C could be viewed as laying the basis for an eventual second phase of an industrialisation drive of the type now being proposed, in our view, prematurely.

Second, it is probable that under Case C, rural foodgrain consumption would rise in the short run. In this strategy, too, state farms would play a crucial part in the transitional phase and beyond. It is necessary therefore to assist them in achieving efficiency quickly, and to overcome the problems of haphazard location and early growth. A period of consolidation might be necessary prior to any further expansion on any large scale.

Finally, we need to turn our focus to the problems of urban poverty and unemployment which are not directly handled in any of the three cases. A separate policy component is therefore called for. A two-pronged approach is necessary. The first of these is to ensure that all low-income earners are covered by the urban rationing system. In the present context, this would require extending the coverage to the smaller urban centres and even in the larger ones to that lowest strata which might not be registered in any urban *kebele*. Thus, the AMC needs to grow greatly and quickly. It is in this context that the current and future role of the state farm sector has to be seen. Even within the framework of Case C, it will be some time before the area of stable grain yields is extended to a point where the urban populations are not held to ransom by the weather all too frequently; in the meantime, the state farms provide an insurance cover which is indispensible. (A corresponding function would be performed in the food-insecure rural areas by the grain banks suggested earlier.) Further, the *kebele* shops need to move more into the inferior cereals, in particular, sorghum, maize and black teff. Improving the storage facilities of the AMC and state farms could achieve the welcome result of lowering cost by anything up to $15-20$ per cent on some crops. All such gains registered should reflect themselves in lower prices for the inferior, rather than for the superior, cereals as appears to have been the case in the recent past.

However, while this would ensure the availability of grain at reasonable prices, the real problem lies in generating the exchange entitlement which would enable the poor to buy their minimum food basket. The problem manifests itself in low real wages of the employed, as well as in the form of open unemployment. For the employed, a minimum wage, which is, at prevailing *kebele* prices, capable of covering the nuclear household's food basket, needs to be guaranteed and maintained in real terms through indexing with *kebele* prices. Alternatively, *kebele* prices could be adjusted to achieve such an end at lower cost to the industrial sector in general. The latter is a more potent method of reaching those who are in part-time, seasonal, or self-employment. The subsidy involved could be partially recovered through taxing the considerable profits of the private grain merchants.

However, this will still require a wide range of programmes to generate entitlements for the unemployed. As far as the new, young entrants into this pool are concerned, the problem should be attempted to be solved at source, that is, within urban *kebeles*. These should be encouraged to provide the institutional framework and initial support for absorbing such young persons into services and production enterprises, ranging from nurseries, infrastructure maintenance, house-repair services, restaurants and, most importantly, small-scale industries. So also the informal sector which exists beneath HASSIDA's floor level should be strongly encouraged and provided material assistance to form co-operative ventures, the production of which could be regulated and partly sold through the *kebele* shops. Food-for-work schemes might be more appropriate for those whom long years of unemployment have rendered unemployable without a lengthy period of rehabilitation and skill creation. The availability of *kebele* rations to such persons could be made conditional upon such work participation. For the increasing members of educated unemployed, there might be avenues to be employed in the field of the school education sector itself while, within the framework of the strategy discussed, there is considerable scope for the productive employment of young campaigners and educators for the purpose of raising the management and accounting skills of the leadership of the producer co-operatives. Such employment could be absorbed at the level of the service co-operative. In the same vein, the new rural industrial development programme suggested could provide a substantial number of productive intermediate level jobs for such persons. In the context of the urban unemployed, the falling off of the rate of rural–urban migration is a source of some satisfaction. However, this must not be allowed to generate the complacent and false presumption that the problem will disappear with development without any special attempts to solve it. Indeed, in none of the alternative strategies available would this happen; in fact, in the absence of such schemes and absorbers as are suggested, the situation is likely to get worse, given the age structure and high growth rate of the population and labour force.

In this study, we have made rather wide-ranging suggestions, most of them calling for a radical departure from the development strategy implicit in the plan now being debated. In formulating this alternative path to socialism from the grassroots, we have indulged in the presumption that our supply of alternatives will not encounter a lack of demand arising from the political entitlement failures of potential buyers. It is the only assumption one is able to or can wish to make; whether it is a realistic one is another matter altogether.

## REFERENCES

Ghose, Ajit Kumar, 1985, 'Transforming Feudal Agriculture: Agrarian Changes in Ethiopia since 1974', this volume, pp. 127–49.
Saith, Ashwani, 1983, 'Distributional Dimensions of Revolutionary Transition: Ethiopia', Working Paper No. 15, Institute of Social Studies, The Hague.
Sen, Amartya, 1981, *Poverty and Famines – An Essay on Entitlement and Deprivation*, Delhi: Oxford University Press.

# Money, Planning and Rural Transformation in Mozambique

*by Marc Wuyts\**

*This article argues that the transformation of the rural economy should proceed on a broad front which links the development of the state sector with the need to transform family agriculture through co-operatisation. In actual fact, planning became concentrated on the state sector which received the bulk of the investible resources. Disequilibria between the planned needs of resources and their real availability destabilised the exchange between the state sector and peasant production and consequently blocked the possibilities of transforming family agriculture. This contradition expresses itself in the form of monetary disequilibrium, but it cannot be solved by monetary policy only. Rather it requires rethinking the nature of planning itself.*

In this article I shall attempt to analyse some fundamental aspects of the agrarian question under socialist transition within the context of the Mozambican experience.[1] Our focus is on the relationship of the state sector to the peasantry within this process of change towards constructing a socialist economy.

The state sector commands considerable economic power within a period of transition: directly, as a major producer, and indirectly, through its control over allocation of material resources and of labour within the economy. This concentration of economic power constitutes a crucial force to propel social and economic change. Planning relates to how this economic power is organised to effect change within the economy, and therefore its starting point cannot but be an analysis of the nature of the social organisation of production within society so as to identify the class forces which can carry the process forward.

In this article I shall argue that planning in actual practice within Mozambique came to be seen as the organisation of the expansion of the state sector in itself with little regard for the wider transformation of peasants' production. As such the issue of establishing the exchange with the peasantry, and of transforming family agriculture through the way in which the state sector organises its exchange with the peasants, became of secondary importance.

---

\* Institute of Social Studies, The Hague.
In writing this article I am indebted to various colleagues with whom I worked at the Center of African Studies of the Eduardo Mondlane University in Maputo. More specifically, I am indebted to Bridget O'Laughlin, Maureen Mackintosh, Helen Dolny, Nuno Castel-Branco, David Wield and to the late Ruth First, research director of the Center.

I shall argue that the pattern of allocation of material resources and its relationship to the circuits of money and commodities are crucial for the question of transforming on a broad front in which the state sector, through the economic power it commands, plays a determining role. The argument is that the absence of such a strategy brings contradictions to the fore which effectively block the process of socialisation of the countryside.

## I. THE COLONIAL LEGACY[2]

The inherited economy was characterised by the following three basic features:

(1)  The economic integration within the Southern African sub-system under the domination of South African capitalism led to a situation in which Mozambique became to a large extent a service economy dependent upon the provision of transit transport services (ports and railways) for the South African and (then) Rhodesian economies as well as of the supply of migrant labour to the South African mining sector and, to a lesser extent, to South African and Rhodesian settler farms.

To show the relative importance of these services in terms of labour utilisation and of foreign exchange earnings we can see that about 25 per cent of total wage labour consisted of migrant labour to the Southern African region (and this is more likely to have been an underestimate) while employment in the ports and railways amounted to nearly half as much as total employment in the manufacturing sector ( respectively five per cent and ten per cent of total wage employment which itself amounted to between 20 per cent and 30 per cent of the active population) [*Centro de Estudos Africanos, 1981b: unit 2*]. With respect to foreign exchange earnings, the ports and railways sector was consistently the major foreign exchange earner with a relative importance of approximately 30 per cent of total income on current account of the balance of payments, which was considerably more than the income from the major cash crops – cashew (roughly 15 per cent of income on current account) and cotton (about 14 per cent). Income in terms of foreign exchange coming from migrant labour is more difficult to assess since no precise statistics are available. However obligatory, deferred payments of miners' wages amounted to about four per cent in the latter phase of the colonial period (its share rising in the 1970s due to the increase in wages on the mines in that period) [*Centro de Estudos Africanos, 1981b: unit 5*].

(2)  The production of primary commodities destined for exports: cashew, cotton, sugar, copra and tea as the major products (respectively 23 per cent, 21 per cent, 11 per cent, six per cent and four per cent of the total exports of goods). Sugar, copra and tea were mainly produced by the plantation sector located in and around the Zambezy valley in the centre of the country. Cotton, initially exclusively a peasant cash crop produced under forced cultivation, was increasingly produced by the growing sector of settler agriculture toward the latter end of the colonial period (in the early 1970s more than half of the output came from this sector). In terms of location cotton was produced mainly in the northern and the central region of the country. Finally, cashew was

exclusively produced by the peasantry along the whole coastal area [*Wuyts, 1978*]. Linked to this process of production of primary commodities was the development of elementary processing industries (cotton ginning, sugar extraction tea preparation as well as some vegetable oils production), destined primarily for exports. Together with the only major export-oriented industry − the petrol refinery (oriented towards the South African market), these industries accounted for about 40 per cent of the total industrial output and were spread over the four provinces of Maputo, Sofala, Zambezia and Nampula with roughly equal relative importance with respect to output [*Centro de Estudos Africanos, 1981b: unit 2*].

(3) A colonialism based on settler immigration which implied a relatively significant development of the internal market centred on the consumption pattern of the growing settler community. Hence, in industry 60 per cent of total output was geared to the internal market and included apart from the production of consumer goods (including certain durables like refrigerators, radios and other electrical equipment, etc.). This industry was virtually wholly concentrated on three towns: Maputo (66 per cent of the output destined for the home market), and the remainder in Beira and Chimoio. It depended heavily on the proximity of the South African industrial complex on which it relied for spare parts, inputs and technical expertise in servicing equipment [*Centro de Estudos Africanos, 1981b: unit 2*].

Within the rural areas settler production concentrated on the supply of food (rice, potatoes, vegetables, dairy products) to the towns; an activity mainly concentrated in the Southern region − the Limpopo, Incomati and Maputo valleys. Rural trade was also largely in the hands of settler shopkeepers (often combined with agrarian production).

Finally, it is necessary to point out the importance of this settler-based colonialism for the structure of the labour market: virtually all administrative and skilled jobs were largely the preserve of the settler community, and hence the racial stratification of the working class was extremely pronounced. Moreover, within this context it is important to note that the plantation and settler farm sectors were largely based on the supply of labour from the peasantry and this system of internal migrant labour grounded in maintaining an organic link between family agriculture and labour supply was an essential feature which determined the conditions of profitability of these sectors.

In terms of the structure of the rural economy, the peasantry directly produced about 70 per cent of the total agricultural output in 1970, of which 55 per cent (of total agricultural output) was production for own consumption and the remaining 15 per cent were cash crops (export crops such as cotton and cashew as well as foodcrops for the internal market). Furthermore, the peasantry supplied seasonal labour to plantations and to settler farms, as well as migrant labour to the Southern African region. Of the total monetary production in agriculture, plantations and settler farms each accounted for about one-third, while the remainder consisted of cash crops production by the peasantry [*Wuyts, 1978*]. Tables 1 and 2 provide the reader with a summary

## TABLE 1
### THE STRUCTURE OF THE COLONIAL RURAL ECONOMY IN 1970

| REGION | PLANTATIONS | SETTLER FARMS | PEASANTRY | | | DOMINANT ASPECTS OF REGIONAL RURAL ECONOMY |
|---|---|---|---|---|---|---|
| | | | MARKETED OUTPUT 1 | SALE OF LABOUR 2 | OWN CONSUMPTION 3 | |
| NORTH [Cabo Delgado, Niassa Nampula] | Sisal (67%) 2% | Cotton (17%) Tobacco (50%) 12% | Cashew (78%) Cotton (37%) Food Crops (see 3) 26% | Seasonal labour to plantations & settler farms, plantations in Tanzania | Cassava (67%) Groundnuts (56%) (+ Sorghum, Millet, Maize) 60% | Cash crop production (in part under forced cultivation) by the peasantry. Later accelerated development of settler cotton farms |
| CENTRE [Zambezia, Manica, Sofala, Tete] | Sugar (73%) Copra (69%) Tea (100%) Sisal (33%) 28% | Potatoes (67%) Tobacco (27%) (& maize, cotton, vegetables) 11% | Cotton (20%) Cashew (9%) Food (see 3) 9% | Seasonal labour to plantations, Tete/Manica: contract labour to Zimbabwe & Malawi. | Rice (28%) Maize (64%) Groundnuts (17%) Cassava (25%) (& other minor ones). 48% | Plantation economy in the Zambezia valley, relying on huge quantities of seasonal labour. |
| SOUTH [Maputo, Gaza, Inhambane] | Sugar (27%) 2% | Rice (56%) Potatoes (32%) (veg., wheat) 39% | Cashew (13%) & food crops (see 3) 10% | 20-30% of male adults worked on South African mines for contract periods of 1-1/2 yrs. Seasonal labour to settler farms & plantation | Maize (16%) Groundnuts (27%) Cassava (8%) 49% | Labour reserve for South African mining & settler farm based granary to feed the towns. |
| NATIONAL | 15% | 15% | 15% | - | 55% | - |

*Source:* Marc Wuyts, 'Peasants and Rural Economy in Mozambique'.

*Notes:* (1) % between brackets refer to % of national production of the particular crop.

(2) % at the bottom of each block refer to relative importance within regional production.

(3) Meat and dairy products are not included (mainly South and parts of central region).

TABLE 2

THE STRUCTURE OF WAGE EMPLOYMENT IN COLONIAL MOZAMBIQUE IN +/− 1970

| Sector | % of Total Wage Employment |
|---|---|
| External Migrant Labour | 24 |
| Agriculture | 17 |
| Fishing | 3 |
| Manufacturing | 10 |
| Construction | 3 |
| Commerce and Finance | 11 |
| Ports and Railways | 5 |
| Public Administration | 7 |
| Domestic Servants | 11 |
| Other Sectors | 9 |

*Basic Source*: *IV Plano de Fomento, Parte III, Relatório Sectoriais, Vol. 8, Mão de Obra e Formação Profissional, pp. 5–6* (adapted).

*Note*:* Statistics on employment were generally of very poor quality and often inconsistent as to data sources. More specifically, large discrepancies existed with respect to data on agricultural employment depending on whether or not seasonal labour was taken into account. As a rough estimate, wage employment accounted for between 20 per cent to 30 per cent of the active population (which is high relatively to countries such as Tanzania with +/− 15 per cent and Zimbabwe with 18 per cent, the main reasons being the dominant feature of external migrant labour as well as the considerable demand for labour coming from plantations and settler agriculture. Since wage labour was mainly (but not exclusively) male labour, it follows that probably +/− 50 per cent of the male active population was well integrated in wage work (although in agriculture the intensity of wage work varied weekly).

* In comparing several data sources (such as the census data, agricultural and industrial statistics, migration, data, etc.) I am heavily indebted to David Wield and Chris Gerry (both CEA members) on piecing together a reasonable picture out of conflicting sources.

overview of the structure of the rural economy and of employment in colonial Mozambique at the time of the early 1970s.

## II. A PERIODISATION OF POST-INDEPENDENCE ECONOMIC DEVELOPMENT

Before turning to the main issue of this article I shall present a tentative periodisation of economic development sicne the instalment of the transitional government in September 1974 so as to provide the background against which the role of money within rural transformation can be assessed. With respect to each period a short discussion of its general features is presented in this section.

### From the Transitional Government to the Third Congress of Frelimo: September 1974 to February 1977[3]

The Lusaka agreements of September 1974 between Frelimo and the Portugese government specified the principle of the unconditional transfer of political power to Frelimo and determined the conditions of this transfer of power. This agreement was quite distinct from the normal classical pattern of decolonisation in Africa since the latter generally implied that a compromise between the colonial power and the nationalist movement(s) is worked out in a constitutional conference which not only shaped the political system of the new post-colonial state, but also worked out the economic and financial obligations and arrangements of the new state *vis-à-vis* its previous colonial power. Frelimo's position that the Lusaka conference could only discuss the conditions of the transfer of power and not the content of the new power was accepted in the end by the Portuguese delegation. Furthermore, no agreements were made with respect to financial and economic ties as a carry-over from the colonial period. The concrete mechanism of the transfer of power was to take place through the immediate instalment of a transitional government in which Frelimo was the majority partner with portuguese officials as the only remaining other partner. The immediate response to the agreements was the aborted attempt on the part of section of the settler population to seize power by means of Rhodesia-type unilateral declaration of independence.

The period of the transitional government (up to independence in June 1975) and roughly the first two years after independence were characterised by the massive emigration of the settler population accompanied by an intense struggle waged by the colonial bourgeoisie and petty bourgeoisie in an attempt to destabilise the economy as well as to export most of its capital (in whatever form). Hence economic sabotage in its various forms − destruction of equipment, and economic infrastructure; killing of cattle stock; large-scale dismissal of workers from productive enterprises and complete production standstills − were practised on a large scale all over the country. The export of capital also assumed enormous proportions and took various forms: the collapse of the (colonial) state apparatus and the fact that banks were privately owned meant that it was easy to arrange for acquiring foreign exchange to import goods without any imports subsequently materialising, or to export cashew, cotton, etc., without the foreign exchange ever returning to the national bank; furthermore, initially no control was organised over the export of personal belongings of returning settlers which led to massive buying in shops and depletion of stock of commodities; finally, the direct illegal exportation across the borders to South Africa and Rhodesia of trucks, tractors, equipment, cattle, etc., further depleted the available means of production in the country.

With this context economic policy was dictated by the necessity to fight against the destabilisation of the economy propelled by the actions of the colonial bourgeoisie and petty bourgeoisie (as well as of skilled and administrative workers). The legal weapon was a decree of February 1975 which specified that in proven cases of acts of sabotage (which included the massive dismissal of workers and deliberate production stoppages) the government could intervene by transferring the management of the enterprise to an appointed administrative council composed of workers and often members of the old management as well. The social force which concretised this policy were the dynamising groups − popular organisations of militants which were constituted at community level as well as in enterprises, public institutions and government administrations.

The outcome of this intense struggle was a sharp production crisis which provoked pronounced falls in output of different sectors: in agriculture, marketed output of export crops dropped by more than 40 per cent in the period 1974–76 in relation to the 1973 levels; foodcrop production by the peasantry dropped by 20 per cent for maize and 61 per cent for cassava, while settler farm production of food went down by 50 per cent in the same period [*Wuyts, 1978*]. In industry production went down by 36 per cent, relatively, that is, from 75 to 73 and dropped further such that in 1979 its output was an estimated 48 per cent of the 1973 level (and this was after a certain recovery took place after 1977) [*Wuyts, 1980a*]. The impact was cumulative in as much as the contraction in output in one sector (especially in the case of key sectors such as transport, servicing and repair of equipment, etc.) provoked spill-over supply constraints on to other sectors. Within this context, the massive withdrawal of the major part of skilled and administrative labour created an enormous shortage with widespread effects on production.

In the immediate post-independence period the government also moved quickly in terms of nationalisations directed at redressing the sharp racial discrimination which existed in the colonial period in terms of access to education, health, land, legal services and housing. Not surprisingly, the nationalisation of housing provoked in its aftermath the virtually complete standstill of production in the construction industry and related industries.

It is important to note, however, that the nationalisation of land and the emigration of settler farmers did not lead to the redistribution of land to the peasantry. That is, no land reform was carried out in this period, and rural dynamising groups were mobilised to prevent the uncontrolled takeover of abandoned settler land. The dominant tendency was, rather, for the state to take over the land with a view to its future consolidation into state farms (and to a much lesser extent – co-operatives). As can be seen in this case the economic policy pursued in this period was responsive not merely to the crisis produced by the colonial bourgeoisie and petty bourgeoisie, but incorporated within this struggle strategic elements concerning the future development of production.

### From the Third to the Fourth Congress: February 1977–April 1983[4]

At the Third Congress the liberation front was transformed into a Marxist-Leninist party and a socialist programme for economic development was adopted as the basic policy. The programme stressed the importance of constructing a planned economy in which the state sector was to assume the dominant position and to constitute the propelling dynamic force within the transitional period. It is important to note, however, that the dominant role of the state sector was not seen to be the exclusive role: the transformation of rural society was to be realised as well through the development of communal villages and the organisation of peasant producers into co-operatives as complimentary aspects of the overall transformation of the economic structure.

The implementation of the policy in practice, however, was heavily concentrated on the development of the state sector:

(1) Investments were virtually exclusively concentrated on the consolidation and development of the state enterprises and related economic infrastructure;

(2) there was strong bias towards identifying the establishment of the socialist sector with nationalisation and mechanisation; and

(3) planning became essentially the planning of the state sector through the elaboration of central plans based on material balances, and little attention was paid in practice to the role of planning and economic policy in providing the conditions for a process of transformation on a more wider front (including the transformation of small producers) which also would require the material backing of the resources of the state.

This development, however, contradicted the basic fact that a considerable part of production of foodcrops and of export crops depended on smallholder production and, hence, constituted a fundamental aspect of the accumulation capacity of the economy, apart from this sector still embracing the greater part of the rural population. Furthermore, the corner-stone of the state farm sector remained the supply of labour from the peasantry and hence the question of transforming the rural economy could not be bypassed through the accelerated expansion of the state farm sector without confronting the nature of the link between wage labour and family agriculture.

Before turning to the discussion on the nature of planning within rural transformation, let us look first at the transformations which took place within the economy at large, and within the rural economy more specifically.

The state sector expanded at a very rapid rate. Table 3 gives us the relative importance of the state sector within monetary production of agriculture as compared with the balance between private (settler farms and plantations) and family production in 1970. The emphasis was on expansion rather than on consolidation of production on the already established farms. By 1978 100,000 hectares had been put under state farm cultivation and this expanded to 140,000 by 1982. Investment concentrated on the state sector: its share of agricultural investment was well over 90 per cent, while to the remainder, co-operatives received two per cent and family agriculture, nil. Hanlon reports that:

> in the four years after the congress, Mozambique imported 50 million pounds in agricultural machinery, including 3,000 tractors and 300 combined harvesters. During the last decade of the colonial period, 700 tractors a year were imported. So the new large importation only served to replace those wearing out naturally and those destroyed or driven over the border by fleeing settlers. But as part of a quest for modernisation, the new tractors tended to be larger and more powerful than the ones they replaced. And the combine harvesters were new; the colonists had depended on semi-forced seasonal labour for their harvests [*Hanlon, 1984: 100*]

In contrast, after independence no hoes were imported and local production of hoes fell to more than half of the 1973 level in the period up to 1981 [*Hanlon, 1984: 100*].

TABLE 3

THE RELATIVE IMPORTANCE OF THE STATE SECTOR IN AGRICULTURAL
PRODUCTION IN 1980 AS COMPARED WITH THE BALANCE BETWEEN
PRIVATE (SETTLER AND PLANTATION) AND FAMILY PRODUCTION
IN 1970

| | 1970 | | 1980 | | |
| | Private (in | Peasant %) | State | Private (in %) | Peasant |
| --- | --- | --- | --- | --- | --- |
| Total: | 69 | 31 | 52 | 10 | 38 |
| Cotton: | 35 | 65 | 45 | 10 | 45 |
| Sugar: | 100 | - | 85 | 15 | - |
| Cashew: | 10 | 90 | - | - | 100 |
| Tea: | 100 | - | 90 | 10 | - |
| Sisal: | 100 | - | 30 | 70 | - |
| Copra: | 80 | 20 | 20 | 40 | 40 |
| Rice: | 60 | 40 | 80 | - | 20 |
| Tobacco: | 80 | 20 | 55 | 40 | 5 |

Source: Hanlon [1984: 100].

Within other sectors of the economy the share of the state sector also became dominant: 65 per cent of production in industry, 85 per cent in transport and communications, 90 per cent in construction and 40 per cent in commerce [Frelimo, 1983b].

Turning now to the evolution of production, in general domestic output increased somewhat in the period 1977–81 as can be seen from Tables 4a and 4b. Agriculture lagged behind the general recovery, and this was specifically the case with monetary output. While industry expanded by 14 per cent, transport by 15 per cent and construction by 25 per cent (which reflects the emphasis on investment), agriculture expanded only by nine per cent, and the latter expansion may well be an overestimate obtained by extrapolating the growth of subsistence production independently of the evolution of monetary output in agriculture. In fact, monetary output more or less stagnated over

TABLE 4a

GLOBAL SOCIAL PRODUCT AT CONSTANT PRICES OF 1980
(million contos)

| | 1975 | 1977 | 1980 | 1981 | 1982 | % Growth 1975/77 | % Growth 1977/81 | 1981/82 |
| --- | --- | --- | --- | --- | --- | --- | --- | --- |
| Agriculture | 26.1 | 30.6 | 33.4 | 33.3 | 32.5 | + 17.2 | + 8.8 | − 2.4 |
| Industry | 26.4 | 27.8 | 30.7 | 31.6 | 27.2 | + 5.3 | + 13.7 | − 13.9 |
| Transport | 9.1 | 7.8 | 81. | 9.0 | 8.4 | − 14.3 | + 15.4 | − 6.6 |
| Others + | 9.5 | 8.8 | 10.0 | 9.8 | 9.8 | − 7.4 | + 11.4 | 0 |
| GSP | 71.1 | 75.0 | 82.2 | 83.7 | 77.9 | + 5.5 | + 11.6 | − 6.9 |

(+ includes construction, commerce and unspecified others)

Source: Commissão Nacional do Plano [1984].

TABLE 4b

AGRICULTURAL OUTPUT ACCORDING TO NAT ACCOUNTS DATA AND
MONETARY AGRICULTURAL OUTPUT

(Million contos – constant 1980 prices)

| Year | *(1)*<br>*Global Product*<br>*in Agriculture* | *(2)*<br>*Monetary Agricultural*<br>*Output (NPC series)* | *(3)*<br>*(2) as % of (1)* |
|------|------|------|------|
| 1975 | 26.1 | 5.5 | 21 |
| 1977 | 30.6 | 4.6 | 15 |
| 1980 | 33.4 | 4.3 | 13 |
| 1981 | 33.3 | 4.3 | 13 |
| 1982 | 32.5 | 4.0 | 12 |

*Source*: Commissão Nacional do Plano [*1984*].

*Notes*:  (1) Global Social product equals the gross value of production.
   (2) In the GSP data, agricultural output includes subsistence production, although this cannot be but a rough estimate since no data were collected on this item. The data are not broken down by components and hence it is impossible to derive monetary output and its evolution.
   (3) However, a separate series on monetary production (specified as integrated within the plan) is given by the NPC. The evolution of this series shows a continuous decline in monetary output (contrary to the GSP national account data). The monetary output series does not include the plantation sector (sugar, tea, coffee) and hence is a good measure of food production and cotton production in the state sector and larger private sector plus official marketing of peasants crops.
   (4) It appears therefore that the subsistence production estimates have been extrapolated independently of the evolution of monetary output.

the whole period despite the heavy investments which went into the state sector. As such exports did not recover at the same rate as the domestic product and its composition changed drastically over the period with respect to relative importance of different items. This is shown in Tables 5 and 6.

Table 6 shows clearly that the basis of expansion of exports in the 1977–81 period was more a result of the expansion of fishing and of petroleum products (not in quality, but in nominal terms). With the exception of tea, the exports based on the state sector performed rather badly (cotton and sugar).

A further element within the stagnant evolution of agriculture was the growing shortfall in food production. This notwithstanding the fact that most investment within the state farm sector was directed towards food production to feed the towns. The major example in this case was the massive undertaking of the agro-industrial complex of Limpopo which was aimed at assuring the self-sufficiency in rice production. Table 7 compares the evolution of rice production with that of maize, the former being exclusively reliant on state farm production with respect to monetary output, while the latter in part is provided through peasant production. As the reader can verify in Table 7, the evolution of rice production was much more problematic than that of maize, despite the heavy investments and the concentration of the state effort in this sector.

The development within the rural economy was compounded by the sharp reduction in the recruitment of mine labour from 1976 onwards. Recruitment

TABLE 5

COMPARATIVE GROWTH RATES OF INDUSTRIAL OUTPUT, OF MONETARY AGRICULTURAL
OUTPUT AND OF EXPORT (CONSTANT PRICES OF 1908)
(in %)

| Period | Industry | Agriculture | Exports |
|--------|----------|-------------|---------|
| 1973–75 | − 33 | − 23 | − 34 |
| 1975–77 | − 1 | − 16 | − 39 |
| 1977–81 | + 12 | − 6.5 | + 6.5 |
| 1981–82 | − 13.5 | 0 | + 2.5 |

Source: Time series data of the Commissão Nacional do Plano [*1984*] for agriculture and industry,
and export data [*Commissão Nacional do Plano 1984*].

Note: The data on industrial output are not exactly identical with the GSP national account
data since they only include sectors integrated in the plan. However, unlike in the case
of agriculture, these data tally well with the national account data.

TABLE 6

THE COMPOSITION OF EXPORTS IN SELECTED YEARS
(% of total exports)

| | 1973 | 1975 | 1977 | 1979 | 1981 | 1982 |
|---|------|------|------|------|------|------|
| Cashew (kernels) | 18 | 15 | 30 | 17 | 19 | 19 |
| Cotton | 20 | 9 | 6 | 9 | 9 | 8 |
| Sugar | 10 | 11 | 5 | 12 | 9 | 4 |
| Tea | 4 | 4 | 8 | 8 | 5 | 11 |
| Prawns | 2 | 5 | 7 | 9 | 19 | 17 |
| Petroleum Products | 5 | 7 | 7 | 15 | 19 | 16 |
| Total Exports of current prices (million contos) | 5.5 | 5.1 | 4.9 | 8.3 | 9.9 | 8.7 |

Source: Commissão Nacional do Plano [*1984*].

TABLE 7

THE EVOLUTION OF PRICE AND MAIZE PRODUCTION 1973–82
(Quantity Indices 1973 = 100)

| Year | Rice | Maize |
|------|------|-------|
| 1973 | 100 | 100 |
| 1974 | 100 | 100 |
| 1975 | 78.33 | 79.16 |
| 1976 | 62.50 | 75.00 |
| 1977 | 50.00 | 28.33 |
| 1978 | 36.66 | 58.33 |
| 1979 | 46.91 | 55.00 |
| 1980 | 35.75 | 54.71 |
| 1981 | 24.08 | 65.25 |
| 1982 | 34.58 | 74.5 |

Source: Commissão Nacional do Plano [*1984*].

Note: Although the precise content of the data coverage was not listed with the published data,
these data appear to refer to monetary officially marketed production. While the monetary
production of rice is mainly state farm production and hence reasonably well recorded,
the data on maize may underestimate the evolution of the latter years since (1) a significant
share is produced by the peasantry, and (2) the parallel markets expanded rapidly over
these latter years (diverting the food surpluses away from official marketing).

levels which normally oscillated between 80,000 and 100,000 per year, and which in 1975 had soared up to 118,000 workers, were sharply reduced to 40,000 thereafter [*First, 1982*]. This mainly affected the southern part of Mozambique by creating massive rural unemployment. The towns had no capacity to absorb this surplus labour since employment was drastically reduced in the towns as well. The latter process was due to the fall in employment in domestic work (servants) and in the tourist sector (restaurants, hotels, bars, etc.). The exodus of Portuguese settlers and the virtual standstill of tourism (which catered for South Africans and Rhodesians) had amplified the problem of structural employment in the towns.

The rural unemployed could not merely fall back on family agriculture since this was heavily dependent on cash income from wage work. Oxen and ploughs, farm implements, water reserves, etc. were normally paid for with wages from mine labour or other wage work. Furthermore, due to this cash inflow from wage income, a more interactive type of division of labour developed within the rural areas of southern Mozambique. Hence, peasants without oxen and plough would rent the services of peasants who did, and pay for it out of wage income. Brick-makers, carpenters, house-builders, tailors, mechanics were to be found among the middle peasantry who relied on these activities (usually acquired through mine labour) to supplement their income from farming. In a similar fashion, local transport and petty commerce were sidelines of middle peasants stabilised by the influx of wage income. The reduction in mine labour employment deeply affected the viability of this internal division of labour within the rural economy.

Finally, the impact of the reduction in mine labour was not evenly spread among the peasantry, since only those who held valid work certificates from the recruitment agency could continue to go to the mines. Other peasants were cut off altogether. This introduced a sharp element of differentiation within the rural econonmy. Those who could continued to go to the mines not only had cash income but also a guaranteed access to commodities (including means of production), while within Mozambique shortages were rapidly turning into a goods famine.

However, rural unemployment was not merely a phenomena of the south. In central Mozambique, wage work to Rhodesia dropped sharply with the closure of the border between Mozambique and Rhodesia since 1976, and as a result of the war situation which developed thereafter.

As stated in above, the concentration of resources on the state sector further weakened the basis of family agriculture at a time when a considerable part of its cash income through wage labour was cut off. While the colonial situation was characterised by persistent labour shortages within the rural economy and continued state intervention to keep labour cheap (through the imposition of forced labour and forced cultivation of crops as well as by fragmentation of labour markets to avoid competition for labour to drive up the wage levels), the post-independence situation became characterised by rural unemployment and an intensified flow of people from the rural areas to the towns in search of wage work.

The priority accorded to investments led to the slow expansion in the supply of consumer goods and in 1981 it actually fell by eight per cent : six per cent in food products and 17 per cent in other products (the major drop being in textiles) [*Frelimo, 1983b*]. The impact of this was felt more sharply in the rural areas where no system of rationing and of allocation of basic consumer commodities existed as operated in the towns.

From 1982 onwards, the economic situation took a turn for the worse, the major factors accounting for this being the escalation of the silent war of aggression by South Africa against Mozambique and the drought. By 1983 the economy itself encountered an acute crisis situation: sharp falls in production, mounting debts and massive destruction caused by the war [*Wuyts, 1984a*].

III. THE QUESTION OF PLANNING FOR RURAL DEVELOPMENT[5]

The sluggish development of rural agricultural production was not first and foremost a technical or managerial problem, although the shortage of technical and managerial capacity was an important factor for the type of development which took place. Rather, as Bridget O'Laughlin argued, the key problem was that planning for rural development was essentially seen to be a question of pursuing a modernisation strategy within the context of a perceived dual economy [*O'Laughlin, 1982*]. Hence, the key problem was the notion itself that the state sector could grow under its own steam and consequently that the optimal path of socialist construction consisted in the maximum expansion of this sector.

Indeed, planning is not only a matter of technique, but rather a question of the social organisation of production and of its dynamic process of change. Therefore planning is informed by the analysis − made explicitly or implicitly − of class forces within a society. The state occupies a crucial position through its control over the allocation of material resources and of skilled manpower. However, these material resources will only propel of process of transformation in so far as they are channelled to mobilise those social forces within society which are the agents of socialist transformation. Social change requires the backing of material resources and the concentration of efforts behind such change, and therefore 'investment' by itself does not bring about change unless it plays into existing social forces capable of transforming production.

The implicit notion of modernisation through the self-propelled development of the state sector which shaped the allocation of material resources within the rural economy effectively disarmed the peasantry as a social force of socialist transformation and left them in the cold awaiting their 'historic' mission of being absorbed by the growing stae sector.

The state farm sector therefore became dominant but untransformed. Indeed, its Achilles' heel consisted of the inherited system of drawing labour from the peasantry on the basis of an internal migrant labour system. The profitability and productivity of the colonial farm and of the colonial plantation was rooted in the organic link which existed between its wage labour (especially, its seasonal labour) and family agriculture. Over the agrarian season labour could be attracted and subsequently expelled in accordance with the requirements of production and, hence, labour costs could be minimised in this way. However, this system implies that family agriculture paid the bill for the costs of adjustment. It needed to provide for a considerable part of the subsistence requirements of the household but its own development was blocked by its subordinate position *vis-à-vis* the settler farm or plantation. Furthermore, it was a key function of the colonial state to assure that the peasantry provided its labour power as cheaply as possible.

The key question in transforming this system therefore becomes the creation of a stable proletariat on the one hand, and simultaneously freeing family agriculture from its subordinate position by raising its productivity through the co-operative movement. The actual policy pursued by the state farms was based on an invalid assumption of an elastic labour supply without much consideration of the problem of wage labour and its link with family agriculture. Not surprisingly, therefore, was the fact that labour shortages became chronic during peak periods of the agricultural season. The old coercive action of the colonial state had fallen away, but no strategic and tactical measures were taken to transform the conditions of productivity and of profitability within a wider context. Planning considered labour supply as a residual factor and answers to problems were sought in mechanisation.

The result was high costs/low productivity conditions of state farm production. Mechanisation was rapid but was not accompanied by an organisational capacity to run and service the newly acquired equipment. Investment was geared towards new equipment, but no funds were earmarked for spare parts and repair capacity.

Planned targets for the farms were generally over-optimistic. These were based on pre-set norms rather than relating to existing productive capacity and organisational strength. Since plans were formulated with hectares as targets the production units would aim at satisfying the area targets independently of considerations of yield or cost. Hence, invariably, the area prepared for cultivation would be superior to the area sown, and the latter superior to the area harvested. Costs accumulated over the smaller area and, hence, virtually all state farms were heavily in deficit.

The co-operatives were perceived not so much as the transformation of family agriculture but rather as a way of organising the cultivation on prior settler land which was not, or could not be, integrated within the state farm sector, due to their more distant location or to other factors. Hence, in this case, too, the link with family agriculture was not explicitly recognised. Co-operatives were planned in much the same way as state farms with little consideration for the effective capacity of the members to supply labour, given their commitment to their own family plots. Excessive targets and the non-correspondence between labour inputs and other inputs also led to the accumulation of costs on feasible production.

As a result, family agriculture was always identified as a sector by itself without consideration for its linkage with either the state sector or the co-operatives. Implicit in this was the assumption that either this sector had no inherent potential for being transformed from within, or that such a transformation could take place only through simple co-operation which necessitate political mobilisation rather than any commitment of resources to support it.

The peasantry, however, did not constitute a passive entity dwelling in its underworld of subsistence production and marginal linkages with monetary production and accumulation. Rather, the peasantry constituted the pillar that underscored rural production through its supply of wage labour and through its production of cash crops both for exports and food for the home market.

After independence, the peasantry did not demand a withdrawal from exchange but, rather, terms of exchange more favourable for allowing them to transform their conditions of existence as producers and as consumers. But this required viable conditions of circulation of money and commodities within the rural areas and an active role on the part of the state sector in establishing this exchange within a dynamic process of change which allowed for the transformation of family agriculture.

Exchange within the rural economy, however, became increasingly characterised by goods famine, the rapid development of parallel markets and depreciation of the currency through inflation of prices in these parallel markets. To understand their impact on production within the rural economy we need to analyse somewhat further the relationship between material planning and monetary policy.

As we have seen, it was after the Third Congress that the construction of a planned socialist economy became the key target of economic policy. To this effect the machinery for central planning was set up: the economic ministries were hierarchically subordinated to the newly formed National Planning Commission (NPC); the banking sector was nationalised and restructured; the state budget became the principal instrument of financial policy and subordinated to the requirements of material planning. Within the economy at large, the key sectors came under direct control of the state and, hence, the state sector rapidly became the dominant sector.

Material planning therefore became the major regulatory force in allocating material resources and manpower over the economy. By 1980 planning was carried out by means of material balances based on a system of production norms. Four aspects came to characterise this system of planning:

(1) The scope of material planning was essentially the state sector as such, and little consideration was taken for the issue of the role of the state sector in establishing the exchange with independent small-scale production. The latter function was generally seen as merely formal: a question of regulation and control, rather than of using the economic power of the state sector to propel the transformation of other sectors.

(2) The state sector was consolidated into relatively large-scale units which were directly subordinated to the respective economic ministries, and hence little scope was left for flexibility in planning and in economic policy at the regional level. This system facilitated the use of material balances, but it implied highly centralised planning. Little scope was left for state intervention and planning which would take the regional interdependences as its starting point.

(3) Targets were generally set with respect to assumed norms which had little or no basis in the actual existing capacities to organise production. Plans therefore were generally taut and consistently under-fulfilled.

(4) The balance between accumulation and consumption was shifted drastically in favour of investment, and in the direction of large infra-structural projects (power lines, irrigation infrastructures and dams) as well as of large-scale projects for the state sector enterprises.

The latter two aspects need some further illustration. Targets were set with reference to potential norms which did not take account of the real existing organisational capacity at the level of enterprises. Table 8 gives us an indication of the degree of plan fulfilment for the year 1979/80 in the state farm sector.

TABLE 8

PLAN FULFILMENT IN THE STATE FARM SECTOR
(major products) 1979/80 − tons

|  | Real output | Planned output | % Fulfilment |
| --- | --- | --- | --- |
| Rice: | 37,483 | 67,070 | 56 |
| Maize: | 32,721 | 50,400 | 65 |
| Potatoes: | 7,395 | 38,950 | 19 |
| Unions: | 1,441 | 8,800 | 16 |
| Vegetables: | 1,552 | 19,750 | 8 |
| Cotton: | 14,820 | 21,200 | 70 |
| Tea: | 16,020 | 17,000 | 98 |
| Citrus: | 16,000 | 38,200 | 42 |
| Copra: | 14,986 | 16,150 | 93 |
| Total: | 155,362 | 315,830 | 49 |

Source: Commissão Nacional do Plano [1984].

In industry the picture was somewhat better. Plan fulfilment at constant prices amounted to 71 per cent in 1980 [NPC, 1981].

Clearly, the result of this consistent discrepancy between planned output and realised output is the imbalances created between projected resource utilisation and its real availability. Production for the internal market consistently falls short of the projected requirements, and foreign exchange income derived from exports and services falls short of projected import necessities. The result is that available resources need to be rationed in function of their planned use, and this requires that a set of priorities are formulated (formally or informally) to deal with rationing within the plan.

De facto, this power to ration the available resources with respect to the options set by the plan was centralised in the hands of the NPC. Hence, when the available resources fell short of the planned needs as formulated within the Central Plan, the NPC would decide which were the priority areas to which such resources were to be channelled. Invariably, the inherent bias of the NPC was to favour the state sector on the one hand, and accumulation on the other.

This power to ration has important political consequences. The Central Plan was to be formulated by the NPC and submitted for approval of the Party at its Central Committee meetings and of the Popular Assembly. Often at these levels the concern with peasant agriculture was versed and allowance was to be made for this within the allocation of resources of the Plan. However, these plans were far removed from the real production potentialities, and hence would not prove to be feasible in practice. This involved a second round of priorities to be formulated so as to ration the plan. This process of rationing was not subject to any political control, but a technical task of the NPC. As such, considerable political power to decide on the allocation of resources was concentrated in the hands of the planning commission.

TABLE 9

ACTUAL PUBLIC INVESTMENT: 1979–83
(million meticais) – current prices

|              | 1978/79* | 1980   | 1981   | 1982   | 1983   |
|--------------|----------|--------|--------|--------|--------|
| Total        | 8,010    | 9,916  | 13,962 | 14,255 | 10,197 |
| Economic:    | 7,290    | 8,027  | 11,827 | 12,291 | 8,803  |
| Agriculture: | 1,095    | 2,271  | 4,181  | 4,826  | 2,560  |
| GDP:         | –        | 66,200 | 70,400 | 73,000 | 68,800 |

Source: Commissão Nacional do Plano [1984].
Note:    *Investments for both years: 1978 and 1979.

The strong drive towards investment can be seen from the date in Table 9. Furthermore, these figures concern only realised investment and, hence, not planned investment. For example, for the year 1980 planned investment of the public sector was projected at 15,147 million meticais. Hence, actual investment only amounted to about two-thirds of the planned level! The reason for this was the unavailability of foreign finance for some projects, the freezing of existing projects due to insufficient construction capacity or lack of materials, etc. The weight of investment over the economy was thus much heavier then reflected in the table due to the frustrated execution of ongoing projects [Wuyts, 1984a].

The financing of investment could not be done from the internal savings of the state sector itself. Over the period concerned, current receipts more or less balanced with current expenditures, leaving at best a small surplus. The main reason for this was the low surplus generating capacity of the public sector due to its low productivity/high cost conditions. As such surpluses of state enterprises contributed little to government income; only by 1981 did the contribution of state enterprises become more significant with 18 per cent of government income, and this mainly as a result of price increases [Wuyts, 1984a]. Hence, investment had to be financed from other internal and external sources.

The foreign resources inflow can best be measured by the deficit on current account of the balance of payments. Table 10 shows us the growing foreign exchange gap from 1978 onwards. From this it can be seen that a considerable share of investment was financed through foreign credits. It should be noted, however, that the profit from the sale of gold balances accumulated by converting the deferred payments of miners ages into gold at the official price of gold in South Africa are not included in the data. Hence, the actual foreign inflow was less than what the data seem to suggest.

TABLE 10

THE GROWING FOREIGN EXCHANGE GAP
(000 million meticais)

| Year | Balance on Visible Trade | Balance on Invisibles | Current Surplus/ Deficit | Import Coverage % |
|------|--------------------------|-----------------------|--------------------------|-------------------|
| 1973 | − 5.9 | 3 | − 2.9 | 79 |
| 1974 | − 4.1 | 4 | − 0.1 | 95 |
| 1975 | − 5.4 | 5.4 | 0 | 100 |
| 1976 | − 4.5 | 4.9 | 0.4 | 103 |
| 1977 | − 5.7 | 3.6 | − 2.1 | 80 |
| 1978 | − 11.1 | 4 | − 7.1 | 54 |
| 1979 | − 10.3 | 4.2 | − 6.1 | 67 |
| 1980 | − 17.2 | 4.7 | − 12.5 | 53 |
| 1981 | − 18.1 | 5.3 | 12.8 | 54 |
| 1982 | − 23.0 | 6.6 | − 16.4 | 48 |
| 1983 (est) | − 16. | 6.1 | − 10.4 | 53 |

*Source:* Commissão Nacional do Plano [*1984*].

*Notes:* Import coverage = ratio of (export earnings + balance on invisibles) over total imports or commodities.

The balance on current account does not include the profit on the sale of gold from mine labour remittance. This was an important cash earner up to 1978.

The issue of domestic money was another source for financing investment as well as financing the deficits of many state enterprises and other enterprises. Indeed, in this respect, the contribution of state enterprises to the budget was somewhat ficticious, since the enterprises in deficit were mainly financed by the banks.

With respect to monetary policy, the implications of this concentration of material resources on the state sector and on its expansion needs to be viewed with respect to the allocation of foreign exchange and to medical payments.

Dollar balances were allocated in the function of the plan and investment received a high priority. As such, it was easier to obtain funds to build new farms and/or factories than to obtain money to buy imported raw materials to keep existing enterprises running at reasonable levels of capacity utilisation. With the sluggish expansion of exports and the priority allocation of foreign funding to investment, the net outcome was that ongoing production was squeezed because of lack of imported inputs, thereby aggravating the imbalances between planned and realised output.

As to the local currency, the supply of money through bank credits was very elastic in respect of investment projects listed in the plan and just as elastic in financing state enterprises. On both counts costs, and especially wage costs, expanded more rapidly than production. For example, the total wage bill expanded by 29 per cent over the period 1980−83 while the gross domestic product only increased by four per cent over the same period.

Hence, the money supply was endogenous in respect of the execution of the material plan in as much as its supply was elastic within the state sector.

The result was a generalised shortage economy characterised by severe monetary disequilibrium. This did not only affect the imbalance between disposable income and the supply of consumer commodities at official prices, but also had a direct impact on production, namely, that part of the national output produced outside the state sector and dependent on the circuits of money and commodities for its integration within the national economy. More specifically, it directly affected the integration of cash crop production by the peasantry and the potentiality to transform this production into increasingly more socialised forms of production.

## IV. MONETARY DISEQUILIBRIUM AND THE EXCHANGE BETWEEN STATE SECTOR AND PEASANTRY[6]

At the 1977 Party Congress the class alliance which would constitute the driving social force in the transitional period was defined as the worker−peasant alliance. Strengthening the worker−peasant alliance within the transition to socialism is a question of politics and economics. Further, regarding the latter aspect, it requires the material backing of the state sector:

(1) The peasantry as cash crop producers are integrated within the national division of labour through market relationships. The state sector therefore needs to show in practice that it is capable of organising and realising this exchange with the peasantry in terms acceptable to them. Hence, the criticality of the terms of trade in the exchange with the peasantry and their effectiveness in terms of relative prices existing not merely nominally (as specified official prices) but being effectively backed up by goods.

(2) Furthermore, to a considerable extent the transformation of social relations of production in the rural economy is propelled by the nature and conditions of the exchange which the state sector establishes with the peasantry. The formation of communal villages and co-operatives requires the material backing of the state both in terms of manpower and of material and financial resources so as to provide incentives for the development of these forms of production and to prove their superiority in production in practice.

Hence, the task of the state sector consists not merely of establishing an exchange with the peasantry, but of organising this exchange in such a manner as to propel the socialisation of the countryside.

Channelling resources through exchange is never neutral but acts upon the social organisation of production − that is, through increased differentiation within the peasantry or through organising poor and middle peasants into associations and/or co-operatives in a process of increased socialisation of production.

We have seen that in actual practice the attitude towards the peasantry is at best ambiguous. Behind the economic policy towards rural development lurks a strongly-held conception of a dual economy − a modern sector (the inherited plantation and settler farm settlers) − and a traditional sector of subsistence production (where in the colonial period mainly extra-economic factors such as forced cultivation or forced labour caused the integration of the peasantry in the market exchange). Socialist development was therefore strongly identified with modernising through the rapid expansion of the state sector, that is, nationalisation and mechanisation on an ever-increasing scale. The peasantry would be gradually absorbed within this expanding sector, and hence, at first, the role of the peasantry was seen as essentially passive with its transformation mainly centring on social aspects. As such, the policy of communal villages became virtually a habitational concept (and was in actual fact the responsibility of the national directorate of housing): a question of social infrastructures (water supplies, schools, etc.) within a concept of communal life without concerning production and its transformation.

This view conflicted heavily with the objective conditions in the rural areas characterised by a deep involvement of the peasantry in market relationships and their dependence on it either as suppliers of labour power or as cash crop producers. This contradiction became more obvious, when the balance of payments became a real constraint (in 1979) and, hence, the question of financing accumulation cropped up more strongly in practice. The peasantry as suppliers of cash crops, of food and of labour power to the state sectors occupied a crucial position in production and accumulation.

However, the crucial question then becomes whether the peasantry only performs the role of supplying part of the accumulation fund or whether the peasantry itself is part and parcel of the process of transformation and hence that accumulation embraces as an integral part the transformation of peasant agriculture into more socialised forms of production. In other words, it poses the question whether the strategy is based on a primitive socialist accumulation on the basis of the peasantry (transferring the agrarian surplus to the development of the state sector), or whether accumulation includes the transformation of peasant agriculture. Clearly, the way this question is posed in practice will influence heavily the nature of the organisation of the exchange between the state sector and the peasantry.

The proposition that the state sector can develop under its own steam (with or without the aid of external borrowing) cannot bypass this crucial question since, on the one hand, a considerable part of foreign exchange earnings and of the food supply to the towns depended on peasant production and, on the other, the very conditions of productivity and profitability in the agrarian state sector depended heavily on the organic link that existed between labour supply and family agriculture.

The monetary disequilibrium originating from the state sector has a severe impact on the organisation of the exchange between the state sector and the peasantry. First, the imbalance between the demand for and the supply of consumer commodities affected rural areas differently from urban areas. The reason was that in urban areas the rationing system guaranteed to each family a minimum quantity of basic consumer necessities at official prices. In the rural areas the principal form of rationing remained the queue! Hence, forced savings were distributed differently over urban and rural areas. Furthermore, the concentration of resources on the state sector also implied that the peasants' demand for producer goods (that is, implements, fertilisers, etc.) was largely left unsatisfied, a fact which eroded the peasants' productive basis.

The exchange with the peasantry became conditioned by the following three interlocking phenomena:

(1) the reduction in relative and in absolute terms of official marketing of crops as result of the rapid expansion of parallel markets;
(2) the galloping inflation of prices in the parallel markets; and
(3) the consequent rapid depreciation of the currency and the increased reluctance to accept the metical in exchange for sale of goods.

Although the surface appearances of these phenomena were generally recognised, the explanation of the underlying mechanisms was by no means clear.

The dominant explanation of the problem came from the ministry of internal commerce which was in its day-to-day operation more directly confronted with the problem. According to this view the nature of the problem was the withdrawal from the market by the peasantry since money no longer bought goods. Hence, the payment of rural wages and the buying of cash crops channelled a volume of money into the economy far in excess of available producer and consumer goods directed to the peasantry. Cash balances therefore accumulated over time and the stimulus to further production was blunted. The fact that the supply of commodities destined to be traded with the peasantry was, in terms of value, far in excess of the official marketing of crops was the often quoted proof that peasants simply ran down cash balances to buy goods and did not produce more for exchange. This view often overlooked the impact of the demand springing from the wage bill and, hence, directly equated the difference between the supply of goods to the peasantry and the goods obtained in return with the running down of cash balances accumulated by the peasantry.

The problem therefore was seen as one of an excessive volume of money being held in the rural areas: peasants had too much money relative to the available supply of goods. Therefore, they withdrew from the market and preferred to buy up any supplies forthcoming with the money in hand rather than through production. Implicit in this view was a conception of a single circuit of exchange between the state sector and the peasantry in which the state buys with money either cash crops or labour power, and subsequently the peasantry buys consumer and producer commodities from the state sector (with or without the intermediation of private trade). If both parts do not balance in value, idle balances of money will build up in the hands of the peasantry and over time blunt the incentive of production. The preoccupation was thus with the stock of money in the hands of the peasantry (as a measure of frustrated demand) and little attention was paid to its velocity since it was implicitly assumed that these balances remained idle (stuck in the peasants' pockets).

Therefore, concerning economic policy, a solution was sought in the direction of neutralising the interference of accumulated balances by linking sale and purchase together. Hence, commodities would be sold to the peasantry only in exchange for the purchase of cash crops. Similarly, state farms would guarantee a certain part of the wage in kind to assure the flow of labour.

*De facto*, this implied that the state imposed limitations on its acceptance of its own currency which it issued abundantly to finance the deficit of the state budget and of state enterprises. Implicit in this is the idea that by freezing the accumulated stock of money balances the state sector could maintain the circulation of commodity flows (within a continued context of excessive issue of currency).

However, the key problem with this conception was that it did not take account of the very dynamic of the parallel markets and the accompanying process of the accumulation of commercial speculative capital. Speculation within this view was seen mainly as the activity of small producers and consumers to bypass the official channels in search of a higher price as far as the producers are concerned and in search for access to commodities as far as consumers were concerned. Money, however, did not remain idle in the hands of the peasantry but rather ended up as money capital in the hands of speculative traders. Speculative trade established alternative circuits of trade with the peasantry and between town and countryside and fed itself on diverting supplies originating from the state sector. Private trade was not merely an intermediary in the exchange between the peasantry and the state sector, but asserted itself as an independent actor propelled by its own capitalist (speculative) accumulation drive. Feeding on the imbalance between supply and demand private commerce accumulated rapidly through the galloping inflation on the parallel markets. The government controlled the issue of money (and attempted to accumulate on the basis of it), but the private traders through their action on the parallel markets effectively dominated the circulation of money and activated the money balances held by the peasantry, functionaries and workers by transforming them into money capital. As a result, real wages and the real terms of trade (*vis-à-vis*) the peasantry deteriorated rapidly, but its impact was much more devastating in the rural areas since in the towns the rationing systems assured access to commodities at official prices with regard to some basic minimum quantities.

The impact on the peasantry was by no means uniform but on the contrary tended to sharpen the differentiation within the peasantry. The key to understanding the way in which the goods famine and the development of the parallel markets acted upon the peasantry and intensified its differentiation lies in how access to resources (especially means of production, but also consumer goods) is differentiated within this context.

In this respect it would be wrong to picture the situation merely as one in which there is an official market and a parallel market, the latter being *de facto* effective. Rather, not all rural producers and consumers confront the same conditions of exchange and, hence, equal levels of money income do not imply equal real incomes. This applies both within a given regional context as well as between regions. A general calculation of a terms of trade index would only provide us with an average trend but would give us little information regarding processes of differentiation. The point can best be illustrated by means of some examples.

In southern Mozambique, access to material resources was very much linked with access to outside wage labour. The latter gave access to hard currency (the rand) and to the commodities markets of South Africa and Swaziland.

Initially, mine workers would be rather reluctant to invest their wages in means of production (in agriculture and in transport) within the Mozambican rural economy. Up to 1980/81, government policies were not favourable to such investments. However, thereafter, miners were specifically encouraged to plough back their wages into production and commerce. Rural unemployment was widespread and, hence, the conditions for private accumulation were favourable on this count. Generally, miners would invest in transport and commerce, but some did invest in agriculture. Indeed, in the latter years, peasants with resources were allowed to operate on unutilised ex-settler farms.

In other cases, the more permanent and better paid state farm workers could use their specific position to strengthen their own farm, often supplemented by hired labour. As mechanics or tractor drivers, etc. they had access to certain resources such as seeds, fertiliser, fuel and consumer goods which they could buy either from the state farm or, not unfrequently, merely take from stocks on the state farms.

Border areas were another such case of differentiated access to resources by means of barter trade cross the border. Due to the political criticality of such areas within a general condition of war, the government distribution policy would grant a certain priority to supplying these areas with commodities which would then provide a basis for further barter trade with the neighbouring country. Further, areas located more closely to the main food markets (either towns or plantations) would be subject to a much more dispersed and intensive barter and money trade, thereby raising the producer prices which would benefit those peasants who had sufficient resources to produce surpluses. More distant food producing areas were much more within the grip of the commercial traders who provided the link with the market.

Hence, while some strata within the peasantry managed to create some room for themselves by producing for the parallel markets, the majority of rural producers (either as wage labourers or small-scale producers) confronted declining real incomes as a result of the inflation on the parallel markets to which they had to turn not only for industrial commodities but also to supplement their food needs. Hence, their problem was not one of having too much money at hand with too few commodities to buy; rather, they experienced an acute shortage of both money and goods.

The poorer peasantry were the main suppliers of seasonal labour to the state sector. However, although rural unemployment was high, the supply of labour was by no means elastic. The reasons for this were the following. First, the pattern of labour demand of the state farms and plantations was in most cases highly seasonal and, hence, did not provide an all-round income for the worker. Second, money wages earned on the state farm did not guarantee any access to commodities, and often did so only at speculative prices. For both reasons, the real basis of security of the rural worker still remained his family farm, however fragile that may have been. The state sector may have become dominant in terms of area and in terms of production (regarding monetary output), but it certainly was not the dominant aspect in securing the livelihood of rural producers.

In most cases, the pattern of peak demand for labour on the state farms coincided with the peak demand for labour in family agriculture. For example, in the Limpopo valley harvest labour was needed for rice production at the agro-industrial complexes at the same time that the peasants needed to harvest their own plots. The colonial settlers had relied on force and on the use of task work to cope with this. Hence, the peasants would start very early in the morning to harvest a designated area at the settler farms and subsequently move on to their family plots. The wage would supplement the income and subsistence acquired from the family plot. However, when the state farms tried to introduce an eight-hour working day (instead of task work), they experienced an immense withdrawal of labour when it was most needed. The wage did not cover the consumption needs of a family throughout the year and, increasingly, money did not guarantee access to goods or did so only at the cost of accepting catastrophic reduction in the real wage. Similar shortage problems of labour were experienced in the plantation sectors, in food production in state complexes of Angonia or Zambezia, on cotton farms in the north, etc.

The co-operative movement, which was never very strong since it had never received the effective material backing of the state, was further weakened by the fact that the development of parallel markets within the rural economy enfeebled the poorer peasantry even further. The latter would have to be the social force to be mobilised behind the co-operative movement; rather, it became economically weakened as a result of its rapidly deteriorating real incomes and the fact that the existing co-operative movement provided no real alternative. The government policy to link up purchase with sale so as to stimulate rural production did nothing to counteract this process of differentiation but, rather, tended to intensify it.

Indeed, rural trade between the state and the peasantry was intermediated by private trade. The policy gave them an increased leverage over the peasantry and allowed them to channel more crops into the parallel markets since they effectively traded at terms of exchange which were less favourable than those laid down officially. Furthermore, the impact was that the supply of commodities became concentrated in the hands of the richer peasantry (who had surpluses to sell) and this gave them leverage over the poorer peasantry.

Finally, this process did not take place within conditions of peace but, rather, within an ever-spreading war situation. The South African-backed MNR was gradually spreading throughout the whole country and its acts of brutal oppression of the population and of sabotage and destruction of the whole network of social and economic infrastructure led to the increased destabilisation of the economy and society. To combat this force, a strong alliance between the army and the peasantry was necessary. But this alliance itself became weakened by the worsening of the economic situation of the peasantry.

Economic investment was concentrated in bis projects within the state sector and these became the target of MNR attacks. On the other hand, the destabilising effect of the concentration of resources on the state sector and of off-loading the burden of the costs on to the peasantry through the inflationary issue of money, unbacked by material resources, weakened the peasantry economically and intensified processes of differentiation.

At the time of the preparation for the Fourth Congress it was not surprising therefore that a critique of the pursued policies was building up at different levels. Economic policy was challenged from within the army, at village meetings and in the towns. The congress itself formulated various elements of a strong critique against the practice of planning for resource allocation within the prior period. The critique itself still remained an addition of part-critiques: the need to support family agriculture; the need to consolidate the state sector before its further expansion; the question of the place of private enterprise within the economy; etc. No clear-cut strategic line and tactical measures were laid down within the congress: rather, many issues remained somewhat vague and therefore set the stage for a further struggle as to the content of economic policy thereafter.

## V. A CONCLUDING NOTE

The arguments presented in this article should not be interpreted as an argument against the state sector and for freeing the market *vis-à-vis* the peasantry. Rather, the point is that the state sector should organise itself so as to constitute a powerful instrument to create favourable conditions for the socialisation of agricultural production by the peasantry. This requires

(1) that the state sector shows itself capable in practice of organising the exchange with the peasantry and this in terms acceptable to the peasantry. Hence, the immediate importance within the process of transition of developing the capacity to organise production so as to raise productivity and to assure the financial viability of state enterprises. This is not merely a question of management since the underlying conditions of productivity and profitability change within a period of transition. Thus, colonial tea or sugar production was profitable because of its reliance on internal migrant labour from the peasantry and the consequent low wages it entailed. Within a transitional period the task consists of transforming the organisation of the labour processes themselves and this implies the reorganisation of the structure of labour markets and of the link between wage labour and family agriculture.

(2) Since this exchange involves commodity production it must necessarily take place within the context of a monetary economy and, hence, monetary stability within this exchange is crucial.

(3) Finally, the task of planning does not consist merely of planning the state sector by itself, but also of planning the intervention of the state sector within the market exchange with the peasantry. As a major economic producer the state has enormous leverage on the markets (compounded by its function as an overall regulator of the economy) and can use this economic power to influence the direction of change within the organisation of production in the rural economy. It is altogether a different matter if resources destined for the rural economy are channelled towards the development of richer peasants or whether they are channelled into the development of peasant associations and co-operatives. A free market is never free for all and the direction of change which is propelled by the market depends on the way in which

access to resources is organised within that market. To transform the peasant economy towards increased socialisation in production requires a state sector capable of organising an exchange with the peasantry which favours such a process of transformation.

NOTES

1. This article was written on the basis of my experience as researcher at the Center of African Studies of the Eduardo Mondlane University in Maputo, where I participated in teaching and collective research projects in the period 1976 to 1983. The reader will notice therefore that most of the reference sources in this article consists of inside material. Unfortunately, most of the basic references refer to texts written in Portuguese and, hence, are not readily accessible to most readers.
2. The literature which underlies this section can be found in First [*1982*], Wield [*1983*] and Wuyts [*1978/1980b*]. More specific case studies on aspects of the colonial economy can be found in various articles of the Estudos Mocambicanos such as Adam *et al.* [*1981a*], Davies [*1981*], de Brito [*1980*], Head [*1980*], Penvenne [*1981*], and Serra [*1980*].
    Two basic references can be given regarding Frelimo's own analysis of the structure of the colonial economy and society, namely Mondlane [*1969*] and FRELIMO [*1977a*]. Statistical analyses of the structure of the colonial economy are the following: Centro de Estudos Africanos [*1981b*], Da Costa *et al.* [*1973*], Direcção de Servicos de Planeamento Económico [*1976*], FAO [*1982*], Pereira de Moura and Amaral [*1978*], and Wuyts [*1978*]. Finally, for the reader interested in a survey of the available literature on colonial and early post-colonial Mozambique, the best references are Darch [*1980, 1981a/b*].
3. The best reference on this period can be found in Wield [*1983*]. The aspect of the dependence on South Africa and of its impact on the domestic economy is dealt with in First [*1982*] and in Centro de Estudos Africanos [*1978*]. Frelimo's analysis of the period up to the Third Congress can be found in FRELIMO [*1977a/b*]. Regarding the statistical analysis of the evolution of production and of the balance of payments, the reader may be referred to Wuyts [*1980a/ 1984a/b*] and for the immediate post-independence period Pereira de Moura and Amaral [*1978*].
4. A good reference book which deals with the major development of the period 1977–83 is Hanlon [*1984*]. Further, regarding more specifically the issue of economic development, the reader should consult Wuyts [*1980a, 1984a, 1984b*]. Further data on the economy and on agricultural development can be found in FAO [*1982*]. Two basic references which provide us with the party's analysis of the developments during the period concerned are to be found in FRELIMO [*1983a/b*].
5. The key reference to this section is to be found in O'Laughlin [*1982*], which provides a sharp analysis of the agrarian question in Mozambique. For further references there are the successive research reports on issues of rural development produced within the Centre of African Studies; see, for example, Centro de Estudos Africanos [*1979, 1980a/b/c, 1981a/c, 1982a/b, 1983*], which provide a series of case studies on the transformation of family agriculture and co-operative development, on state farm and plantation production, and on the context of the development of communal villages. An interesting account of the agrarian question in Mozambique which draws on this literature as well as other sources is provided in Hanlon [*1984*]. The question of the development of the co-operative movement is analysed in more depth in Dolny [*1983*]. With respect to the analysis of the system of planning and its impact on resource allocation, the basic theoretical references are Griffith-Jones [*1981*], Kornai [*1971, 1979*], and Lavigne [*1978*]. The arguments were developed more specifically within the Mozambican context in Wuyts [*1983b, 1984a*]. Two important readings on the Party's analysis of planning are the following presidential speeches: Machel [*1979, 1980*].
6. The key references to this article are Mackintosh [*1983*] and Wuyts [*1983a*]. Specific examples used in this section were taken from case studies carried out by the center of African studies (see the references listed in note 5). The analysis made by the party of the problems of planning in the 1977 to 1983 period can be found in FRELIMO [*1983a/b*].

REFERENCES

Adam, I., Davies, R. and J. Head, 1981a, 'Mão de Obra Moçambicana na Rodésia do Sul', in Centro de Estudos Africanos, *Estudos Moçambicanos*, No. 2, pp. 59–72.
Adam, I., Davies, R. and S. Dlamini, 1981b, 'A Luta pelo Futuro da Africa Austral: as Estratégias das CONSAS e SADCC', in Centro de Estudos Africanos, *Estudos Moçambicanos*, No. 3, pp. 65–80.
Centro de Estudos Africanos, 1978, *Relatório sobre o Desemprego em Maputo*, Maputo.
Centro de Estudos Africanos, 1979, *Problemas de Transformação Rural na Província de Gaza: Um Estudo sobre a Articulação entre Aldeias Communais selecionadas, cooperativas agricolas e a Unidade de Produção do Baixo Limpopo*, Maputo.
Centro de Estudos Africanos, 1980a, *A Transformação da Agricultura Familiar na Provincia da Nampula*, Maputo.
Centro de Estudos Africanos, 1980b, *O Sector Estatal de Algodão – Força de Trabalho e Produtividade: um Estudo da U.P. II Metochéria*, Maputo.
Centro de Estudos Africanos, 1980c, *Macassane, Estudo de uma Cooperative Agrária no Distrito de Matutuine, Provincia de Maputo*, Maputo.
Centro de Estudos Africanos, 1981a, *Cotton Production in Mozambique: A Survey: 1936–1979*, Maputo.
Centro de Estudos Africanos, 1981b, *Métados Empíricos*, Syllabus 3, Maputo.
Centro de Estudos Africanos, 1981c, *A Trabalhador Sasonal na Transformação duma Economia de Platações*, Maputo.
Centro de Estudos Africanos, 1982a, *Agricultural Marketing in the District of Alto Molócue, Zambezia Province*, Maputo.
Centro de Estudos Africanos, 1982b, *O Papel Dinamizador da Emochá na Transformação Socialista de Alta Zambezia*, Maputo.
Centro de Estudos Africanos, 1983, *Famílias Camponesas da Angonia no Processo de Socialização do Campo*, Maputo.
Commissão Nacional do Plano, 1979, *Informação Estatistica*, Maputo.
Commissão Nacional do Plano, 1980, *Informação Estatística*, Maputo.
Commissão Nacional do Plano, 1984, *Economic Report*, Maputo.
Da Costa, P. *et al.*, 1973, *Moçambique na Actualidade*, Lourenço Marques.
Darch, C., 1980, 'Escritos e Investigacão sobre Moçambique', in Centro de Estudos Africanos, *Estudos Moçambicanos*, No. 1, pp. 111–20.
Darch, C., 1981a, 'Trabalho Migratório na Africa Austral: um Apontamento Crítico sobre a Literatura existente', in Centro de Estudos Africanos, *Estudos Moçambicanos*, No. 3, pp. 81–96.
Darch, C., 1981b, 'As Publicacões da FRELIMO: Um Estudo Preliminar', in Centro de Estudos Africanos, *Estudos Moçambicanos*, No. 2, pp. 105–20.
Davies, R., 1981, 'O Comité Luso-Rodesiano para Assuntos Económicos e Comerciais: 1965–1970', in Centro de Estudos Africanos, *Estudos Moçambicanos*, No. 2, pp. 73–8.
de Brito, L., 1980, 'Dependência Colonial e Integração Regional', in Centro de Estudos Africanos, *Estudos Moçambicanos*, No. 1, pp. 23–72.
Direccão dos Servicos de Planeamento Económico, 1976, *Moçambique – Dependência Económica*, Centro de Documentacão Tecnico Económica, Lourenco Marques.
Dolny, H., 1983, *Agricultural Producer Cooperatives*, Centro de Estudos Africanos, Maputo.
FAO, 1982, *The Agricultural Economy of Mozambique*, Maputo.
First, R., 1982, *Black Gold*, Brighton: Harvester Press.
FRELIMO, 1977a, *O Partido e as Classes Trabalhadores Moçambicanas na Edificação da Democracia Popular*, Third Congress Documents, Maputo.
FRELIMO, 1977b, *Directivas Económicas e Sociais*, Third Congress Documents, Maputo.
FRELIMO, 1983a, *Out of Underdevelopment to Socialism*, Fourth Congress Documents, Maputo.
FRELIMO, 1983b, *Directivas Economicas e Sociais*, Fourth Congress Documents, Moputo.
Griffith-Jones, S., 1981, *The Role of Finance in the Transition to Socialism*, London: Frances Pinter.
Habermeier, K., 1981, 'Algodão: Das Concentrações a Produção Colectiva', in Centro de Estudos Africanos, *Estudos Moçambicanos*, No. 2, pp. 37–58.

Hanlon, J., 1984, *Mozambique, The Revolution under Fire*, London: Zed Press.

Head, J., 1980, 'A Sena Sugar Estates e a Mão de Obra Migratório', in Centro de Estudos Africanos, *Estudos Moçambicanos*, No. 1, pp. 53–72.

Kornai, J., 1971, *Anti-Equilibrium*, Amsterdam: North Holland.

Kornai, J., 1979, 'Resource-constrained versus Demand-constrained Systems', in *Econometrica*, Vol. 47, No. 4, pp. 801–19.

Lavigne, M., 1978, 'The Creation of Money by the State Bank of the USSR', in *Economy and Society*, Vol. 7, No. 1.

Machel, S. M., 1979, *Façamos de 1980–90 a Década da Vitoria sobre o Subdesenvolvimento*, FRELIMO, Palavras de Ordem, Maputo.

Machel, S. M., 1980, *Desalojaremos o Inimigo Interno do nosso Aparelho do Estado*, FRELIMO, Palavres de Ordem, Maputo.

Mackintosh, M., 1983, 'Economic Tactics: Commercial Policy and the Socialization of African Agriculture', in *World Development*, Vol. 13, No. 1, pp. 77–96.

Mondlane, E., 1969, *The Struggle for Mozambique*, Harmondsworth: Penguin.

O'Laughlin, B., 1982, 'A Questão Agrária em Moçambique', in Centro de Estudos Africanos, *Estudos Moçambicanos*, No. 3, pp. 9–32.

Penvenne, J., 1981, 'Chibalo e Classe Operária: Lourenço Marques 1870–1962', in Centro de Estudos Africanos, *Estudos Moçambicanos*, No. 2, pp. 9–26.

Pereira de Moura, F. P. and F. Amaral, 1978, *Estimativa do Produto Interno de Moçambique: 1970–1973–1975*, Universidade de Eduardo Mondlane, Curso de Economia.

Serra, C., 1980, 'O Capitalismo Colonial na Zambézia', in Centro de Estudos Africanos, *Estudos Moçambicanos*, No. 1, pp. 33–52.

Wield, D., 1983, 'Mozambique – Late Colonialism and early Problems of Transition', in G. White *et al.*, *Revolutionary Socialist Development in the Third World'*, Brighton: Wheatsheaf, 1983.

Wuyts, M., 1978, *Peasants and Rural Economy in Mozambique*, Centro de Estudos Africanos, Maputo.

Wuyts, M., 1980a, *Statistical Note on Post-Independence Economic Development in Mozambique*, Centro de Estudos Africanos, Maputo.

Wuyts, M., 1980b, 'Economia Política do Colonialismo Português em Moçambique', in Centro de Estudos Africanos, *Estudos Moçambicanos*, No. 1, pp. 99–122.

Wuyts, M., 1981a, 'The Question of Mechanisation in Present Day Mozambican Agriculture', *Development and Change*, Vol. 12, No. 1, pp. 1–28.

Wuyts, M., 1981b, 'Sul de Save: Establização e Transformação de Força de Trabalho', in Centro de Estudos Africanos, *Estudos Moçambicanos*, No. 3, pp. 33–44.

Wuyts, M., 1983a, *Dinheiro a Economia Rural*, Centro de Estudos Africanos, Maputo.

Wuyts, M., 1983b, *A Organizacão das Financas e o Desenvolvimento Económico em Moçambique*, Centro de Estudos Africanos, Maputo.

Wuyts, M., 1984a, 'Money and the Balance of Payments in Mozambique', Working Paper – Subseries on Money, Finance and Development, No. 11, Institute of Social Studies, The Hague.

Wuyts, M., 1984b, 'A Statistical Note on Trends of Economic Development in Mozambique', mimeo, Institute of Social Studies, The Hague.

# Agrarian Reform as a Model of Accumulation: The Case of Nicaragua since 1979

*by E. V. K. FitzGerald\**

*Despite the fact that the historical experience of the construction of socialism has taken place in predominantly agrarian societies, it is notorious that the 'agrarian question' remains unresolved and constrains their progress to a greater or lesser degree. This is all the more crucial for those revolutions of the second half of the twentieth century which, generated in the Third World by the 'liberation struggle', not only seek an increased food supply as the basis for raising popular living standards, but also greater exports from the primary sector to secure imports of producer goods. Thus the agrarian question becomes central to the accumulation model, not only as a source of investible surplus but also as part of the articulation between the different forms of production which underlie the inherited social structure. An account of the Nicaraguan experience of agrarian reform in its first five years (1980–84) should have some intrinsic interest; it also serves to illustrate this central problem of the economics of the transition to socialism.*

## I. INTRODUCTION

The revolutionary transformation of economy and society in Nicaragua, since the overthrow of the Somoza dynasty in 1979 by the Frente Sandinista de Liberacion Nacional,[1] has necessarily involved a profound Agrarian Reform. Agriculture provides three-quarters of exports; over two-thirds of industry is engaged in processing the products of, or providing inputs to, agriculture; and well over half the population is rural. The future development of productive forces and the emergence of socialist social relations are clearly linked to the transformation of agriculture; at least for the rest of the century.

It is not the object of this article to give a full account of Nicaraguan economic development, but rather to characterise the main elements of agrarian transformation in order to make a preliminary assessment of the Nicaraguan experience. This we shall do from the point of view of agrarian reform as a model of accumulation, so as to look beyond the short-term redistributive consequences, towards the implications for future development, particularly the articulation of different forms of production, the relation to the international division of labour and the expansion of productive capacity.

\* Professor of Development Economics, Institute of Social Studies, The Hague. The author would like to thank colleagues, particularly at the CIERA, for stimulating discussions on this topic. The views expressed here should not be taken to reflect those of the Nicaraguan government, which the author has served as economic adviser.

Despite the fact that the historical experience of the construction of socialism has taken place in predominantly agrarian societies, it is notorious that the 'agrarian question' remains unresolved and constrains their progress to a greater or lesser degree [*White and White, 1982*]. This is all the more crucial for those revolutions of the second half of the twentieth century which, generated in the Third World by the 'liberation struggle', not only seek an increased food supply as the basis for raising popular living standards, but also greater exports from the primary sector (albeit in processed form) to secure imports of producer goods.[2] Thus the agrarian question becomes central to the accumulation model, not only as a source of investible surplus but also as part of the articulation between the different forms of production which underlie the inherited social structure.

An account of the Nicaraguan experience of agrarian reform in its first five years (1980–84) should have some intrinsic interest. It also serves to illustrate this central problem of the economics of the transition to socialism.

## II. THE INHERITED MODEL

By 1979, Nicaragua was neither a 'feudal' nor a 'plantation' economy, although it retained traces of both from its historical origins.[3] The Somoza dynasty had, during the previous 40 years, transformed a coffee, banana and mining economy by the introduction of cotton, sugar, cattle and fishing as new export activities, and built up a manufacturing base of simple wagegoods. The process had largely relegated food production to the peasantry forced off the fertile Pacific plains towards the land-surplus agricultural frontiers in the mountains. However, sufficient foreign exchange was generated to satisfy the agrarian bourgeoisie and provoke a steady process of urbanisation, although little was invested in infrastructure or the industrialisation of agriculture itself. What is more, the reliance on these export products led to a deepening economic dependence on the USA, Western Europe and Japan for markets and as sources of producer goods. The model, therefore, led to growth rather than development, and in the 1970s most of the agrarian surplus was being consumed unproductively or transferred abroad rather than being devoted to mechanisation, irrigation or herd improvement, let alone technical assistance or social services.

Essentially, the model had been a dualistic one where the capitalist export sector generated the realised surplus and concentrated investment, serving also as the 'Department I' of the economy through exports to finance imported producer goods. The peasant sector not only acted as 'Department II' by producing food, but also supplied the seasonal labour force required on the export estates on a migratory basis. This peasant sector was thus doubly exploited: both as a source of cheap labour and as a supplier of cheap food. Reproduction of the labour force was thus achieved at a minimum cost and released a maximum of surplus as work intensity on the estates was kept high by various forms of coercion. Moreover, much of the surplus was strictly speaking differential rent generated at an international level by the fertility of Nicaraguan soils and its favourable geographic location.

The Somoza group (that is, the family plus business associates, political allies and the military) had not only large landholdings, but also direct control over strategic elements of the 'circuit of agrarian capital' such as agroindustry, processing facilities, foreign trade, manufacturing and all the banks. The monopolistic control not only excluded direct participation by foreign firms but also reduced the rest of the bourgeoisie to a subordinate position. Above all, the monopoly in banking (which provided virtually all the working capital for export agriculture in the form of annual loans backed by pre-export credits from foreign banks, preserving classical monetary stability) [*FitzGerald, 1985c*] gave the Somoza group indirect control over commercial farmers, directing their production decisions and siphoning off much of the investible surplus. In a country with a high cultivable land to population ratio (two hectares per head) and a social structure which guaranteed labour availability, the scarce resource was credit, especially in export agriculture which requires considerable working capital for inputs and the harvest wagefund. Agroexports in 1976 used 47 per cent of the cultivated area but received 75 per cent of the credit; most of the rest went to the two modernised foodgrains, rice and sorghum [*IFAD, 1981*].

As we shall see, this inherited model has had a profound effect upon the particular form of 'mixed economy' in agriculture that has been adopted in this transitional stage. The resulting land tenure pattern is indicated in Table 1. In 1978, the large (over 500 mz) units included 36 per cent of the farmed area, of which about one-half was the property of the Somoza group. This was concentrated predominantly in agroexport production of sugar, cotton, coffee and cattle. The medium and small farmers (50–500 mz) included some 46 per cent of the land, using a lower technology and with a balance of food and export crops. The peasantry proper had only 18 per cent of the land, predominantly in foodcrops, much of this of a subsistence nature. The data

TABLE 1

LAND TENURE IN NICARAGUA
(thousands of manzanas)*

|  | 1978 | | 1984 | |
|  | Area | % | Area | % |
|---|---|---|---|---|
| Individual farmers | 8073 | 100 | 5232 | 64 |
| › 500 mz | 2920 | 36 | 1026 | 13 |
| 200–500 mz | 1311 | 16 | 1021 | 13 |
| 50–200 mz | 2431 | 30 | 2391 | 30 |
| 10–50 mz | 1241 | 16 | 561 | 7 |
| ‹ 10 mz | 170 | 2 | 127 | 1 |
| Co-operatives |  |  | 1431 | 17 |
| Credit-Services (CCS) | - | - | 804 | 10 |
| Production (CAS) | - | - | 627 | 7 |
| Agrarian Reform Enterprises (APP) | - | - | 1517 | 19 |
| TOTAL | 8073 | 100 | 8073 | 100 |

*Source*: MIDINRA [*1985*].
* one manzana (mz) = 0.7 ha.

on relative productivity are not clear, but post-1979 results would indicate that the large farmers were responsible for at least half agricultural and livestock production and as much as three-quarters of exports [*IFAD, 1981*]. The middle farmers were probably supplying about half of the marketed food supply. The only exceptions to this division of labour were capitalist production of rice and sorgum on the one hand, and peasant coffee production on the other.

The labour requirements of the export sector were (and still are) highly cyclical. Agroexports consume the greatest volume of wage labour in Nicaragua: about three times the equivalent of factory employment on yearly average, and double that figure in the peak harvest months of November to January when coffee, cotton and sugarcane overlap.

The structure of the rural labour-force, and thus that of agrarian classes, was the direct product of this model of accumulation, a structure which is still essentially maintained today, for although ownership patterns have been radically altered since 1979, the production system itself has yet to be transformed. As Table 2 indicates, some five per cent of the rural population are proprieters and their families, in the sense of employing year-round wage labour and a minimum commercial holding that permits accumulation. These are basically 'middle farmers' for the rural bourgeoisie as such was no more than one per cent of the total. The classical division between 'rural proletarians' and 'peasants' is not a very meaningful one in Nicaragua because as 'pure' classes they are not dominant. The permanent labour force is roughly 20 per cent of the total, while independent peasants and their family labour are another 25 per cent. The remaining 50 per cent (the division between the two activities in Table 2 is in proportion to their labour time) are semi-proletarians, seasonal workers at harvest time and sub-subsistence peasants the rest of the year. Whether these are essentially peasants who sell their labour power at harvest to achieve subsistence or essentially rural proletarians who survive the rest of the year on microfundia is a subject of considerable academic debate and is of practical relevance for the design of the agrarian reform. This debate also had political implications for the revolutionary struggle before 1979, between those who argued for a prolonged peasant war, and those who stressed labour organisation. The balance of opinion is now in favour of the basically proletarian nature of these workers (derived from their origins as well as their behaviour) although as we shall see, since 1979 there has occurred a process by which, as a result of the agrarian reform itself, they are becoming stabilised as either peasants or proletarians [*Baumeister, 1984*].

Within the peasantry, moreover, there has occurred a considerable process of differentiation, as the land tenure structure indicates. 1980 estimates[4] indicated that while some 60 per cent are the impoverished peasantry forced to engage in seasonal wage labour on a migratory basis, another 42 per cent are middle peasants who may both buy and sell labour (usually in reciprocal form) but who are essentially dependent on family labour power. The marketable suplus provided by both these groups is not large. It is the six per cent of rich peasants (of 10–50 mz) who, with the middle farmers, produced the bulk of marketed foodstuffs and thus sustained the labour force in the capitalist sector. The poor peasants helped to keep both wages and food prices down.

TABLE 2

COMPOSITION OF AGRICULTURAL LABOUR FORCE, 1982

(thousands)

| | Commercial Sector | | Peasant Sector | Total |
|---|---|---|---|---|
| | State | Private | | |
| Propietors | | 21.2 | | 21.2 |
| Latinfundists | | .4 | | .4 |
| Agrarian Bourgeoisie | | .7 | | .7 |
| Petty Agrarian Bourgeoisie | | 13.4 | | 13.4 |
| Family Labour | | 6.7 | | 6.7 |
| Peasantry | 22.1 | 44.6 | 192.6 | 259.3 |
| Self-employed | | | 42.9 | 42.9 |
| Family Labour | | | 53.6 | 53.7 |
| Semi-proletarians | 22.1 | 44.6 | 96.1 | 162.7 |
| Agrarian Proletariat | 56.8 | 110.1 | | 166.9 |
| Permanent | 31.1 | 58.5 | | 89.5 |
| Seasonal | 25.8 | 51.6 | | 77.5 |
| Total Economically Active Population | 78.9 | 175.9 | 192.6 | 447.4 |

Source: CIERA [1985].

Notes:   The 'semi-proletariat' are peasants working less than nine months for wages, but have access to land. The 'seasonal proletariat' are those working for wages less than nine months a year, but without access to land.

The classification of the 'propietors' is as follows (in mz):

| | Latinfundist and Agrarian Bourgeoisie | Agrarian Petty Bourgeoisie | Peasant Farmers |
|---|---|---|---|
| Basic Grains | › 500 | 50– 500 | ‹ 50 |
| Coffee | › 65 | 15– 65 | ‹ 15 |
| Cotton | › 200 | 50– 200 | ‹ 50 |
| Grazing | › 1000 | 200–1000 | ‹ 200 |

This class structure, which denied land or adequate wages to the mass of the rural population, was essentially unstable and a root cause of the collapse of the former accumulation model; although the circumstances of its over-throw are naturally more complex [Walker, 1985]. As an accumulation scheme, it displayed a remarkable capacity for expansion but by the 1970s had reached two unsurmountable barriers. First, the labour-intensive growth of export agriculture based on low wages and cheap food from outside the capitalist sphere had reached the limits in terms of suitable unimproved land and available labour. Second, the resulting social structure had become progressively more difficult to control, mainly because it generated a mass of displaced and mobile workers but also because of the resentment of the rest of the agrarian bourgeoisie against the ruling Somoza group.

The identification of peasants and rural labourers with the struggle of Sandino against US Occupation between 1912 and 1933, their role as a social base for the FSLN in its formative years between 1961 and 1972, and their widespread participation in the final insurrection of 1977–79 gave an agrarian political legitimacy not only to the revolutionary leadership but also to the Sandinista rural organizations which subsequently formed the Asociacion de Trabajadores del Campo (rural labourers' union) and the Union Nacional de Agricultores y Ganaderos (small farmers' association).

III. FIVE YEARS OF AGRARIAN REFORM (1979–84)

Agrarian Reform had been a central element of the Sandinista political programme since its foundation [*FSLN, 1982*], not just in the sense of breaking the power of landlords and overestimating peasant poverty but also in that of developing the national economy. Two practical considerations prevented an immediate distribution of land in 1979: first, that division of land, particularly on agroexport estates, would limit the future potential for accumulation, productivity growth and social transformation; second, that the state should not absorb more land in each stage than it could reasonably administer with its limited administrative resources; and third, that it was necessary to maintain a 'production alliance' with non-Somocista agrarian capital in order to sustain production and a certain degree of national political unity against external aggression [*Wheelock, 1983*]. Both these considerations were regarded as lessons from other agrarian reforms, where 'normal' production tends to fall sharply in the early stage as commercial firms are expropriated before the state sector is able to manage them, or else 'potential' production is limited subsequently by a fragmented peasant landholdings which resist collectivisation. The strategic concept for the long run was (and is: see section V below) that of the absorption of capitalist agriculture into state farms (Area de Propiedad del Pueblo) and of small peasant farms into co-operatives. However, the possibility of effective transformation of social relations was considered by the FSLN to be subject to economic development, as well as to the need to restore existing production levels, for only in that way could the economic roots of backwardness, poverty and dependency be overcome.

This approach was feasible due to the nature of the previous agrarian model. The expropriation of the domains of the Somoza group alone would give the state about half of large-scale agriculture, while the nationalisation of the banks would permit control of the rest of commercial farming. The semi-proletarian nature of the peasantry would reduce the immediate demand for land distribution, while the centralisation of credit and inputs could be used to encourage co-operativisation.

In effect, the expropriation decree of 1979 created a state property sector (APP) of 1.6 million manzanas grouped in over 100 multi-unit enterprises. On this basis, a phase of rationalisatin and recapitalisation of this area was started, including the building of a new sugar mill, irrigated grain production, mechanised cotton harvesting, cattle herd improvement, palm oil plantations, coffee renovation and vegetable processing. The control of all the slaughter-houses and grain silos, and about half the capacity of sugar milling, cotton ginning and coffee processing, plus the monopoly of the export trade and a predominant position in the distribution of basic grains gave the state enterprises considerable control over output. On the production side, the APP had control over imports of agricultural inputs and their marketing and a virtual monopoly of new machinery through its machine service enterprises. Thus the APP could form an integrated economic system which, without itself accounting for the bulk of output, could effectively control the rest of the modern sector, at least [*Wheelock, 1983*]. The APP became subject to centralised production and investment planning while initiating a process of worker participation in management through the ATC at farm, regional and national levels.

Between 1979 and 1981 there sprang up spontaneously various collective forms of peasant organisation, predominantly service cooperatives (Cooperativas de Credito y Servicios, CCS) of middle peasants with their own land; and some production co-operatives (Cooperativas Agrarias Campesinas, CAS) of landless peasants on state lands too small to operate centrally as part of the APP [*CIERA, 1982*]. There was some land invasion but this was not a major source of conflict because it took place mainly on the properties of absentee landlords. The first Agrarian Reform Law was decreed in October 1981, two years after the Revolution which defined the new 'social' property forms and declared expropiable large estates not under adequate cultivation. The Law had considerable potential because the concept of 'adequate' could include compliance with territorial production programmes set by the government.

In fact, this second expropriation process made little apparent headway until the end of 1983. ONly 0.4 million manzanas had been entitled to co-operatives, benefiting 17,000 out of approximately 250,000 rural families. However, it would appear that a considerable informal usufruct of latifundia land was already taking place, mainly by peasants previously renting such lands or seasonal workers living nearby. Government economic support was largely confined to the massive extension of rural credit which benefited individual peasants as well as co-operatives. By 1983, the crop area so financed was ten times greater than in 1978 and some 80,000 families were receiving credit for inputs, machine services, improvements and even as a form of wage-fund. Moreover, the extension of social services to the countryside had a considerable impact on living standards: the 1980 literacy campaign reduced national illiteracy rates from over 60 per cent to 12 per cent; infant mortality was reduced from 12 per cent to seven per cent by public health campaigns; housing schemes and organised distribution of basic consumer goods reached peasants for the first time; and labour legislation reduced labour exploitation considerably [*CIERA, 1984*].

The upsurge of US aggression in 1983–84 was based on the organisation of armed incursions by ex-members of Somoza's National Guard who had fled the country in 1979. This affected, above all, the impoverished and mountainous northern border and central regions where about a third of the population, mainly peasants, live. To consolidate the social base of the Revolution, the government undertook a sudden acceleration of the land reform programme and a change in its nature. In 1984 alone, some 1.4 million manzanas were entitled (bringing the total to over 2.0 millions) of which 1.1 millions were essentially in the form of individual holdings. Although much of these lands were already effectively under peasant control, this legislation made it possible to extend services to them and implied that collectivisation would be postponed to the future. By early 1985, nearly 80,000 families had benefited from the land reform, of which about two-thirds were in co-operatives. Some state lands were transferred in this way but for the most part latifundia in the mountain regions were affected.

The exigencies of war in the frontier regions prevented this part of the land reform process from being properly planned or accompanied by investment, organisation and training [*FitzGerald, 1985d*]. Moreover, the military defense strategy adopted involved the relocation of a considerable part of the mountain population in the new settlements (asentamientos) where health, education and communications can permit integrated development around the production co-operatives. Unfortunately, the war has undermined the peasant economy in most of this region, delaying further development until peace returns. None the less, it could be argued that had agrarian reform been implemented in the mountains earlier one, if only on the basis of individual land distribution, then the social base for military defence would have been stronger, and collectivisation could have been achieved later on through differentail access to credit, machinery and so on.

The quantitative changes in land tenure are summarised in Table 1. The impact of the expropriation of the Somoza group properties in favour of the state and subsequen distributions of unused latifundia to co-operatives is reflected in the decline in the proportion of land held by the agrarian bourgeoisie (› 500 mz) from 36 per cent in 1978 to 13 per cent in 1984: it is programmed to fall to 11 per cent in 1985. In contrast, the APP held 19 per cent of the land in 1984, slightly less than in 1982 due to the co-operativisation of the smaller state farms. The co-operative sector had expanded to 17 per cent of land (programmed for 20 per cent in 1985), the CAS mostly on the basis of expropriated latifundia and the CCS mainly on the voluntary grouping of small farmers so that the proportions of individual properties of 50 mz or less also fell, from 18 per cent in 1978 to eight per cent in 1983.

Although large individual holdings have been almost eliminated, the 'middle farmer' group (50–200 mz) has been virtually untouched; it held 46 per cent of land in 1978 and 43 per cent in 1984. In other words, it is the upper and lower strata of the distribution that have been affected to provide a substantial socialised sector of about one-half of agriculture, leaving the agrarian petty bourgeoisie (about a third of the rural population, as we have seen) with the other half.

The balance of crop production by ownership is indicated in Table 3. The APP and co-operatives control nearly half (48 per cent) of arable land and large capitalist farmers only 22 per cent. In export crops, the state controlled 26 per cent of the cropped area in the 1984–85 season, and the large farmers another 40 per cent, for here the modern sector predominates. In foodcrops, the balance is distinct for the co-operatives control 39 per cent and small producers 41 per cent, with traditional production methods dominating. None the less, if we take the APP and the co-operatives together as at least potentially a 'socialised' sector, then together they control 46 per cent of the export crop area and 50 per cent of that for foodcrops. This, of course, reflects the

TABLE 3

AGRICULTURAL PRODUCTION BY PROPERTY FARMS, 1984–85

| | Large Private Producers | Small and Medium Farms | Co-operative | State Farm | Total |
|---|---|---|---|---|---|
| Area (thousand mz) | | | | | |
| Export Crops | 164.6 | 58.8 | 82.4 | 105.1 | 410.9 |
| Internal Consumption Crops | 61.1 | 256.7 | 247.9 | 65.6 | 631.3 |
| Total Area | 225.7 | 313.5 | 330.3 | 170.7 | 1042.2 |
| Shares (%) | | | | | |
| Export Crops | 40.1 | 14.3 | 20.1 | 25.5 | 100 |
| Internal Consumption Crops | 9.7 | 40.6 | 39.3 | 10.4 | 100 |
| Total | 21.6 | 30.3 | 31.7 | 16.4 | 100 |

Source: MIDINRA [1985].

Notes: 'Large private farmers' in this table is more than 500 mz.

historical accumulation model, but it provides the basis for an articulation of the state farms and the co-operatives on the one hand, and sufficient weight to counterbalance the private sector on the other. Unfortunately, the co-operative units tend to be very small with an average of 20 families and about 200 manzanas of unintegrated land so that as a production form they are more peasant than an enterprise.

Although the fundamental agrarian political alliance was to be between the revolutionary state (representing the proletariat) and the organised peasantry, during these first five years of agrarian reform, success in production still depended on the response of the private sector and thus on profitability. A system of guaranteed purchase prices based on a stable mark-up over average production costs was established which de-linked farm-gate prices from both international and consumer prices. The state banks supplied credit and state importers the inputs; machinery services or sales came from state enterprises; rents were legally limited; and the agrarian labour unions ensured social stability.

For large capitalist farmers, this was equivalent to a gradual reduction in their role to that of an 'administrative bourgeoisie' in that their access to foreign exchange and the possibilities for accumulation were severely limited. Moreover, their political power was largely gone, but neither was there much risk involved in production and the land reform protected those who went on producing, which most of them did. Medium farms and rich peasants, outside the war zones, expanded their production rapidly in response to new opportunities; to some extent they came to replace the bourgeoisie as the dominant expression of commercial agriculture – petty capitalism within a planned economy.

This 'mixed planned economy' strategy of articulating different forms of production under state guidance was quite successful in output terms, indeed extremely so, if compared with the experience of other countries in similar situations. As Table 4 indicates, by 1984–85 almost all the main crops had recovered pre-revolutionary levels and in many cases (such as coffee, sugar, rice and agriculture) considerably surpassed them. The three products that failed to recover were cotton, beef and milk, the first because of poor world prices and high costs, the latter two because of the indiscriminate slaughter during the 1978–79 insurrection which would take ten years to replace. However, supply was very badly affected by the war from 1983 onwards, particularly coffee, maize and beans (produced in the war zones) while the foreign exchange shortages also affected the output of import-dependent crops such as sugar and cotton. The general lack of 'business confidence', logical under the circumstances, also had a negative effect. The main achievement, therefore, was to maintain a reasonable level of production at all.

TABLE 4

PRODUCTION OF MAJOR AGRICULTURAL PRODUCTS

|  | 1977/1978 | | 1979/1980 | | 1984/1985 | |
|---|---|---|---|---|---|---|
|  | Area | Production | Area | Production | Area | Production |
| Coffee | 120 | 1251 | 143 | 1228 | 128 | 1253 |
| Cotton | 311 | 2774 | 64 | 407 | 164 | 1792 |
| Sugarcane (M.T.) | 57 | 2485 | 53 | 2149 | 64 | 2948 |
| Maize | 303 | 3942 | 240 | 3168 | 270 | 5069 |
| Beans | 88 | 930 | 76 | 1329 | 123 | 1287 |
| Rice | 35 | 1050 | 51 | 1387 | 64 | 2297 |
|  | 1977 | | 1979 | | 1984 | |
| Beef (million lb.) | 108 | | 119 | | 106 | |
| Milk (million gals.) | 21 | | 12 | | 9 | |
| Eggs (million doz.) | 12 | | 14 | | 17 | |

Sources: CIERA [1984], MIDINRA [1985].

Note:    Area in thousands of manzanas.
         Production in thousands of quintals (cwt.).

IV. ARTICULATING THE MODEL: PROBLEMS OF THE AGRARIAN REFORM IN ITS FIRST STAGES

The Revolution disarticulated the historically specific social relations which underpinned the former accumulation model, particularly the system of peasant exploitation to provide productive and cheap labour and an adequate food supply for the towns, as well as the investible export surplus. This disarticulation has had serious consequences for the economic model in the transition stage: the old production system must be maintained while the new one is constructed which does not require such exploitation – which essentially implies investment as well as ownership reform.

One of the principal problems was the increasing scarcity of harvest labour for the export sector, particularly coffee and cotton. This was partly a consequence of the Central American situation, which cut off traditional seasonal labour supplies from Honduras and then required drafts of a substantial proportion of the young male rural force for the army and militias. To a certain extent, they were replaced by the volunteer labour of students and civil servants from the cities for coffee and the mechanisation of cotton. None the less, the causes of the shortage seemed to be structural too, for traditional semi-proletarian field workers were not arriving at harvests from 1981 onwards, while rural labour productivity had also declined to about half its previous level.

Two explanations were put forward which reflected different interpretations of the dynamics of the agrarian reform. The first hypothesis was that the access of semi-proletarians to land and credit removed the need to seek harvest wage income to survive, in other words, that a process of 'peasantisation' was taking place. Indeed between 1981 and 1983 this analysis was used to justify the slow process of land distribution. The second hypothesis was that the problem lay in the relatively low wages, for in real terms they were much the same as before 1979, even though the social conditions had improved considerably. The removal of coercive labour discipline had caused the low labour productivity and no new system of incentives – either moral or material – had been established. However, by 1983, the second view had become dominant and led to both land distribution and the establishment of strong wage incentives for piece-work in 1984; by 1985 the rural basic wage had been brought up to its urban equivalent. The solution had recognised the fundamentally proletarian nature of the rural workforce.

This was not just a conjunctural problem, for it reflected the disarticulation of the old link between production forms. Although it was not entirely clear how a new articulation was to be achieved, the tendency was towards the stabilisation of the labour force in the two sectors separately, with higher productivity and earnings in both.

However, it also appeared that migration [*CIERA, 1985*] towards the cities had accelerated since 1979, particularly towards the area of the capital, Managua, which by 1984 held nearly one-third of the national population. The war conditions in the north undoubtedly acted as an impulsive factor, but the attraction of the towns was even stronger. The new 'basic needs package' – of health, housing, education, transport etc. – reached the urban slums faster than the countryside. Moreover, conditions of import shortages and inflationary government expenditure [*SPP, 1985*] stimulated the expansion of petty commerce. Here, too, the elimination of the former repressive mechanisms permitted the rural labour force to establish its own economic self-improvement in the towns. The response of the government was to eventually freeze urban infrastructure investment from 1983 onwards, accelerate co-operative development, raise rural wages and severely limit entry to urban commerce. However, a new articulation between town and country, particularly the small rural towns where half the agrarian population lives, had yet to be established.

Despite the considerable increase in production (see Table 4), food supply also became a serious problem from 1982 onwards [*CIERA, 1984*]. This caused the government to establish a limited urban rationing system, regulate public markets, fix basic consumer prices (which came to involve extensive subsidies) and import deficit items. To a considerable extent, this reflected an enormous increase in effective demand as popular incomes in town and country rose, and the poor attained not only purchasing power but also social entitlement to basic wagegoods. This was underwritten by new channels of food distributions: commissaries, neighbourhood committees and rural stores supplied from state warehouses with basic goods at fixed prices. These prices were held between 1981 and 1984, even though farm-gate prices had more or less doubled. This not only stimulated consumer demand further and swelled the inflationary budget deficit, but also led to many export estates ceasing to sow foodcrops for their own workforce. Finally, the population itself was growing all the while, rising by some 25 per cent between 1978 and 1984.

Although food production did recover, and average per capita consumption levels in most basic products were higher than before the Revolution (see Table 5), the levelling out of consumption between social classes left extreme shortages in the towns, especially for the urban middle class, exacerbated by the absence of non-basic consumer goods due to the import restrictions. Consumption per head of food products from the modern farm sector (such as sugar, rice, chicken and eggs) rose particularly rapidly, but cooking oil and milk, for instance, which both required imports, could not.

TABLE 5

CONSUMPTION PER HEAD OF MAJOR FOOD ITEMS

|              | 1977  | 1981  | 1984  |
|--------------|-------|-------|-------|
| Meat (lb.)*  | 26.5  | 32.1  | 29.9  |
| Eggs (doz.)  | 5.3   | 11.7  | 12.8  |
| Rice (lb.)   | 45.2  | 55.1  | 76.1  |
| Beans (lb.)  | 38.6  | 38.1  | 45.1  |
| Maize (lb.)  | 174.4 | 173.9 | 152.1 |
| Oil (lt.)    | 19.4  | 22.9  | 22.9  |
| Sugar (lt.)  | 103.9 | 91.1  | 101.1 |

Sources: SPP [1985]; CIERA [1984].

* Includes beef and chicken.

The most serious problem was the difficulty in securing an adequate supply of the two 'peasant' grains, maize and beans, for the towns. The reasons were varied, including greater on-farm consumption as a result of the land reform and, from 1983 onwards, the effect of the war. None the less, the disarticulation of the peasant economy from the industrial sector was also crucial. The Agrarian Reform demolished the traditional private commercial links that provided tools, clothing, etc. and even credit in exchange for harvests at the farm-gate and transporting them to market, albeit as part of an exploitative relationship. This integrated relationship was not reconstructed in the first five years; the multiplicity of state institutiosn involved became too bureaucratic and inflexible. The shortages of industrial goods (particularly imported items, but also clothing etc., in high demand in the towns) turned the internal terms of trade against the small farmer. Only in 1985, as the deteriorating situation of the mountain peasantry became a defense problem, did this question of 'rural exchange' receive high priority in the Economic Programme of the government [*SPP, 1985*].

Agrarian investment in the 1980–84 period was maintained at a high level, equivalent to about half the national total. This was almost exclusively concentrated on the APP: that is, in about half the modern sector or about a quarter of the whole of agriculture. This investment included extensive irrigation works, imports of tractors and combine harvesters, coffee renovation, a sugar mill, palm oil plantations, intensive dairy and beef breeding units, as well as the recapitalisation of the new state farms ruined by their previous owners. It formed part of a long-term strategy discussed below and thus did not itself add much to production during the first five years, although it did help compensate declines in the large private production sector.

Given the external terms of trade (which had deteriorated by 40 per cent between 1977 and 1983 [*CEPAL, 1984*]) and the gradual recovery of production, the agricultural sector was not in a position to generate a sufficiently large surplus to finance its own investment. Even though the sector generated three times more exports than it absorbed imports [*MIDINRA, 1985*], the foreign exchange thus released was needed to maintain basic consumption elsewhere in the economy. Similarly, food supplies over and above the requirements of the agrarian workforce were needed to maintain the rest of the population; there was no significant capital goods sector to absorb these wagegoods [*FitzGerald, 1982*]. Thus, this investment was basically financed from abroad, initially with long-term development loans from multilateral institutions, but as US agression increased these funds were cut off and replaced by commercial credits from both capitalist and socialist suppliers. This was economically justifiable in that the increment in exports (or substituted imports) would have a compensatory balance of payments effect within a few years. Eventually, however, a net exchange surplus would have to be generated so that agroexports should expand more rapidly than domestic foodstuffs rather than the reverse, as had been the case between 1980 and 1984, when popular living standards had a higher priority than the trade balance.

None the less, the major shortcoming of this accumulation model was undoubtedly its almost exclusive concentration on the APP as the focus of modernisation. Large private farmers might not wish to invest, but the middle farmers and the co-operatives were also neglected in machinery assignment, cattle restocking, and irrigation equipment. The political objective of preventing the re-emergence of capitalist accumulation or the reconstruction of a rural bourgeoisie (albeit on a petty scale) appears to have been the main justification. However, the cost in terms of production was high, and in any case such a sector could have been simply controlled through the existing fiscal, banking and commercial mechanisms, let alone the eventual application of the Agrarian Reform laws.

V. AGRARIAN REFORM AND ECONOMIC DEVELOPMENT IN NICARAGUA

An agrarian reform cannot be properly evaluated after so short a period. However, an analysis of the official strategy for the medium-term development of agriculture [*MIDINRA, 985*] serves to indicate the expected directions the Agrarian Reform will take, and thus permits an evaluation of the degree to which the limitations indicated above could be overcome. This will only reflect, of course, the current intentions of the government; external or internal developments might well force a change of course.

The national development strategy[5] is based upon the capitalisation and modernisation of the primary sectors (agriculture, livestock, fishing, mining, forestry and energy) as the basis of accumulable export earnings and basic consumption goods. Industry would be subordinate to agriculture, processing its products for export or wagegoods while building up a capacity to supply inputs and even simple equipment. Popular living standards would rise with the greater supply of wagegoods, universal primary education and basic health care, better housing and collective transport. The development of rural towns at the expense of the capital would halt internal migration while the urban informal sector would be gradually absorbed into production co-operatives. In essence, this is a continuation of the strategy already applied in the first five years.

The agrarian development strategy is thus obviously central to the new national accumulation model. The MEDA (Marco Economico de Desarrollo Agropecuario) has two main objectives. The first is the food security programme [*UNRISD, 1982; CIERA, 1984*], based on the provision of a minimum recommended diet for the whole population by 2,000 which requires that food output be doubled in the 1980s and raised by a further 50 per cent in the 1990s. This will require very rapid expansion (virtually tripling between 1985 and 2000) in meat and milk products, although basic grains self-sufficiency is much nearer to achievement. Vegetable oil (based on african palm and sesame rather than the traditional cottonseed) will also have to triple. Food security in this sense is understood as not only meeting these consumption targets, but also maintaining adequate reserves so a small export surplus in products such as rice may well develop as well.

The second objective is to generate sufficient foreign exchange to maintain the long-term import levels implied by such basic consumption targets and undertake debt service. This would not be just a question of greater volumes, but also the diversification of markets (especially socialist countries offering preferential prices), the introduction of new export products (such as tobacco, cacao, rubber and processed fruits), then further industrialisation of traditional products such as cotton (yarn, textiles), and specialisation in products with the highest net yield of 'dollars per hectare'. This would imply a doubling of the value of agroexport production in the 1980s and a further doubling in the 1990s.

The expansion of production required to meet this ambitious (however logical) targets would have to come from irrigation and mechanisation on the Pacific plain. At present, less than 100,000 manzanas are under irrigation, out of the 160,000 that could be supplied from subterranean sources, while

Lake Nicaragua alone could irrigate another 170,000 around its shores. It is planned to raise the irrigated area to 175,000 manzanas by 1990 and 250,000 by 2000. Most of this would be in the APP or CAS. The raising of the technological level of each production process would require machinery, inputs (fertilisation, pesticides) and more skilled manpower on a not much greater land area. The investment required for this rate of accumulation would be equivalent to about $150 millions a year, about 20 per cent of value added in agriculture and roughly proportional to the overall national rate of investment between 1980 and 1984; over half of this would be in the form of imported equipment financed from abroad.

The main constraint (assuming that the external resources are forthcoming, which is feasible if US aggression ceases) foreseen by the MEDA is that of labour supply. The production pattern, in so far as it moves away from crops such as cotton and coffee with high seasonal labour requirements, organises land use more rationally, introduces multiple cropping under irrigation, and mechanises harvesting, should raise not only the productivity of land but also that of labour. It is also planned to 'fill in' the troughs in the seasonal labour demand schedule, allowing the labour force to be stabilised around export production in specific rural settlements. As a result, overall labour requirements should grow at a rate little more than that of the rural population as a whole, rising abotu 50 per cent between the 1980–82 mean and 2000.

In sum, the development of productive forces is based upon a strategic basic needs target (with food security as a central element) and the surplus generation (with agroexports as a central element) required to finance it. With underused land and water resources and a shortage of 'free' labour, rapid elevation of technical levels is held to be the only way forward. Moreover, the absorption of modern agricultural technology, even if this can only be done in the large farm sector, is seen as the only way to 'industrialise' Nicaragua, develop linkages with other sectors, create a large and educated proletariat, achieve a new insertion into the international division of labour, and so on: in other words, to develop.

As far as the different ownership forms are concerned, the MEDA sets out a 'two-track' strategy, summarised in Table 6. The state farms would not expand their landholdings, but rather their productivity would raise their share of output from 16 per cent of output to 30 per cent by 2000. The APP would be the 'axis of accumulation', developing activities of longer maturity, higher technical complexity and greater capitalisation, but also acting as a point of diffusion of modern technology to the co-operatives. The proportion contributed by the co-operatives would rise from 21 per cent to 40 per cent, mainly by the inclusion of new land area, associating peasants with individual holdings in the CCS and the elimination of large private landholdings to form CAS. Within this category, it is also expected to shift the balance in favour of the CAS, which with the APP should contribute half of production by 2000. Production co-operatives would expand their share faster than all other ownership forms, partly because of the voluntary conversion of CCS to CAS, but also because they would, after the APP, receive the greatest mechanisation. Small and medium individual producers would have declined to 25 per cent of production and large private farms to an insignificant five per cent. These

TABLE 6

PROJECTED EVOLUTION OF PRODUCTION SHARES AND LAND TENURE (%)

|  | Farm Area | | | Production | | |
|---|---|---|---|---|---|---|
|  | 1981–82 | 1990 | 2000 | 1981–82 | 1990 | 2000 |
| State farms | 18.3 | 22.3 | 27.4 | 16.0 | 23.0 | 30.0 |
| Production co-operatives | 1.3 | 11.8 | 25.1 | 2.6 | 11.0 | 20.0 |
| Credit and service co-operatives | 13.6 | 17.9 | 23.3 | 18.0 | 16.0 | 20.0 |
| Large private farmers | 12.0 | 9.4 | 6.0 | 14.0 | 10.0 | 5.0 |
| Small and medium farmers | 54.8 | 37.8 | 18.2 | 49.4 | 40.0 | 25.0 |
| Total | 100.0 | 100.0 | 100.0 | 100.0 | 100.0 | 100.0 |

*Source*: MIDINRA [*1983*].

*Notes*:   The base figures differ slightly from others in this article which are more recent.
The underlying assumptions for the change in land tenure to 2000 are as follows:

(a) half of large private farms is expropriated, passing in equal shares to state farms and production co-operatives;
(b) two-thirds of small and mediuim farms pass in equal shares to state farms, production co-operatives and credit and service co-operatives;
(c) a third of the credit and service co-operatives become production co-operatives;
(d) a third of the state farms is transferred to co-operatives, in proportion of one-third to Credit and service co-operatives and two-thirds to production co-operatives.

'Large private farmers' in this table is more than 500 mz.

two latter categories are expected to maintain a third of production which itself should have tripled by the end of the century so that their absolute production level would not decline.

How feasible is this project to achieve a radical agrarian transformation in less than a generation? The first unknown is, of course, the military and economic aggression directed by the USA against Nicaragua. The longer this continues, the more will production and investment be held back, although the experience of other similar situations indicates that social transformation may be accelerated. External recources will be limited and domestic surplus will inevitably be chanelled towards defence.

None the less, it is worth contrasting the MEDA with the problems identified above. Broadly speaking, the material limitations imposed by the dual economy are anticipated and supposedly overcome. The peasant sector supplies of food would be supplemented by large irrigated grains and intensive livestock schemes while production co-operatives supply vegetables and fruit to nearby towns. The stabilisation of production patterns, mechanisation, and the association of labour-short APP estates to labour-surplus CAS should overcome the problem of the agroexport workforce. Thus, the problems of the real wage in the towns and the creation of a rural proletariat (which should reach half the rural population by 2000) are to be resolved as part of a new model of agrarian accumulation.

The strategy contains, however, an internal contradiction.[6] In overcoming the exploitative relationship of capitalist agriculture with the peasantry (which was a root cause of its collapse) the MEDA does not define a new role for this class in the model. The strategy concentrates on modern farming as the most rapid way of resolving the agrarian accumulation problem – food and investible surplus. At most, assuming that there is sufficient administrative capacity and skilled labour to implement the strategy, it will benefit the APP and the CAS, about half of agrarian production but only a quarter of the rural population. It would take place, moreover, basically on the irrigated and fertile Pacific plain where two-thirds of the population resides. Meanwhile, the land reform itself has effectively established a middle farmer and service co-operative group which occupies over half the rural population and provides the other half of production; this group has no specific part to play in the MEDA. Depending on the circumstances, this group might either develop into a 'kulak' class dependent on the market and opposed to further agrarian reform or else collapse and migrate to the towns in the long run. But in any case, it will be responsible for the bulk of the food production in the short term (which may well last for a decade) and thus requires specific attention.

To overcome this contradiction, which is already apparent, the APP would have to restore part of the role of estate agriculture in the rural economic formation, acting as a point of articulation for small and medium farmers instead of acting as a competitor to them. This articulation essentially implies subordinating them to the state rather than marginalising them, but also means shifting input and investment resources towards them in exchange for guaranteed production sold to the state.

VI. CONCLUSIONS

It is too early to make a definitive characterisation of the Nicaraguan agrarian reform, not only because the Sandinist Revolution is still in an initial transitional stage, but also because of the current war conditions which, depending upon external political factors, could change the direction of social change. None the less, the nature of the agrarian reform project, the experience of its implementation to date, and the long-term agricultural development proposal do provide elements for some tentative conclusions.

First, that the three lessons learned from other agrarian reform experiences were applied to some effect. Namely: (a) that production must be maintained throug the reform period, in order to avoid collapse of exports or falling urban living standards; (b) that the process of nationalisation should not proceed faster than the capacity of the state to assimilate the private sector; (c) that while individual land distribution should be avoided, co-operativisation should be voluntary and gradual. In this way, the collapse of productive forces as production relations are transformed was avoided.

Second, that it is possible to effectively remove the control of agrarian capital over the economy without land expropriation as such, if the 'surrounding' mechanisms such as commercialisation, credit and inputs are used effectively. Indeed it might even be suggested that social control of the relations of exchange in agriculture are as important as ownership of the means of production, especially land. It is true that the Nicaraguan experience, where the strategic Somoza group holdings passed directly to the state without threatening the rest of the private sector, was especially conducive to this solution. None the less, the experience of post-reform agriculture in a number of socialist countries indicates that this is in practice the best way of articulating such disparate forms of production.

Third, that the process of capitalist agricultural development does generate a large proletariat, even though it is disguised in the form of impoverished peasantry. This means that the agrarian reform can proceed in socialised production forms in the 'capitalist' sector without direct peasant ownership of land. It is true that in the Nicaraguan case, the relatively high land endowment per head reduced this pressure, but it is also important not to overestimate the 'peasant' nature of agriculture in Latin America [*Goodman and Redclift, 1981*], because this tends to lead to agrarian reform proposals which ignore the inevitable role of agriculture as the base of the national accumulation model in almost all underdeveloped economies in transition.

Fourth, that in the case of Nicaragua, this logic has probably been carried too far. In implementing a project to eliminate the exploitative relationship between capitalist export agriculture and the peasantry (cheap labour and cheap food) by establishing a stable rural proletariat and secure food supplies, the revolutionary state has effectively undermined the remaining peasant economy without providing a coherent alternative. This has produced a new contradiction in the agrarian development model proposed for the rest of the century, when the revolution not only depends upon the mountain peasantry for defence against external aggression but also for food supplies during the transitional accumulation period.

A successful agrarian accumulation model, above all during the transition, must provide for an adequate articulation of distinct forms of production as part of the process of rural transformation.

NOTES

1. For a general survey of the Nicaraguan revolution, see Walker [*1985*].
2. In other words, in the absence of heavy industry, agriculture contains not only 'Department II' (reproduction of the labour force) in food production as in the classical model, but also a surrogate for Department I (production of the means of production) in raw materials exports. This problematic is discussed in FitzGerlad [*1985a*] and developed more formally in FitzGerald [*1985b*]. The concept of 'articulation' used in this paper is essentially that of Wolpe.
3. Wheelock [*1976*]. Commandant Wheelock, a noted rural sociologist, is a member of the National Directorate of the FSLN and Minister of Agriculture and Agrarian Reform.
4. Based on the Literacy Campaign of that year; see IFAD [*1981*].
5. Gobierno de Nicaragua [*1983*]; see also FSLN [*1984*] for election commitments in this respect.
6. This was clearly foreseen in FIDA [*1981*].

REFERENCES

Baumeister, E., 1984, 'Estructuras y Reforma Agraria en el Proceso Sandinista' (mimeo), Managua: CIERA.
CEPAL, 1984, 'Notas sobre la Economia de America Latina: Nicaragua', Mexico: United Nations.
CIERA, 1982, 'Produccion y Organizacion en el Agro Nicaraguense', Managua: Centro de Investigaciones y Estudios de la Reforma Agraria.

CIERA, 1984, 'Estrategia Alimentaria en Nicaragua', Managua: Centro de Investigaciones y Estudios de la Reforma Agraria for the Canadian International Development Agency.

CIERA, 1985, 'Problemas y Perspectivas de la Migracion Campo-Ciudad', *Revolucion y Desarrollo*, No. 3.

FitzGerald, E. V. K., 1982, 'The Economics of the Revolution' in Walker [*1982*].

FitzGerald, E. V. K., 1985a, 'The Problem of Balance in the Peripheral Socialist Economy: A Conceptual Note', *World Development*, Vol. 13, No. 1.

FitzGerald, E. V. K., 1985b, 'The Problem of Balance in the Small Peripheral Economy', in Martin [*1985*].

FitzGerald, E. V. K., 1985c, 'Problems in Financing a Revolution: The Case of Nicaragua 1979–84', The Hague: ISS Working Papers Series, 14.

FitzGerald, E. V. K., 1985d, 'An Evaluation of the Economic Cost to Nicaragua of U.S. Aggression', paper presented to Latin American Studies Association, Albuquerque.

FSLN, 1982, 'Programa Historico del FSLN', Managua: DEPEP (a reprint of the original document issued in 1969).

FSLN, 1984, 'Plan de Lucha del FSLN', Managua: DAP.

Gobierno de Nicaragua, 1983, 'Lineamientos de Politica Economica 1983–87', Managua: Fondo Internacional para la Reconstruccion.

Goodman, G. and M. Redclift, 1981, *From Peasant to Proletarian: Capitalist Development and Agrarian Transitions*, Oxford: Blackwell.

IFAD, 1981, 'Report of the Special Programing Mission to Nicaragua', Rome: International Fund for Agricultural Development.

Martin, K., 1985, (ed.), *Readings in Capitalist and Non-capitalist Development Strategies*, London: Heinemann.

MIDINRA, 1983, 'Marco Estrategico del Desarrollo Agropeculario', Managua: Ministerio de Desarrollo Agropecuario y Reforma Agraria.

MIDINRA, 1985, 'Plan de Trabajo: Balance y Perspectivas, 1985', Managua: Ministerio de Desarrollo Agropecuario y Reforma Agraria.

SPP, 1985, 'Programa Economico 1985', Managua: Secretaria de Programacion y Presupuesto.

UNRISD, 1982, 'A Preliminary Analysis of the Nicaraguan Food System', Geneva: United Nations.

Walker, T., 1982, (ed.), *Nicaragua in Revolution*, New York: Praeger.

Walker, T., 1985, (ed.), *The Nicaraguan Revolution: Five Years On*, New York: Praeger.

Wheelock, J., 1976, *Imperialismo y Dictadura*, Mexico: Siglo XXI.

Wheelock, J., 1983, *El Gran Desafio*, Managua: Editorial Nueva Nicaragua.

Wheelock, J., 1984, *Entre la Crisis y la Agresion*, Managua: Editorial Nueva Nicaragua.

White, C. P. and G. White, 1982, 'Agriculture, the Peasantry and Socialist Development', *IDS Bulletin*, Vol. 13, No. 4.

Wolpe, H. (ed.), 1980, *The Articulation of Modes of Production*, London: Routledge & Kegan Paul.

# REVIEW ARTICLES

# Does De-industrialisation Beget Industrialisation which Begets Re-industrialisation?

*by Raphael Kaplinsky**

**The Military Origins of Industrialisation and International Trade Rivalry.** By Gautam Sen. *London: Frances Pinter*, 1984. Pp. 204. £16. ISBN 0 86187 357 2.

**The De-industrialisation of America: Plant Closings, Community Abandonment, and the Dismantling of Basic Industry.** By Barry Bluestone and Bennett Harrison. *New York: Basic Books*, 1982. Pp. x + 323. $8.95. ISBN 0 465 01591 3.

**Industry in a Changing World: Special Issue of the Industrial Development Survey for the Fourth General Conference of UNIDO.** By United Nations Industrial Development Organisation. *New York: United Nations*, 1983. Pp. xvii + 369. UN Publications Sales No. E.83.11.B.6.

**Industry Strategy in a Changing World.** By Robert Ballance and Stuart Sinclair. *London: Allen & Unwin*, 1983. Pp. xix + 218. £15 and £5.95. ISBN 0 04 338107 3 and 338108 1.

**Multinational Corporations, Technology and Employment.** By Edward K. Y. Chen. *London: Macmillan*, 1983. Pp. xv + 247. £25. ISBN 0 333 31995 8.

**Japanese Manufacturing Technique: Nine Hidden Lessons in Simplicity.** By Richard J. Schonberger. *London: Collier-Macmillan*, 1982. Pp. 260. £19.95. ISBN 0 02929 100 3.

**Industrial Renaissance: Producing a Competitive Future for America.** By W. J. Abernathy, K. B. Clarke and A. M. Kantrow. *New York: Basic Books*, 1983. Pp. 206. £16. ISBN 0 465 03254 0.

'There are no obsolete industries, only obsolete technologies .... There are no condemned sectors. Innovation allows all sectors to be competitive'.[1]

It is important to maintain a sense of historical perspective in assessing the changing order of dominance in the global manufacturing sector. After all, a mere two hundred years back industrial production in south Asia probably exceeded that of the whole of Europe; and the American industrial sector was largely confined to the households of a sparsely settled subcontinent. Who would be prepared to put money down on the distribution of global manufacturing production in one hundred years time, or even half that period (that is, if we can avoid nuclear incineration in the interim)?

Yet, working on more limited time scales it is possible to detect trends of change, and it is tempting to project these into the future. For example, in the 1963–73 period,

*Institute of Development Studies, University of Sussex. Thanks are due to David Booth and David Lehmann for their comments on an earlier draft of this review.

manufacturing value added in less developed countries grew at an annual average rate of 2.5 per cent *over* that achieved in the developed market economies; in 1973–80, this superiority in performance rose to 3.4 per cent per annum (UNIDO, Table 11.2). The Second General Conference of UNIDO (held in Lima in 1975) projected these high LDC growth rates into the future and thought it feasible that the Third World's share of global manufacturing value added would rise from around nine per cent in the mid-1970s to around 25 per cent by the year 2000. Even academics, who perhaps are less susceptible to the hype of international forums, have been drawn in to similar exercises. Focusing on a particular mode of industrial growth – namely, export-oriented industrialisation – Hughes and Waelbroek [*1981*] conclude (albeit with reservations): 'For developing countries future prospects seem rather optimistic. Their penetration of industrial-country markets is still low. Room for further penetration exists even in the traditional products ...' [*144*].

It is not our task here to judge whether the optimistic or a more pessimistic scenario is appropriate (see rather the various contributions in the recent Special Issue of *The Journal of Development Studies* [*Kaplinsky, 1984d*]). However, there are a number of factors which suggest caution in projecting the experience of the East Asian 'Gang of Four' for the Third World in general. These include the specificity of the political conditions which underlay these countries' industrial performance, problems of access to developed country markets, the resolution of the international debt-crisis, the impact of the New Cold War on industrial performance in the periphery, and the effects of radical technical change on comparative advantage, particularly as reflected in unit wage costs.

Two themes widely represented in this body of analysis, speculation and presentation are relevant to the books under review. The first is the growing interconnectedness of industrial growth, reflected in the fact that the expansion of trade in manufactures has consistently exceeded that of output over the past three decades. It makes little sense nowadays to discuss industrial policy in isolation from global production and markets. Second, there has been increasing recognition since the early econometric studies on the sources of economic growth in the developed countries in the late 1950s, of the key role played by technological innovation in facilitating industrial growth and international competitiveness.

It is in this context that we can see the direct link between industrial development in the Third World and Japan (both ascendant in the past few decades) and de-industrialisation in the industrially advanced economies. For in a situation in which the income elasticity of demand for industrial goods is static or begins to decline, or where consumer incomes in the major markets grow at a lower rate than industrial output in the expanding economies, industrial growth in the Third World and Japan must necessarily occur at the expense of industrial output in the remaining OECD economies.[2] What happens, though when other, non-industrial sources of employment and growth begin to slacken, as they have in the post-1973 period, and when there exists little opportunity to 'restructure' (the keyword of the late 1970s)? Are the industrially mature economies likely to keep their markets open, trading high rates of unemployment and stagnating incomes for low-cost manufactures? Or are they more likely to close off their markets, and thus arrest the process of de-industrialisation, at the same time inhibiting export-oriented industrialisation in the expanding economies?

The answer is uncertain, partly because the resolution depends upon political processes, involving actors such as the State, labour, transnational corporations and 'national capital'. But it is also indeterminate because there is an alternative apart from de-industrialisation/market-access versus the maintenance of industrial structures/ protectionism, namely a strategy of *re*-industrialisation. This has now become a key policy discussion, particularly in France but also in the USA and other OECD countries.

The question is whether in the face of an increasingly rapid rate of technological progress, the industrially mature economies will be able to reform established industrial practices and thereby reverse the trend towards de-industrialisation.

The seven books considered in this review are all, in one way or another, concerned with the combined theme of industrialisation, de-industrialisation and re-industrialisation. They consider not only the interconnectedness of industrial growth but also the impact of radical technical change on comparative advantage. Their content ranges from discussion to analysis to prescription; from the Third World to the Socialist bloc to the industrially advanced market economies; from abstract theorisation to empirically-based investigation; and from the macro to the micro. Inevitably, therefore, the range of issues covered in vast. In this review we concentrate on the relevance of the books to a general concern with the international division of labour in manufacturing, focusing particularly on the pattern of industrialisation in the mature industrial economies, the rise of industrialisation in LDCs and Japan, and the contemporary discussion on re-industrialisation strategies in the USA and Europe. Before considering seven major issues which emerge from the books under consideration, we offer a brief summary of their content.

THE SUBJECT MATTER OF THE BOOKS

The UNIDO volume and the Ballance and Sinclair book have much in common,[3] and both provide useful overviews of the pattern of post-war industrial development. The UNIDO book sets out 'to document, describe and analyse recent trends' in industry (p. 1) particularly in the light of the objectives set for the Third World by the Second and Third General Conferences of UNIDO. In the two most useful chapters of the volume ('The Changing Map of World Industry' and 'The Relationship Between Trade in Manufactures and The Industrialisation Process'), *Industry in a Changing World* illustrates that the attainment of this objective now seems highly unlikely. Despite the fact that the LDCs' share of global manufacturing value added rose from 8.1 per cent in 1963 to 11 per cent in 1982, even on an optimistic and high-growth scenario, the share of LDCs in the year 2000 is only likely to reach 19.2 per cent. On an only slightly less optimistic projection of historic growth rates, the Third World share falls to only 14.9 per cent. Yet, as the UNIDO book points out, the rising share of the Third World was largely a phenomenon of the period between 1963 and 1975; after that it effectively stabilised, suggesting that even the low-growth projection of a 14.9 per cent share may be too optimistic.[4]

Overall, the two most striking trends to emerge from the UNIDO analysis are (a) that the sharp fall in the share of the 'mature market economies' — that is, effectively the US and the EEC excluding Germany — was largely taken up by the advance of the centrally planned economies, rather than by the rise to prominence of Japan, Germany or the NICs; and (b) the heavy concentration of shares in value added and manufacturing exports, both as between the First and Third Worlds, and within both of these two sets of economies. For example, ten LDCs account for 72.3 per cent of the total increase in LDC manufacturing value added in the 1973–80 period, and five countries account for more than two-thirds of all DC manufactured exports and 54 per cent of global manufactured exports. In addition to this aggregate analysis, the UNIDO book provides invaluable source material (much of it based on unpublished data), a unique data base on China's industrialisation, global case studies of five sectors, and a useful overview of eastern Europe's trade with the Third World. Its weaknesses are that it comprises a somewhat curious amalgam of subject matter, not always linked together in a coherent manner. Its comprehensiveness is also somewhat limited by the omission of Taiwan from the statistical data base, but that is a fair price to pay for the inclusion of mainland China.

Although Ballance and Sinclair's book has a much narrower appeal than the UNIDO volume, it is a much more tightly argued text. It documents the growing competitiveness and changing face of international industry in the post-war period, and argues that unlike agriculture, the industrial sector comprises a very heterogeneous set of 'special interest groups'. These exert a variety of forms of pressure on the State, making it difficult to generalise on policy formulation at the firm, industry or national levels. The authors are thus driven to a series of excellent sectoral case studies covering two 'Ageing Poles of Growth' (automobiles and steel) and three 'Engines for Growth and Survival' (consumer electronics, advanced electronics and oil refining).[5] These set the scene for a final chapter which considers the future role of the TNC and 'suggests that the more conventional interpretations of the TNCs' post-war importance may need to be refined although by no means abandoned' (p. 180). It also questions the proposition that State intervention makes adjustment more difficult, and discusses the 'de-maturity' strategy which is the subject matter of the book by Abernathy *et al.* In this reviewer's opinion the value of Ballance and Sinclair's highly readable and serious book transcends the limitations of some of its analysis as encapsulated in the following somewhat anodyne conclusion:

> [W]hat has been suggested is that the well publicised interruptions to this process of growing industrial prosperity should not blind us to the enormous changes that are taking place in world industry; to ignore these changes, or to attempt to thwart them, and in the process keep the price of manufactured goods unnecessarily high, would be of benefit to no one in the long run (p. 199).

Bluestone and Harrison, Abernathy *et al.*, and Schonberger, are all concerned with the space created for industrialisation in the Third World and Japan by the onset of de-industrialisation in the USA. Each not only offers an attempt to analyse the causes of industrial decline in America, but also moves from description to prescription. Abernathy, Clark and Kantrow all hail from a Harvard Business School background; each has played a part in pushing the issue of re-industrialisation (if not Industrial Policy) to the forefront of public discussion in America. Their thesis is clear and well stated.

> Our starting point in the discussion that follows is a single harsh but inescapable fact: the nation's lackluster industrial performance in recent years is, in large part, the result of the failure of many of its traditional manufacturing industries to adjust to a troubling new set of competitive realities (p. xi) .... American competitors in each of these industries are not experiencing a temporary loss of their share in once-and-for-all established markets. Their weakened condition has pushed them towards the sidelines as the industries in which they compete undergo technological and structural upheavals (p. 12).

This process of industrial decline is charted for the US automobile industry by comparison with productivity levels and product quality in the Japanese industry: 'Although constant harping on the economic challenge that Japan now presents to the West tends to numb the mind, to make us feel that when we have admitted the fact we have done enough, a close exposure to the inner mechanics of that challenge is like a splash of cold water. This is scary stuff' (p. 58). The details of the competitive weakness of the US automobile industry are well presented and striking. The major explanation offered is the trend towards 'maturity in American industry in which either technological innovation is absent, or it is conservative and non-disruptive'. However, in moving from description to prescription the authors dispute the 'conventional assumption that with manufacturing operations as with anything resembling a biological organism, the process of ageing is irreversible': 'Rather we would argue for the possibility of industrial "dematurity"' (pp. 20–21), so that ... '[i]t is our strong belief that properly understood, the possibilities of a restored technology-based competition ... can turn the threat of de-maturity into an attractive program for industry renewal' (p. 29).

This transition to de-maturity involves ...

> a movement away from productive unit standardisation − [this] means an increase in the diversity of product technology actually offered in the market as well as an increase in the competitive viability of that technology. Innovation once more carries a premium, as the focus of innovation shifts back from the reinforcement of existing concepts towards disruptive change in the concepts themselves (p. 28).

The key in moving towards industrial 'de-maturity' is a fundamental change in managerial attitudes and the removal of conflict from the work-place ('The imperatives of quality and productivity, which lie at the heart of this new industrial competition, are impossible to satisfy without the active, loyal, and committed participation of a well-trained and constantly improving workforce', p. 90). How the American political economy is to move to this new pattern of class relationships is largely unstated (except by brief reference to the experience of 'Quality of Worklife' programmes in the US automobile industry) and forms the major weakness of an otherwise well-argued and well-written book.

Schonberger's book − easily the best available text on best-practice Japanese manufacturing techniques − is an important adjunct to the study by Abernathy *et al.* Written in a somewhat loose, polemical and exhortative style, and largely in the realm of production engineering, it might be considered a strange acquisition for a reader interested in development studies. Yet this reviewer regards it as perhaps the most interesting (if not academic) of an excellent pack of material. It explains how the organisation of work in Japanese factories, largely in the automobile sector, enables quality cars to be produced at 30−40 per cent lower cost than their American counterparts. With similar capital equipment, labour productivity in equivalent tasks is often double that in Western factories. The key to this, Schonberger argues, is to be found in the following sets of practices. First, organisation is built around 'just-in-time' (JIT) rather than just-in-case methods, which reduces levels of inventory for both inputs and final products. Second, the reduction in inventories depends upon a zero-defect policy, in which each worker assumes responsibility for quality control of each part and operation, as opposed to the Western method of specialised random inspection. Third, flexibility is a key component; machines are rapidly converted to other specifications and all workers are expected to perform multiple tasks, combining machine-operation with machine-repair. Output composition thus changes frequently and production lines are flexible.

Referring to the pioneering Japanese investors in America, Schonberger argues that these manufacturing techniques are easily transferable. However this involves new relationships, not only between suppliers and assemblers, but also between capital and labour. Again, as with Abernathy *et al.*, the author is less clear under what set of social relations American entrepreneurs might move from conflict to co-operation at the point of production.

Bluestone and Harrison's analysis (commissioned by a coalition of trade unions and community organisations) focuses on the impact of industrial job losses on the American social fabric and suggests that the political transformation required to re-industrialise America may not be as painless as Abernathy *et al.* and Schonberger might wish. The authors adopt a rather idiosyncratic definition of de-industrialisation as incorporating all forms of job loss, whether resulting from international relocation, relocation within America, or bankruptcy. This job loss has a high multiplier-effect (with a value of one to two, though for unexplained reasons, it is only 0.2 for job creation) and hence an extremely high social cost, for which extensive evidence is cited.

The central, but largely unstated, analytical explanation for this major wrench in contemporary America is the retreat by productive capital into the speculative and financial spheres, which Bluestone and Harrison characterise as the 'conglomerate destruction of viable businesses' (p. 57) by the 'hypermobility of capital' (p. 204). Capital 'has been diverted from productive investment in our basic national industries into unproductive speculation, mergers and acquisitions and foreign investment' (p. 6). Thus '[t]o understand deindustrialization requires a careful analysis of modern corporate managerial strategies in the context of an increasingly interdependent and competitive global economic system' (p. 112). This requires recognition of three inter-related phenomena, namely, the struggle for global market shares, conflict between capital and labour, and the role of the State in mediating these sets of conflicts.

The authors then consider, and dismiss, a variety of responses to this crisis in the American economy, namely, a conservative strategy of doing nothing, a corporatist strategy involving some form of Industrial Policy, a liberal strategy in which market forces are tempered by regulation, the Japanisation of the American economy (with a MITI-type coordinating ministry), small-business led industrialisation and Thatcherite-type Urban Enterprise Zones. Instead the authors present an alternative strategy of 'Re-industrialisation with a Human Face' which recognises that 'productivity is a *social* relation': 'To promote it requires *more*, not less, social security' (p. 232). But to succeed, it requires, *inter alia*, worker participation and a consequent restructuring of social relations at the point of production.

At various points all of the above-mentioned books recognise the central importance of the transnational corporation (TNC, or MNC, hereafter) as a determinant of industrial location. Perspectives on the changing role of the TNC in an epoch of industrial restructuring are provided by Chen and Sen. Chen's book is a gem; clearly written, well structured, incorporating original research and providing very helpful literature surveys on the theory of direct foreign investment, on Third World TNCs, on the diffusion of technology, and on TNCs and employment. Its primary concern is with MNCs in Hong Kong, particularly their transfer of technology, their impact on employment and their role in exporting. The book also includes an analysis of Hong Kong MNCs investing in surrounding developing economies.

Chen's fieldwork is based on questionnaire research with 369 firms in the four major sectors (textiles; garments; electronics; and plastics, toys and dolls) which account for more than 70 per cent of Hong Kong's exports, as well as interviews with 25 locally-registered MNCs. Briefly, seven major results emerged from the research. First, whilst local firms were more likely to undertake R & D than MNCs, the intensity of this R & D as a percentage of sales was much lower; in general MNC R & D was in process rather than product and they also tended to invest more in training than their local counterparts. Second, Chen observed a close link between the higher propensity of MNCs to innovate and their tendency to diffuse technology. Third, there was little evidence to support the assertion (based on research elsewhere) that MNC subsidiaries were more labour-intensive than their locally-owned counterparts. Fourth, MNCs did appear to adapt technology, particularly in sub-processes, to local conditions. Fifth, the performance of MNCs as exporters was no better than local firms, though Chen predicts that as NICs attempt to diversify their export base, so the share of MNCs in exports will increase. Sixth, for South-East Asia as a whole the choice of technique was more influenced by product choice (especially where exports were concerned) than by the ownership of the enterprise. And, finally, the major factors influencing Hong Kong MNCs to invest abroad were the cost of land, diversification of risk and market access.

Notwithstanding these various strengths of Chen's book, it is not without flaws.[6] Most significantly these arise from two related factors, namely, the labour process involved in the fieldwork, and the ideological blinkers of the analysis. In one way or another, whether through the use of aggregate production function analysis or the critique of the theory of foreign investment, Chen writes within the neo-classical mould. Hence the analysis of foreign investment as a global phenomenon, as well as the motivations of Hong Kong MNCs, are considered in a highly particularistic and non-systemic fashion. This leads Chen, for example, to an endorsement of Dunning's eclectic theory of foreign investment despite his own observation that '[i]n a sense the eclectic theory is no theory' (p. 35). This ideological myopia leads to a research methodology involving the distribution of questionnaires which suggest answers to the respondents; is it surprising, therefore, that the failure of the author to generate his own systemic theory of direct foreign investment finds its reflection in a result which ascribes foreign investment by Hong Kong MNCs primarily to the high cost of land? Even so, Chen's research, with its attendant literature surveys and econometric analyses, provides much food for thought.

Sen's book potentially spans many of the issues raised in the volumes considered here. His concern is to analyse the emergence of trade conflict in the global manufacturing sector, for, he argues, both neo-classical and Marxist theoretical frameworks fail 'to address the issue of international trade disputes over the same products between several countries simultaneously' (p. 6). His alternative takes the following form. Industrial development follows a clearly-defined pattern, in relation to both cross-section and time-series analysis (in Marx's terms, '[t]he country that is more developed industrially only shows, to the less developed, the image of its own future'). This involves the development of six strategic industries, namely, iron and steel, chemicals, textiles, machinery, paper and paper products, and transport equipment. Each is characterised by economies of scale, such that 'with the spread of industrialisation, the duplication of production structures implied by imitation unavoidably leads to the emergence of world-wide capacity in the group of strategic industries' (p. 252). Given 'the primacy of politics' (pp. 67–8), '[t]he dominant reality of the international political system is the competition between national sectors' (p. 66). The currency of this rivalry is power, 'and the highest denomination of this currency of power is military capability' (p. 66). But for military power to be credible it needs a sound industrial base – 'it is therefore argued that industrialisation in most major countries has been rooted, historically, in the attempt to acquire a military capability' (p. 71).

Sen then examines the emergence of industry in the USA, Japan, individual European countries and India and Brazil. These short country sketches are not wholly convincing and particularly in the case of the USA they fail to make use of many of the better-known case studies of the link between military requirements and mass production.[7] The analysis of changing world shares of manufacturing value added and trade is, by contrast, comprehensive and a valuable adjunct to the more limited data presented in the UNIDO volume. Finally the book considers the TNC, and rather unusually sees little conflict between international capital and the nation state, with the TNC, through its international trading operations, being 'opposed to the collapse of the liberal international economic order' (p. 253).

The primary value of Sen's book lies in bringing the link between the military imperative and industrialisation to the forefront of discussion. However, this has to be weighed against a failure to consider the role played by the military in inhibiting industrialisation. Moreover, some of the specific analysis is questionable – for example, the tortuous discussion which attempts to draw a link between the textile sector and national security. The links between this sector and the army may have been instrumental in the development of early industrialisation in Europe (a subject not adequately covered by Sen), but the case is considerably weaker for contemporary economies, whether in the Third World or the First.

SOME COMMON ISSUES WITH REGARD TO INDUSTRIALISATION,
DE-INDUSTRIALISATION AND RE-INDUSTRIALISATION

Despite their diversity, all of these books revolve in a rather interesting way around the theme of global industrialisation. Are the advances in global market share of the LDCs, Japan and the Eastern bloc to be sustained in the face of de-industrialisation in the mature industrial market economies? Or, in the face of exemplary best-practice Japanese production techniques, will the mature industrial market economies be able to introduce radical technical change and institute the changes in work-practices required to re-industrialise successfully? What sets of social relations are required for these best-practice techniques to be implemented successfully, not only in relation to the historic divide between capital and labour, but also in relation to the composition and role of the State, and the specific features of the hegemonic capital? These and other questions are of key importance if re-industrialisation strategies (as exemplified by the French strategic planning approach described by Ballance and Sinclair) are to be implemented successfully.

These issues, of course, are extremely complex and the books under consideration could not be expected to offer comprehensive perspectives even if this had been their direct intention. Nevertheless each of the books, in one way or another, illuminates various aspects of the problem and with this in mind, we draw out seven major themes. In each case we shall briefly attempt to reflect the diversity of views contained in the books rather than to offer a definitive view of our own, or of some other author whose work is not under consideration.

*(a) Economic Interdependence and Crisis*

The growing interdependence of the world economy, particularly in the manufacturing sector is clear from almost all the contributions. As Ballance and Sinclair note:

> Decisions about new auto assembly capacity in Spain − or even in South Korea − will have an effect upon other producers in Europe, Japan and the USA. These effects, which will ultimately make themselves felt on pricing, design and trade policy decisions in the firms in the industry and their suppliers, inevitably impinge upon the welfare of Detroit's assembly workers and Sao Paulo's engineers (pp. xvii−xviii).

This growing interdependence, as the UNIDO volume points out, shows up in the global distribution of value added, since the VAGOR (value added as a ratio to gross output) fell in most industrial branches and in most sectors in the 1968−78 period.

Yet, curiously in view of the recognition given by all the authors to the internationalisation of production, only Sen and Bluestone and Harrison attempt to offer explanations for the phenomenon; and these differ markedly in approach. For Sen internationalisation takes place in the sphere of circulation, since trade is an inevitable consequence of economies of scale in the six key, strategically important industries. By contrast Bluestone and Harrison characterise internationalisation as occurring in the sphere of production as conglomerate American capital relocates production from the American industrial heartland to sidestep the power of organised labour. They quote the President of the American Bulova watch company was saying: 'We are able to beat the foreign competition because we *are* the foreign competition' (p. 114).[8] Yet, the internationalisation of production, argues the UNIDO volume, has little to do with relative wage rates, thus drawing the analysis on to stonier ground, particularly with respect to policy formulation − 'A major conclusion emerging from this survey [of international wage rates] is that differences in wage levels are, at best, ambiguous determinants to use when deciding on the location of an industry or, more generally, charting or predicting changes in the world industrial map' (p. 227).

This divergence of views on the causes of internationalisation is in sharp contrast to the recognition by all the books (with the exception of Chen) that the global manufacturing sector is undergoing a profound structural change, which cannot accurately be characterised as recession. Ballance and Sinclair used the term 'crisis' to describe the competitive threat being faced by the mature industrial market economies, and each of the other books recognises the persistence and systemic nature of uneven rates of technological progress and innovation. These have led to high rates of unemployment and trade conflict, and the attendant problems of coping with these changes have brought industrial policy, trade restrictions and restructuring to the forefront of public debate, not just in the LDCs or the Socialist bloc, but also in the heartlands of the global capitalist system. In order either to allow this industrialisation to take place, or alternatively to provide respite from the competitive pressures towards de-industrialisation, some measure of trade protection is recognised as inevitable by all of the books under review.

## (b) Protectionism

The UNIDO survey charts in detailed statistical form the growing share of LDCs in world manufacturing value added and trade until the mid-1970s. It accompanies this analysis with the judgement that '[t]he steady growth of new protectionism since the mid-1970s has marked a turning point in the industrial relations of the developed market economies' (p. 151). The question is whether this advance of protectionism is temporary or more long-lasting. Ballance and Sinclair, analysing the development of protectionism in the automobile industry, suggest that it may be of a cyclical nature. By contrast Bluestone and Harrison argue that protectionism is endemic to the capitalist system, such that faced with economic insecurity, '[t]he entire history of capitalism ... provides evidence that the dominant response to heightened insecurity is protectionism, *not* more virulent forms of cutthroat competition' (p. 204).

However, whatever the differences concerning the nature of protectionism, with the exception of Chen all of the books would seem to lean towards the following judgement by Ballance and Sinclair, made in relation to the steel industry, but of wide relevance to the manufacturing sector as a whole.

> The protectionist approaches adopted by American and European steel interests have obvious consequences for new producers in LDCs. Even though the European or Japanese exporters were the initial target of the American campaign, trade restrictions were soon applied to secondary suppliers as well ... The prospect of additional export-oriented capacity in LDCs can only heighten the potential for conflict with producers in advanced countries so long as a defensive strategy prevails in the latter markets (pp. 124–5).

It is readily recognised, then, that protectionism, being a response to radical structural change ('crisis'), will not easily go away; the question is whether structural adjustment (re-industrialisation) will successfully take place behind these pervasive protectionist barriers. Before considering re-industrialisation strategies, though, we briefly address the analysis of the causes of industrial decline.

## (c) The Causes of Industrial Decline

The industrial decline of the mature industrial economies is well surveyed by both Sen and UNIDO. Sen is particularly helpful in this regard in that he charts not just the changes in aggregate shares of exports and manufactured value added, but also those within six key sectors. Japan shows up particularly strongly in this more disaggregated context, such that between 1950 and 1971 its share of world exports rose from 0.5 to 13.9 per cent for machinery; from 8 to 19.7 per cent for textiles and clothing;

from 0.2 to 9.2 per cent for chemicals; from 1.4 to 15.7 per cent for transport equipment; and from 5.9 to 21.6 per cent for metals.

In public perception the recent industrial success of Japan has been identified with the greater utilisation of electronics-based automation equipment. This is echoed by Ballance and Sinclair who observe: 'In 1981, Japanese manufacturers were reported to be using over 14,000 industrial robots. Less than one-third of this number was found in American factories, whilst West Germany was the only other country with a robot population that exceeded 1,000' (p. 148). Yet on the basis of detailed studies of the automobile industry, Abernathy *et al.*, Schonberger and others have found that the very significant competitive advantage of the Japanese is barely explained by the degree of automation involved. Indeed, Abernathy *et al.* offer evidence to illustrate that '[t]he Japanese advantage rests not on substitution of capital for labour or labour for capital; it rests, instead, on diligent control of the whole system of production' (p. 62), that is, management. Thus working on a matrix of two types of analytical distinction, micro vs. macro and embodied ('hardware') vs. disembodied ('software'), they conclude that ' "micro software" – what management does – is essential to the renaissance of a beleaguered American industry' (p. 5).

This emphasis on the need for a managerial revolution if re-industrialisation is to proceed successfully, is shared by Bluestone and Harrison and Schonberger, though there is a sharp disagreement concerning the social relations of production required to carry through these managerial changes effectively. Bluestone and Harrison conclude that '[i]n one way or another, most of the existing explanations of deindustrialisation ... revert to the time-honoured practice of blaming the victim' [that is, Labour] (p. 111). They thus argue that without some form of genuine worker-participation, effective organisational changes are unlikely to occur. In contrast, Schonberger would seem to favour the reintroduction of upper-level managerial control, even though he recognises that Japanese-style manufacturing techniques require more participation at the shop-floor level.

Despite the evidence adduced in support of the need for changed managerial practices, it is, nevertheless, the theme of technology and innovation which is dominant in almost all of the books under review. As the French policy statement argues, 'there are no obsolete industries, only obsolete technologies .... Innovation allows all sectors to be competitive'. Similarly Ballance and Sinclair, in discussing four major industry strategies for survival, consider the role of technical change to be crucial in three of them; that is, with respect to the substitution of new products, the extension of existing product life-cycles, and changes in process technology (the fourth being the extended maturity of existing products). In this context the major contribution of the Abernathy *et al.* book is to switch the focus of discussion from the rate of technical change to its quality. A key distinction is made between conservative and disruptive technical change. In order to measure the relevant qualities of technical change they develop an interesting methodology around the concept of 'transilience', which reflects the innovation's 'capacity to influence production systems and their linkages with the market' (p. 110). Transilience requires a shift 'from the regular to the revolutionary phase of innovation'.[9]

*(d) The Replicability of Japanese Production Techniques*

The competitive superiority of Japanese manufacturers, particularly with respect to the organisation of production, is widely acknowledged in all the books under review. The question is whether the industrially mature market economies can adopt them successfully and in so doing withstand competition not only from Japan, but also from low-labour-cost LDCs. Yet the manufacturing techniques in question have clear institutional and, arguably, cultural roots. Thus:

What is important ... is that MITI and its ancillary agencies are part of a wider social and economic fabric. Such an organisation would be unlikely, if replicated elsewhere to be successful unless it was firmly rooted in a culture where competing claims on the proceeds of economic growth are resolved (Ballance and Sinclair, p. 34).

Again: 'The system of production and quality management that the Japanese have developed has cultural roots. That is, Japanese social behavioural tendencies, which are products of the unique Japanese economy, have accommodated the development of highly effective production systems' (Schonberger, p. viii).

Can these radically different work practices be transferred to the mature market economies, or are past attitudes so entrenched that such transfers would be ineffective? Schonberger believes that transfer is possible ('... the systems themselves consist of simple procedures and techniques, most of which do not require a particular environment or cultural setting for their implementation', p. viii) and he points to the successful adoption of just-in-time production techniques by the handful of pioneering Japanese firms in the USA. Abernathy *et al.* agree − 'If future efforts can only fulfil current promise, the last decades of this century will see a true renaissance of American industry' (p. 14).

Yet these judgements are surely premature. Bluestone and Harrison, making the voice of labour heard, argue that '[m]any Japanese intellectuals and Western scholars of Japan worry about the strong pressure for conformity in the Japanese system that can easily restrict dissent and stifle individualism' (p. 218): 'The Japanese system is therefore a two-edged sword. It offers economic prosperity and material progress. But it exacts a price in terms of regimentation and institutionalised inequality. Such a form of social organisation is surely not what we want for the United States ...' (p. 220). Perhaps, therefore, Ballance and Sinclair are correct when in the light of their sectoral study of the automobile industry, they throw doubt on the potential of this re-industrialisation strategy:

[A]lthough an assault on higher unit costs is underway in the USA, there are doubts as to whether this strategy will be sufficient .... [Difficulties stem from the past industrial strength of the USA and the power of existing suppliers, unions, etc. − R. K.]. All this power invites obligation. And the signs in the early 1980s are that powerful interests want to retain as much of the US-owned automobile industry within that country's borders as possible. These circumstances may prevent US firms from implementating their cost-cutting strategies to the extent required if they are to match the Japanese in competitive ability (p. 93).

*(e) Locational Implications of Best-practice Japanese Techniques*

According to the thesis of the New International Division of Labour [*Fröbel et al., 1980*] the industrial advance of the newly industrialising countries in the 1960s and 1970s was predicated on a change in the labour process. The historic tendency towards the deskilling of work was continued and extended on an international basis such that components were increasingly transported around the world and then assembled into final products. However, in contrast to the tendency in the 1960s and 1970s,[10] the new Japanese-style just-in-time production techniques threaten this emerging international division of labour by changing the economics of location, particularly when the NIDL takes place between separate firms.

This happens in two ways. First, the new techniques call for a relationship between component-suppliers and assemblers in which design and equity links are more close-knit; and second, just-in-time involves the close proximity of plants. This leads Schonberger to ask about decentralised production techniques. 'How far can just-in-time deliveries of raw materials and purchased parts be feasible given the vast shipping distances [involved]?'. Abernathy *et al.* conclude from their study of the introduction of these techniques in the US automobile industry:

> The emerging commitment is reflected as well in the closer linkages now being developed between producers and suppliers in the scheduling of parts shipments, in product design, and in quality. Where suppliers are located in close proximity to the plants, they have been integrated into the manufacturer's daily production schedule – that is they receive daily information from the relevant plants and invoice daily deliveries of parts (p. 82).

Thus the world's largest auto producer, General Motors is cutting the number of suppliers by around 50 per cent – 'GM will be picking as winners in this selection process the steelworkers with the highest-quality products, closest proximity to GM fabrication plants, and greatest commitment to remain steel producers – just what Japanese manufacturers look for in suppliers' (Schonberger, p. 179). All this bodes ill for the role of the LDCs as component producers in the international division of labour, with the possible exceptions of Mexico (linked to the USA) and South Korea (linked to Japan).

*(f) The Political Economy of Re-industrialisation*

Without accompanying changes in the pattern of social relations, it must be doubted whether these industrial strategies are likely to be viable, with or without substantial and prolonged protection. The books under review tend to see this political economy of industrialisation as revolving around two issues, the relationship between capital and labour, and the role of the State.

Bluestone and Harrison are clearly in the ideological minority amongst these books. They argue that 'neither supply-side reliance on the wonders of the "free-market" nor corporatist models of consensual planning after the manner of Japan can be expected to achieve the *democratic* reindustrialisation of the American economy' (p. 231); 'all the [non-participatory alternatives] share a studied unwillingness to question the extent to which conventional private ownership of industry and the more-or-less unbridled pursuit of private profit might be the *causes* of the problem [of deindustrialisation]' (p. 230).

> Thus, before Americans can embark on any major planned structural transformation of the economy, they must reject the claims of those who would deliberately promote insecurity as a matter of policy, find ways to re-establish the social safety net, and *extend* the range of the regulatory system to make that net even more secure for more groups in the population. These are the preconditions for any fundamental restructuring of the American economy (p. 232).

This analysis and prescription stands far outside the implicit and explicit perspectives of the other books under review. Ballance and Sinclair come closest to raising similar issues when they point to the underlying cultural and political conditions of the Japanese model, but there is clearly a distinct difference between this analysis which is tinged with social democratic hesitancy and the participatory socialism explicit in Bluestone and Harrison. The UNIDO volume, perhaps for obvious reasons, declines even to discuss the implications of dynamic comparative advantage and steers clear of 'value judgements on 'non-economic' issues such as the role of military expenditure in industrialisation, arguing that these problems 'deal with issues beyond the scope of economic analysis' (p. 336).

The political economy of re-industrialisation, particularly in relation to the pattern of social relations at the point of production, is considered more directly by

Abernathy *et al.* They foresee the possibility of capital *qua management* reinvigorating itself, and the key to this lies in the adoption of Japanese-style manufacturing organisation. Although they acknowledge, that '[t]he modern Japanese system of production is not some manufacturing Nirvana, free of all the tensions and problems that beset such systems elsewhere' (p. 84), they argue that it forces a spirit of cooperation rather than conflict between capital and labour: 'The imperatives of quality and productivity which lie at the heart of this new industrial competition, are impossible to satisfy without the active, loyal, and committed participation of a well-trained and constantly improving workforce' (p. 90). Moreover, they believe that this transition is possible, precisely because it harks back to the Fordist production techniques of the early twentieth century. The latter's introduction faltered because '[w]hen the commitment to such enlightened practices [as job security and higher wages]evaporates as it did at Ford after World War I, benevolent paternalism can quite rapidly turn into heavy-handed authoritarism, vigorous anti-unionism, and a reliance on the morally repugnant activities of the justly infamous Service Dept' (p. 81). Japanese-style production techniques, they argue, may in fact be merely an extension of the interrupted progress of American management technique and hence more susceptible to innovation. Schonberger, of course, shares this perspective but one might question his judgement that American corporations can move to a non-conflictual relationship between capital and labour in the light of his further observation concerning the labour-processes involved: 'I have been astounded by statements I have heard from some American "authorities" to the effect that the Japanese reject Taylorism, supposedly in favour of a more humanistic approach ... but the Japanese out-Taylor us all' (p. 193).

So much for the relations between capital and labour, but what of the theorisation of the State in the various books under review? The short answer must be that there is little. Only Sen addresses himself directly to this issue and his perspective is one which imbues the State with an overwhelming degree of autonomy; indeed he presents a theory of industrial accumulation which largely omits its primary actor, capital.

In the light of these comments on the political-economic content of the re-industrialisation strategies covered in the various books under view, it would be fair to conclude that this constitutes their prime collective weakness. Unless these issues are argued through in a coherent manner it is difficult to foresee how the restructured organisational techniques required to re-industrialise can be implemented successfully.

SOME MAJOR ISSUES OF INDUSTRIALISATION AND THE BOOKS UNDER REVIEW

The books under review are each addressed to specific concerns which, as we have seen, relate in one way or another to the current restructuring of the global industrial economy. They also bear on some wider or more particular issues of industrialisation, of which six stand out in significance.

The first concerns the orientation of industrial strategies in LDCs [see *Kirkpatrick and Nixson, 1983; Schmitz, 1984*]. In the first two decades after the Second World War these were primarily concerned with deepening the import-substitution of the inherited structure of industrial output; thereafter the dominant mode has become that of export-oriented industrialisation directed towards developed-country markets, giving rise to the increasing level of interconnectedness noted above. But are these the only two feasible types of industrial strategy? What of a strategy of inward-looking industrial growth designed to meet an altered structure of demand, and to use different types of techniques? And what of an outward-focused strategy which involves greater trade between LDCs, rather than exports directed towards industrially advanced economies? Clearly these possibilities have important implications for the extent to which Third World industrial growth involves de-industrialisation in developed countries. For example, expanded intra-Third World trade in manufactures, perhaps organised on a barter basis to escape the problem of foreign-exchange liquidity, might enable global industrial growth to continue, with continued interconnectedness but with a reduced impact on industrial development in developed countries.

Second, there is the question of the duration of the economic crisis at the centre of the world economy, the resolution of the international debt problem and the links between crisis and technological change. If — as now seems increasingly unlikely — we are through the worst of the economic crisis and the problems of LDC debt can be resolved without significant insolvency (amongst Western banks or LDCs themselves), then economic growth will allow continued industrialisation in both the First and Third Worlds. However, if the economic crisis endures, the conflict between the existing forms of industrial growth in the Third World and in the advanced economies will necessarily persist. Of related interest is the theorisation of the link between technological change and economic crisis. Is the diffusion of the New Technology a response to Crisis, albeit exacerbating emerging trends [*Kaplinsky, 1984a*], or is it better seen as a cause of Crisis [*Jenkins and Sherman, 1979*]? If the latter, does this not suggest that the resolution of current difficulties lies in resistance to the New Technology, in the Third World as much as in the advanced economies?

The third issue of particular relevance to the current global industrialisation debate is an understanding of the nature of best-practice technique. To what extent can this be seen as the introduction of physical, embodied technologies, the dominant topic of discussion in the technology-transfer literature of the 1960s and 1970s? Should not the focus be on information as a commodity, and hence the transition to the software-intensive information economy? This conceptualisation of information as a commodity has wide currency, but it is often forgotten that commodities (for example, iron-ore, but also basic steels) tend to be homogeneous items; 'information', by contrast, is extraordinarily diverse (or else it would hardly qualify as 'information') and is often difficult to appropriate. How then can we really characterise the 'information economy' in relation to industrial development? Of equal significance in the discussion of best-practice technique is the distinction between technology, incorporating both software and hardware, and management. Is the real task of industrial competitiveness to reduce X-inefficiency [*Liebenstein, 1978*], that is, to secure the optimal use of physical technology? More particularly, in the light of the significant organisational implications of the Japanese JIT manufacturing processes discussed above, is Liebenstein's concept of X-efficiency adequate to cope with the social context in which these JIT procedures have developed?

This leads discussion to a fourth major issue affecting current industrial strategy, namely, what is the link between technology, considered in its broadest sense to include JIT-type modes of organisation as well as hardware and software, and social relations? Can technology be theorised in terms of some form of technological-Darwinism [*Kaplinsky, 1984a: Chapter 10*], or must it be seen as a social product? If the latter is the case, it puts the issue of replicability to the forefront, as a problem rather than a solution, for industrial strategy.

Fifth is the question of market closure. The maintenance of market access relates back to our earlier discussion of the durability of the crisis; if crisis persists in the industrially advanced economies, it is a relatively sure bet that protectionism will become increasingly significant. On the other hand there is the question of the decline of Pax Americana in the 1980s — as Nye has argued in a recent contribution to the debate on TNCs, 'the theory of hegemonic stability [states that] unless one nation has the capability and will to stabilize the international economic system, it will tend towards closure under the diverse pressures of domestic nationalistic politics' [*Nye, 1983: 13*]. Thus even an end to the 'crisis' will not necessarily mean an end to protectionism.

Finally, unless the industrialisation discussion is firmly rooted in an institutional – and hence political-economic – context, it becomes difficult to provide convincing analysis of what is likely to occur, and why. This necessarily directs analysis beyond the three broad categories of capital, labour and the State, to a more complex discussion of the different components of each of these three major actors in industrial accumulation.

CONCLUSION

Our concern in this review has been twofold. First, we have considered the extent to which the books under review have considered the relationship between past problems of de-industrialisation in the mature, industrially advanced economies and industrialisation in the Third World. Second, we have queried whether the attempts to re-industrialise in the mature industrial economies are likely to succeed and, to the extent that they are, is this likely to have a negative impact on industrial growth in the Third World in the future. These concerns directly raise the problems of comparative advantage and trade reversal and it was with some anticipation that we scoured the various books to see whether they had directly confronted these issues. Disappointingly, only the UNIDO volume raises the issues and, even then, considers the problem as arising in the realm of technology alone; the potential impact on TNC decision-making (hinted at by Schonberger and Abernathy *et al.*) is ignored, as is the theorisation of 'national capital' and the State. Thus, to end with a quotation from the UNIDO book:

> Technological latitudes, however, may also offer a possibility for adjustment at existing locations. The breakthrough in microelectronics and its application to industrial robots has raised the possibility that standardised lines of production – located in developing countries precisely because of their standardisation – may be shifted again: this time back to the developed market economies (p. 245).

Moreover, LDCs may be relatively disadvantaged in the diffusion of this new technology, and only 'some of these producers [of electronically controlled machine tools] will be able to shift their production lines towards advanced machines and manufacturing systems. Thus, further polarization of the industry is to be expected' (UNIDO, p. 302). Does this suggest an agenda for future research?

NOTES

1. Extracts from French planning directive, quoted in Ballance and Sinclair, pp. 9, 187.
2. For example, *automobile* production in DCs fell between 1970 and 1980 from 27.3 m to 25 m, whilst in LDCs it grew from 0.9 m to 2.3 m; *steel* production in the same period rose imperceptibly in DCs from 389 to 395 m +, but climbed sharply in LDCs from 20 to 50 m +; *colour TV* output in LDCs rose from 6.3 m to 19.7 m in LDCs between 1970 and 1979, compared with a much smaller rise from 30 m to 34.3 m in DCs; *radio* production in LDCs climbed from 49 m in 1970 to 83 m in 1979, compared to a fall in DCs from 62.6 m to 34.6 m (all data drawn from Ballance and Sinclair).
3. This is not surprising for Robert Ballance is the head of the Statistics and Survey Unit of the Division of Industrial Studies at UNIDO, which was responsible for producing *Industry in a Changing World*.
4. The optimistic projection implies a GDP increase of 7 per cent p.a., and an annual increase of 8.7 per cent for manufacturing value added, in the LDCs, and corresponding rates of 4.3 per cent and 5.2 per cent in the DCs; the historic projections imply respective growth rates of GDP of 4.9 per cent in LDCs and 6.2 per cent in DCs. In the light of the post-1979 recession both sets of targets seem unrealistically high.

5. The choice of these two sets of headings is open to question since for many countries – as diverse as Taiwan and the USA – the automobile industry is seen as a dynamic sector, whilst oil refining was in the early and mid-1980s in a state of stagnation in most of the advanced industrial economies.
6. That is, of a non-trivial nature. Both Chen's and Sen's books could have benefited from more careful proof-reading.
7. See, for example, Chandler [*1962, 1977*].
8. However, they neglect to point out, as does Chen, that in the early 1980s the American Bulova watch company had 25 per cent of its equity purchased by a Hong Kong firm determined to maintain access to US markets.
9. In this sense the Abernathy book is highly relevant to much of the technology literature in Development Studies – see M. Fransman's survey [*1985*].
10. As Chen illustrates, the advance of the NICs was only partly due to an internationalisation of production within the TNC.

## REFERENCES

Chandler, A. D., 1962, *Strategy and Structure: Chapters in the History of the American Industrial Enterprise*, Cambridge, MA: MIT Press.
Chandler, A. D., 1977, *The Visible Hand: The Managerial Revolution in American Business*, Cambridge, MA: Harvard University Press.
Evans, D. and P. Alizadeh, 1984, 'Trade, Industrialisation and the Visible Hand', in Kaplinsky [*1984d*].
Fransman, M., 1985, 'Conceptualising Technical Change in the Third World in the 1980s: An Interpretive Survey', *Journal of Development Studies*, Vol. 21, No. 4, July.
Fröbel, F., J. Heinrichs and O. Kreye, 1980, *The New International Division of Labour*, Cambridge: Cambridge University Press.
Hughes, H. and J. Waelbroek, 1981, 'Can Developing-country Exports Keep Growing in the 1980s?', *The World Economy*, Vol. 6, No. 2, June.
Jenkins, C. and B. Sherman, 1979, *The Collapse of Work*, London: Eyre Methuen.
Kaplinsky, R., 1984a, *Automation: The Technology and Society*, London: Longman.
Kaplinsky, R., 1984b, 'Microelectronics and the Onset of Systems Facture: Some Implications For Third World Industrialisation', *World Development*, Vol. 13, No. 3, pp. 423–40.
Kaplinsky, R., 1984c, 'The International Context for Industrialisation in the Coming Decade', in Kaplinsky [*1984d*].
Kaplinsky, R. (ed.), 1984d, 'Third World Industrialisation in the 1980s: Open Economies in a Closing World', Special Issue of the *Journal of Development Studies*, Vol. 21, No. 1, Oct.
Kirkpatrick, C. H. and F. I. Nixson (eds.), 1983, *The Industrialisation of Less Developed Countries*, Manchester: Manchester University Press.
Leibenstein, H., 1978, *General X-Efficiency Theory and Economic Development*, Oxford: Oxford University Press.
Nye, J. S., 1983, 'The Multinational Corporation in the 1980s', in C.P. Kindleberger and D. B. Audretsch (eds.), *The Multinational Corporation in the 1980s*, Cambridge, MA: MIT Press.
Schmitz, H., 1984, 'Industrialisation Strategies in Less Developed Countries: Some Lessons of Historical Experience', in Kaplinsky [*1984d*].

# Managing the World Economy: Old Order, New Order or Disorder?

## by Graham Bird*

**The New International Economic Order: An Overview.** By P. N. Agarwala. *Oxford: Pergamon Press*, 1983. Pp. xiii + 351. £17.50. ISBN 0 08 028823 5.

**Third World Strategy: Economic and Political Cohesion in the South.** Edited Altaf Gauhar. *London: Praeger*, UK distributor Holt-Saunders, 1984. Pp. xvi + 220. £24.95 and £12.95. ISBN 0 03 069713 1 and 069712 3.

**The New International Economic Order: Conflict and Cooperation in North-South Economic Relations, 1974–77.** By Jeffrey A. Hart. *London: Macmillan*, 1983. Pp. xviii + 180. £25. ISBN 0 333 34525 8.

**The Management of the World Economy.** By Evan Luard. *London: Macmillan*, 1983. Pp. xxvii + 270. £25. ISBN 0 333 34236 4.

**The Challenges of South-south Co-operation.** Edited by Breda Pavlič, Raúl R. Uranga, Boris Cizelj and Marjan Svetličič. *Boulder, CO: Westview Press*, UK distributor Bowker, 1983. Pp. xii + 455. £21.75. ISBN 0 8653 601 5.

**The Oil Crisis and Economic Adjustment: Case Studies of Six Developing Countries.** By Andrew MacKillop. *London: Frances Pinter*, 1983. Pp. xi + 180. £16.50. ISBN 0 86187 301 7.

**Controlling the Economic Future: Policy Dilemmas in a Shrinking World.** By Michael Stewart. *Brighton: Wheatsheaf Books*, 1983. Pp. ix + 192. £15.95 and £5.95. ISBN 0 7108 0182 3 and 0187 4.

INTRODUCTION

In many key respects, the international economic order which characterised the 1950s and 1960s broke down during the 1970s and 1980s. An international trading system that had experienced considerable liberalisation became affected by growing protectionism, even though most of the new protectionism took the form of non-tariff barriers. At the same time the world's monetary system, previously based on the rules worked out at the Bretton Woods conference in 1944 and operating under the auspices of the institutions conceived there, effectively collapsed. The world moved away from fixed exchange rates towards flexible ones, and came to rely much more heavily than before on the private international banks as a source of balance of payments finance.

Along with — though not necessarily because of — the breakdown in key facets of the old order, the performance of the world economy began to falter. For the world as a whole, the rate of inflation accelerated, the level of unemployment increased, the rate of economic growth declined, and balance of payments disequilibria became much larger than those with which anyone had previously had to deal. This is not to deny

* Visiting Professor of International Economic Affairs, the Fletcher School of Law and Diplomacy, Tufts University, Medford, MA 02155.

that individual countries or groups of countries — the 'newly industrialising countries' for example — did quite well during the 1970s, but overall there was an observable deterioration.

These events generated a great deal of thought and discussion covering many aspects of economic performance. Two major topics of debate were, first, the chances of replacing the old Bretton Woods order with a new international economic order (NIEO) which would be less dominated by the industrial countries of the North; the second, the search for an explanation for the apparently quite rapid deterioration in the world's economic fortunes. Leading on from this second question was the additional issue of what might be done to improve matters.

The books reviewed here tend to fall into one or other of these areas of debate. However, the two questions are not independent. A major theme of the Brandt Report, for example, is the mutuality of interests between the South and the North, with increased real resource flows from the North to the South being seen as a means by which greater employment, higher levels of output and stronger export performance can be achieved in the North.

While there has been plenty of discussion of the issues mentioned above there has been much less solid achievement. The rise in protectionism has continued unabated, there has been little if any increase in real flows, there has been only slow progress towards an Integrated Programme for Commodities, there has been a continuing decline in the terms of trade of many non-oil primary-producing countries, and there have been no really fundamental changes in international financial arrangements.

Furthermore, while the economic achievements of the United States in the 1980s cannot be denied, it is still perhaps too early to say how durable they will be. In any event there is little evidence that recovery in the US has been transmitted to other industrial nations or to developing countries. While the strength of the dollar has provided foreign producers with a competitive advantage, the dollar's strength has, in part, been caused by the bond-financed fiscal deficit in the US which has pushed up interest rates world-wide, thereby deterring consumption and investment. Moreover, it has exacerbated the problems of those countries whose debt is based on floating interest rates. The kind of recovery pursued by the US may thus have been more contractionary in its world-wide implications than it has been expansionary.

Nor is there much evidence that the global balance of power has altered very much. While OPEC clearly exploited its position when there was a rising market for oil, subsequent events have shown just how quickly the bargaining strength of such a grouping can evaporate when there are no excess demand pressures. More broadly, the era of powerful commodity cartels foreseen by some commentators has simply not materialised and the relevance of the market as a principal determinant of political and organisational changes has been underlined. There have, of course, been some relatively minor achievements. Certainly there is a more general awareness of global distributional issues than prior to 1973. Furthermore, some modifications have been made to the operation of the international financial system, but this is hardly evidence of a NIEO — more the continuation of a trend that was well established long before the 1970s. A question arising from all this — and one which has been only partially answered above — is how can the lack of achievement be explained?

The rest of this article is organised around the questions that have been raised above. Where appropriate, the arguments and ideas contained in the books listed at the beginning will be drawn upon and commented upon, but what emerges is not a full critical review. Without doubt many of the books deserve much fuller scrutiny than space permits here.

MANAGING THE WORLD ECONOMY

World economic performance after 1973 caught economists with their theories down. Contrary to conventional economic theory which predicted an inverse relationship between economic growth and employment on the one hand, and inflation and balance of payments disequilibria on the other, economies seemed to be experiencing at the same time rising inflation, deepening balance of payments difficulties, increasing unemployment and falling economic growth. There seemed to have been a fundamental qualitative deterioration in economic performance.

It shows much for the inventiveness of economists that it was not long before not just one but a series of theories was being offered to explain what was going on. Suggestions included: first, that it was all to do with long waves in economic activity, or business and political cycles; second, that it was simply monetarism at the global level, with rising unemployment reflecting a response to faster inflation and an increase in the natural rate; third, that it reflected not so much excess monetary demand but falling real supply as the size of the producing sector relative to the service sector or government sector fell; fourth, that it resulted from changes in the terms of trade between primary products and manufactures, with rising primary product prices in the early 1970s leading to cost inflation in industrial countries and a demand-deflationary response; fifth, that it was evidence of the world economy's being in transition, adjusting to the emergence of the NICs; and sixth, that it was the direct result of the collapse of the Bretton Woods financial regime and the introduction of generalised floating. These explanations are not central to the books reviewed here, but two further propositions are.

The first is that the deterioration in global economic performance after 1973 may be linked specifically to the increase in oil prices in that year. The increase is seen as having been administered by OPEC, and as causing cost inflation and demand deflation. The latter is explained by the argument that the oil price rise redistributed world income away from high spenders, namely the OECD countries, towards high savers, namely, the OPEC countries, and thereby reduced the world's average propensity to spend. The oil price rise is also used to explain growing payments difficulties, the move to the market place as a way of financing payments deficits, the resultant debt problem, and so on. In short it is seen by its advocates as offering a fairly comprehensive explanation of macroeconomic aspects of the 1970s and 1980s.

Andrew MacKillop investigates the impact of rising oil prices on the economies of six developing countries. His book clearly catalogues the problems with which these countries have had to deal and the pressures for economic and social adjustment that have been generated by a worsening balance of payments situation. However, while enough evidence is presented to confirm that large changes in energy prices create serious problems for countries that rely on imported energy, it is another matter to attribute the entire spectrum of global macro-economic ills to energy-related factors. MacKillop wisely rejects such a temptation and argues that additional factors have been at work; indeed, the intention of his study 'was to show that the increase in oil prices was not the sole reason for the economic malaise of the developing countries'. The logic of this view is supported by the fact that falling oil prices have co-existed during the 1980s with a severe industrial recession. Surely rising oil prices and falling oil prices cannot both be used to explain recession. Nor can one ignore the argument that oil prices are not administered at all but instead are the result of world demand levels. On this view it was the expansion in aggregate demand in the early 1970s which caused oil prices to rise and the recession of the 1980s which caused them to level off. At any rate it would seem right to examine other factors in addition to oil.

The second of our further explanations maintains that many observed macro-economic problems reflect governmental economic mismanagement, albeit mismanagement set against a changing, and sometimes dramatically changing economic background. Failure to manage the world economy appropriately is the underlying theme of both Michael Stewart's and Evan Luard's books.

Stewart investigates in considerable detail what he sees as a neglected dimension of macro-economic policy, namely, the spatial and temporal aspects. To concentrate here on the former, he argues that economies have become much more interdependent over the last 15 years both through trade and, perhaps more so, through capital flows. Even flexible exchange rates, which are in principle supposed to insulate individual economies from the rest of the world, have in practice largely failed to do so. However, there has been no increase in the synchronisation of macroeconomic policy to match this increased interdependence. Instead governments have continued to formulate macroeconomic policy in a unilateral fashion. The result of this policy approach has been to impart a demand-deflationary bias to the world economy, since governments have been preoccupied with reducing inflation and avoiding balance of payments deficits. Any isolated attempts at expansion have encountered the hostility of the international financial community, the exchange-rate repercussions of which have led to their reversal.

The options for countries in this demand-deflationary environment are either to de-link themselves from the rest of the international community through a framework of trade and exchange controls, or to co-ordinate their policies more closely, thereby implicitly agreeing upon a particular distribution of payments disequilibria. Stewart, probably wisely, prefers the second course of action, though rightly he points to the lack of success that has been had up to now by world economic summitry. His hope is that disillusion with monetarism and concern about the high levels of global unemployment will provide sufficient incentive for a co-ordinated expansion. On the basis of the figures published by the IMF in its *World Economic Outlook*, there is little real sign of any change as yet amongst many of the most powerful economic nations. Fiscal impulses appear to be fairly uniformly contractionary – although the US is something of a special case. As Stewart implies, the lack of a positively co-ordinated expansion seems almost inevitably to lead to an uncoordinated, yet fairly universal, recession.

While Stewart leaves to one side the precise mechanisms and organisational structures under which co-ordinated expansion might be arranged, such arrangements are a central concern of Luard's book. His proposals amount to a multi-faceted programme of international institutionalisation. In order to encourage balanced world growth there would be 'a kind of international economic council' which 'would meet, at least quarterly, to discuss the state of the world economy'. To oversee investment and aid there would again be a 'new body ... that would maintain a general oversight of the development process all over the world and of the transfer of resources ... taking place for that purpose'. For trade 'a new joint supervising council' would bring together representatives of GATT and UNCTAD and would 'set up new joint committees or activities where appropriate'. For the international banking system 'better international supervision ... is ... required' and the IMF needs to be expanded. Similarly there would be a new International Commission on National Resources, a new international energy agency, and so on.

Without doubt there are times when it is appropriate to argue for and feasible to establish new international agencies. Blanket acceptance of the institutional status quo is clearly a misguided philosophy. However, it also needs to be recognised that forces which generate what may be seen by some as the inefficiencies and inequities of the existing institutional system are also likely to inhibit the establishment of new agencies designed to remove them. Having identified deficiencies, the easy and soft answer is, in many respects, to propose a new agency which will miraculously correct them. What is more likely in fact is that the new agency will never get off the ground because of political wrangling, or that if it does, it will be subject to many of the same deficiencies as those that it replaces or complements. Furthermore the proliferation of agencies may simply obscure many of the important issues, particularly if time is spent arguing as to whose responsibility it is to do what. Even apparently clearly-defined terms of reference do not eliminate this possibility, as experience with the IMF reveals.

A more interesting question is the political economy of institutional operation and reform. How do institutions work, how do they reach decisions, why do they often do things that to outside observers seem misguided, and why do they often seem inflexible and unresponsive? Once these issues are better understood there may be scope for improving the institutions that already exist rather than replacing them with others which may turn out to be no better.

Furthermore, the scope for institutions to manage the global economy is strictly constrained by both internal and external factors. Internally there are bound to be bureaucratic and administrative delays in decision taking which mean that when the decisions become effective they may no longer be appropriate. For example, attempts to use SDR creation in a counter-cyclical fashion may be subject to a lag structure which would result in variations actually being pro-cyclical.

Even where decisions that might be generally seen as sensible are taken, it is difficult for institutions to make them effective if the outside world is reluctant to accept them. For example, there are good grounds for establishing the SDR as the world's principal reserve asset, and the IMF has set this as a target for international financial policy. However, the world has in practice moved towards a multiple currency reserve system rather than towards the SDR. It is clearly not enough merely to take the right decisions; the means by which they can be made effective also needs to be examined.

In conclusion, the benefits from a new spate of institution building are unlikely to exceed the costs. In circumstances where world economic summit meetings fail to articulate and activate certain policies it is unlikely that an international economic council will achieve much more. What is needed is a change in the attitudes of the participants at such forums. It would be nice to think that scholarly works such as Stewart's and Luard's have a part to play in such a process but one may remain sceptical.

## THE NEW INTERNATIONAL ECONOMIC ORDER

The New International Economic Order figures as the title of two of the books, one by Jeffrey Hart and the other by P. N. Agarwala. Hart sets out to explain the policies of the major participants and the outcomes of the negotiations between 1973 and 1977. He focuses on a series of questions: why did the negotiations assume importance; why did the developing countries manage to maintain greater unity than the developed countries; why did the negotiations fail to achieve much; and finally what are the prospects for the future?

While Hart's book is a fairly narrow study of the politics of economics, Agarwala's is a wide-ranging overview of all aspects of the NIEO. Indeed it synthesises the main findings of a 15-volume study published by UNITAR in collaboration with the Centro de Estudios Económicos y Sociales del Tercer Mundo (CEESTEM) in Mexico, which covers regional issues, sectoral issues — trade, industrialisation, finance, food and agriculture — and socio-cultural and political-institutional issues, as well as general surveys on the objectives of and obstacles to the NIEO.

From the range of questions that these texts raise, two will be examined here. One relates to the lack of achievement in terms of fundamentally restructuring the international economy and altering the distribution of power within it. The other concerns the alternative of South–South co-operation.

A number of factors may be combined to help explain the lack of success, although in short the answer is that the bargaining position of those seeking a new order was insufficiently strong. First the North–South distinction is too simplistic. It cannot be argued that the South, containing as it does OPEC, the Newly Industrialising Countries and the low-income countries, is an homogeneous entity. Different countries within the South − and indeed within the North − have different interests and different views as to how these interests are likely to be best served. Even for individual Southern countries or groups of countries there may be internal inconsistencies in their position with regard to reform. Debt relief, for example, may have some short-term appeal, but at the same time recipients of such relief will worry about damaging their long-run creditworthiness. Or again, while many developing countries may stand to gain from a more structured system of international liquidity creation based on the SDR, they may be reluctant to give up the flexibility that the Euro-currency market offers, or to abandon the scope for reserve management.

Second, the international environment most conducive to evolutionary reform is a structured one. In practice the world moved away from a 'system' in the 1970s. The old order was replaced by no order rather than a new order. Yet in the mid-1970s this move was probably more the result of expediency than of deep ideological beliefs in the superiority of the market.

Third, commodity market conditions changed. There was a move from excess demand to excess supply, and from a sellers' to a buyers' market. To the extent that bargaining strength reflects market position, it is not surprising that the momentum for a NIEO initially generated by the increase in oil prices subsequently petered out. In effect the responses of the developed world to the claims for a new order were to move into recession, economise on the use of oil, adopt more inward-looking trade policies, and thereby undermine the bargaining strength of the South. Of course this was probably not the motivation for these policies. Instead they reflected a pre-occupation with reducing the rates of inflation and payments deficits.

With respect to inflation, many elements of the NIEO, such as the SDR link and the Integrated Programme for Commodities, were seen by countries of the North as making it worse. Furthermore, it is interesting to note that the increase in oil prices which stimulated the South's interest in a NIEO, and which initially improved their bargaining position, also contributed to world-wide inflation and to attitudes which were hostile to the proposals for a new order.

As far as the balance of payments is concerned, it may be noted that measures taken to strengthen the North's position almost inevitably weakened the South's and pushed many developing countries into a situation where they had little option other than to turn to the Fund, an institution which many of them see as a bastion of the old order. The strength associated with being a surplus country and one of the Fund's creditors was really attained only by Saudi Arabia − a country whose attitude towards the NIEO might be seen as somewhat ambivalent. It is only under the threat of a debtor's cartel that deficit countries may improve their bargaining position and, as already explained, debtor countries may feel that carrying out such a threat would involve more costs than benefits in the long run.

Fourth, the 'mutuality doctrine' that is so much a part of some (though by no means all) of the proposals for a NIEO has essentially been rejected by governments of the North. It is seen as being based on Keynesian notions that have been rejected in favour of a more monetarist approach to economic management. In any case, governments have no doubt viewed many aspects of the NIEO, for example, increased aid, as politically infeasible in circumstances where the thrust of domestic economic policy is contractionary.

Given the rejection of mutuality, Northern governments have seen nothing for them in the NIEO, particularly after oil became of less pressing concern. Their short-term interests appeared to be best served by participating in discussions from which nothing much would emerge. What has in fact happened is therefore consistent with the view that the balance of economic power has not changed and that the interests of the most powerful groups continue to dominate.

FUTURE PROSPECTS: THE SOUTHERN ALTERNATIVE

The above factors make it unlikely that a 'grand design' approach based on global negotiations will prove successful. Indeed there is a fundamental 'Catch 22' dilemma. For the South to be in a strong bargaining position it needs to have been relatively successful economically. However, economic success under the old rules will reduce the desire to change them. The motivation to change the system will only be strong in conditions where the South's bargaining position is weak.

If there is not much mileage left in global negotiations involving the North and South, what about the scope for South–South co-operation? In one sense the heterogeneity of the South in terms of comparative advantage provides the opportunity for intra-South trade and investment, yet by the same token the heterogeneity of interests makes it likely that a South–South dialogue will generate as few positive benefits as the North–South one has done. When, for example, thought is given to schemes for an exclusively Southern version of the IMF or the World Bank, a key question is where is the finance to come from? The short answer is that it will have to come from countries that have been relatively successful under existing arrangements. But will these countries be anxious to foster Southern arrangements? They may of course be rather more interested when they themselves become less successful, but then they are unlikely to possess the necessary finance.

The conclusion is that while frustration with the lack of action on the North South front is understandable, the chances of success on the South–South front can easily be exaggerated. It should be emphasised that this general conclusion does not mean denying that there may be opportunities for greater Southern co-operation than has been achieved in the past. What it does imply, however, is the need to get away from the banner-waving type of advocacy of vague South–South solutions and towards a more reasoned and thorough analysis of specific proposals for reform. One cannot escape the fact that attempts to apply the logic of co-operation, as can be found in various Southern trading blocs, have often been rather less than successful. It should not simply be assumed, therefore, either that Southern solutions are automatically desirable on economic grounds – some may be, others may not – or that they can easily be made to work.

Two recent books which examine various facets of the Southern solution are the compilations edited by Altaf Gauhar and Breda Pavlič and others. The former brings together various articles previously published in *Third World Quarterly* and covers a range of issues. Both illustrate nicely, and in various ways, the large gulf that has to be bridged between the desire of some commentators for more co-operation within the South and the practicalities of actually specifying and implementing reforms.

CONCLUDING REMARKS

Does all this mean that talk of managing the world economy and of establishing a NIEO represents just so much wishful thinking by their advocates? Is the world economy doomed to muddle along in a disordered fashion, lurching from crisis to crisis? Not necessarily. There are alternative scenarios which may not be completely implausible. For example, dissatisfaction with flexible exchange rates and concern over unemployment could result in closer policy co-ordination and in a resurgence of neo-Keynesianism. To the extent that such policy changes were successful, they might create an international environment more conducive to at least some of the reforms that are now elements of the proposals for a NIEO. However, these reforms seem more likely to be made in a piecemeal fashion, much as they have been in the past.

The most probable response to the disorder of the 1970s and early 1980s would therefore seem to be a return to a version of the old order — albeit somewhat modified — rather than the establishment of a new order of things. Yet this would not imply a complete failure for the Third World. Indeed the return to a more structured international financial system, a reduction in the variability of exchange rates, an increase in the rate of economic growth, falling interest rates, increased world trade, and reduced protectionism, would all be to the general advantage of developing countries. A case may therefore be made that in present circumstances it would be more sensible for developing countries to focus on trying to encourage such changes in the world economy than to continue with claims for a NIEO which themselves stand almost no chance of success but which may reduce the likelihood of the other reforms being introduced. Rhetoric, no matter how fine, and plans, no matter how grand, stand much less chance of improving the lot of the population of the Third World than a more hard-headed and pragmatic approach which shows a keen awareness of what is, and what is not, possible.